Trix

KIPLING'S FORGOTTEN SISTER

Trix
KIPLING'S FORGOTTEN SISTER

Previously unpublished poems and prose

by Trix Kipling

Plus memories of Trix by relatives and friends

With biographical introduction and research by

Lorna Lee

Foreword by

Michael Smith of The Kipling Society

Pond View

Edited by Roger Wickham

ISBN 1 871044 76 6

Pond View is an imprint of Forward Press Ltd.

Printed in Great Britain

First published in 2003
2nd Edition published in 2004 by

Forward Press Ltd. Peterborough, England
www.forwardpress.co.uk

In memoriam

S.C.W.

&

Margaret Elizabeth MacDonald

A Pond View Biography

Other titles in the series include:

The Pater: John Lockwood Kipling
Everybody's Heard of Blondin
John Frith: Scholar and Martyr

Contents

(continued next page)

List of Illustrations

Foreword

Trix Kipling has ever been a shadowy figure, peripheral to those absorbed by the life and works of her elder brother. Occasionally her flame has burnt brightly, as when she showed an early co-operative talent in writing as part of the family quartet, or when she enjoyed being part of the social scene in Simla. But for much of her troubled life she bewildered those with whom she came in contact, sometimes infuriating, sometimes charming, but always enigmatic. The 'down' side related to frequent and protracted mental illnesses which so beset her. She sought solace in attempting to come to terms with the paranormal, a side of her nature which so disturbed her brother.

Now the veil has been lifted in a most remarkable way by the appearance of this new insight, drawing upon previously published memories of relatives and friends, and with the welcome addition of the first publication of her own verses and short stories. We must be grateful to the Misses Betty and Helen Macdonald, her nieces, for making the material so readily accessible to Lorna Lee who has assembled it with skill and sympathy, and to Pond View Books who were prepared to publish it.

Perhaps Trix's instability in later life can be traced to the experiences which she and her brother were subjected in an enforced foster relationship with the Holloway family in a bleak Southsea so far from the warmth and light of Bombay. This traumatic period affected Rudyard deeply, but eventually he rid himself of the hurt in his autobiographical short story *Baa Baa, Black Sheep*. Trix, it was always thought, escaped mentally unscathed, an assessment which, in light of her later difficulties, might prove not to be true. Although she was not subject to the vicious persecution suffered by her sibling, nonetheless she was indoctrinated by the odious 'Auntirosa'. Just as Rudyard recreated detail in *Baa Baa, Black Sheep,* Trix similarly used this autobiographical material in one of her novels, *The Pinchbeck Goddess*.

Later in adolescence, her captivating of the Viceroy's son resulted in his removal from the scene and may well have shattered her dreams of the grand life. Her marriage to John Fleming, at the age of 21, after their re-engagement, not only confirmed her father's doubts as to the suitability of the match but also provided personal detail in her second novel *The Heart of the Maid*. There is something, too, in it of the dissipation of sympathy between mother and daughter, for Alice seemed determined on a course which put her own needs first. Trix's unconventional relationship with her husband is also mirrored in her treatment of her heroine, May Trent.

At the height of her breakdowns, Trix's conduct varied between sullen silence and destructive outbursts, but those whose memories are recorded here paint a picture of a much more reasonable life - if slightly eccentric. They stress the warmth and kindliness of her nature, and this is a very welcome feature which goes a long way to redressing the balance. The book is very well illustrated with the inclusion of family photographs and, as it covers more specifically the later stages of her life, when her nieces knew her. It also deals with her 'Mrs Holland' persona involved in the world of psychical research and her skill with 'automatic writing' and 'cross correspondence'.

The final section brings to light her later poetry and a number of monologues and stories set in the India she knew and loved. The monologues are reminiscent of the style employed, much later, and with such effect, by Joyce Grenfell. They are light and amusing, reflecting perhaps the stresses of daily life between an incompatible husband and wife. The sketches are set with very detailed stage directions which certainly allows the reader to picture the scene. They, too, poke gentle fun at the foibles of the contemporary social scene.

For Kipling enthusiasts, the book adds poignancy and detail to the life they know so well, and it has the added interest in the enthusiastic support which Trix gave to the early years of the Kipling Society. It is undoubtedly a most acceptable addition to sum total of Kiplingiana, and we should be indebted to Lorna Lee for her very successful presentation.

Michael Smith
Brighton, East Sussex, 2003

Introduction

This book is an attempt to restore the balance of what Trix's mother, Alice Kipling, called 'the family square'. Biographical and critical studies of the life and work of Rudyard abound; John Lockwood Kipling and Alice Macdonald, the parents, have also been written about at some length, but Trix, Alice Macdonald Kipling, has, in her own right, been neglected. Where her life is intertwined with that of Rudyard, as in childhood and the years when the family was together in Lahore before her marriage, it is well documented, and later, after her brother's death and the formation of the Kipling Society, she becomes visible once more as a lively apologist for

Miss Helen Macdonald (sitting) showing the author, Lorna Lee, some of her photographs.

Rudyard. The years between have been largely ignored, except for brief references to her long period of mental illness and her interest in dabbling in the occult. In trying to bring the fourth member of the square into the foreground, I hope to be able to show that she was in many ways the most attractive member of the group.

I have not gone into great detail about the facts of her life that are well known already, and can be found in the various biographies of her brother and Professor Thomas Pinney's edition of Rudyard's letters (see Bibliography). I have concentrated, instead, on information which seems not to have been widely available hitherto.

This book would not have been possible without the help and enthusiastic support of the Misses Helen and Betty Macdonald, daughters of Trix's first cousin, Julius. Sadly, Betty, the family archivist, died before the book had taken its final shape, but her work over the years and the warmth of Helen's welcome and co-operation have made the research a constant pleasure. In addition to my biographical notes, there is a wealth of previously unpublished writings by Trix herself. Most of this has been reproduced in facsimile, exactly as she typed it, to enable the reader to share some of the excitement that I felt when I was first handed these typescripts.

Michael Smith of the Kipling Society assured me of his interest from the beginning, and I would also like to thank Elizabeth Inglis of the Manuscripts Department at the University of Sussex Library, and Professor Thomas Pinney of the Department of English, Pomona College, California, for their support and helpful suggestions; Anne Morrison and Rosamond Brown in the libraries at Edinburgh and Selkirk searched the records on my behalf; the staff at The Society for Psychical Research was extremely helpful, and I am grateful to Notting Hill and Ealing High School for Girls for allowing me the freedom of the archive cupboard. I am also indebted to my daughter, who, reading the biographical notes as a non-Kiplingite, suggested many clarifications.

Lorna Lee
Sevenoaks, Kent, 2003

Lockwood seated extreme left, Trix and Alice seated second and third from right. None of the others has been identified. The style of the building, and the Indian servant in the background, suggest that the photograph was probably taken in Lahore. The clothes suggest the early 1890s; Lockwood and Alice retired to Tisbury, in Wiltshire, in 1893.

Part One

Biography
of
Trix Kipling

BIOGRAPHICAL NOTES

by

Lorna Lee

Trix, aged 4, in 1872.

1868 -1871

Born June 11th 1868 at 'The Grange', North End Road, Fulham, London, in England, the home of her mother's sister, Georgiana Burne-Jones.

Christened Alice Macdonald, but always known as Trix or Trixie because her father called her a 'tricksy baby'.

Early childhood in Bombay. An idyllic period, doted on and spoiled by parents and native servants.

1871 - 1877

Although they had many Macdonald and Kipling relatives in England, the two small children (Rudyard then aged six) were left, totally unprepared for the separation, with complete strangers, Mr and Mrs Holloway, at Lorne Lodge, Southsea, in Hampshire. This is the period of 'The House of Desolation', used by Rudyard in the story, *Baa, Baa, Black Sheep*. There has been much discussion about the accuracy of Rudyard's recollections of his miserable time there and how much he adapted the facts in the service of art, but Trix, at least in public, always supported her brother's version (see her unfinished piece, *Through Judy's Eyes*), and there is no doubt that the children felt themselves rejected and bereft.

In 1875, their parents had moved from Bombay to Lahore, where Lockwood became Principal of the School of Art (really crafts) and Curator of the Museum. His increased salary enabled Alice to come back to England in 1877 to organise - after a rumbustious holiday in Essex, shared by their cousin Stanley Baldwin - the next stage in the children's education.

1878 - 1883

In January, Rudyard began school at Westward Ho!, on the north coast of Devon, whilst Trix, after her mother had returned to India, lived with the Misses Mary and Georgiana Craik and Miss Winnard at 26 Warwick Gardens, in London, and attended Notting Hill High School for Girls. She was there from the beginning of the Summer Term 1878 until July 1883.

It seems she must have returned to Mrs Holloway for visits, as Rudyard met Flo Garrard (the girl who haunted his teenage years and was finally exorcised in *The Light that Failed*) when he went to collect Trix from Southsea in the summer holidays of 1880. Flo and her sister, the latter described by Trix as 'common enough to bring fur to one's teeth', were paying guests at Lorne Lodge.

1883 - 1884

There is a story, which I have been unable to verify, that Notting Hill High School hoped Trix would stay on to do university entrance, but she left, aged fifteen, and returned with her mother to Lahore. The reason was probably financial (Rudyard was already in India, learning his trade on the *Civil and Military Gazette*) although in 1880, Alice wrote to a friend,

> *I long to hear from you when you have seen Trix. I feel the loss of that sweet bright creature even worse than I thought I should.*

Trix's presence always seems to have brought an extra dimension to Alice's life. In Rudyard's letters, there are references to his mother's happiness when Trix is visiting. In the final months of her life, when the presence of a nurse at 'The Gables' in Tisbury made the cramped accommodation even worse, Alice insisted that Trix should have a bed in her own room rather than lodge with a neighbour.

1884 - 1887

The 'Family Square', together for a very happy and successful three and a half years. The period when there were pens and ink in every room of their bungalow, and all four were engaged in writing articles, stories, poems, and reviews.

Echoes, Trix and Rudyard's joint book of parodies, was published in 1884, and *Quartette*, by all four, appeared at Christmas 1885. Writing and literary pursuits were very important.

In a letter to his favourite cousin, Margaret Burne-Jones, in September 1885, Rudyard has this to say,

> *And writing of the Maiden [Trix] reminds me that her bust is in the Simla Fine Arts Exhibition and she is even more admired than her bust and has Goodness only knows how many new dresses. But I rejoice with exceeding great joy to think how these trifles disturb her not and she clings healthily to the inkpot as of yore.*

This was also the period of the apotheosis of the Kiplings in Simla society.

In 1884, probably because Trix was so young, and Simla had a rather raffish 'smart set', the family spent the hot weather at Dalhousie ('Dullhouses'), and Trix earned the title 'Rose in June', but from 1885 they went to Simla, and, with the patronage of the new Viceroy, Lord Dufferin and his wife, moved in the highest social circles.

A description of the family in 1886 by E. Kay Robinson, later to be Rudyard's

Signed photograph, in Trix's possessions, of Lord Dufferin,
Viceroy of India 1884-1888.

superior on *The Pioneer,* shows why they were so popular:

John Lockwood Kipling, the father, a rare, genial soul, with happy artistic instincts, a polished literary style and a generous, cynical sense of humour was, without exception, the most delightful companion I had ever met. Mrs Kipling, the mother, preserved all the graces of youth and had a sprightly, if occasionally caustic wit, which made her society always desirable. Miss Kipling, the sister . . . inherits all her mother's vivacity and possesses a rare literary memory. I believe there is not a single line of Shakespeare's which she cannot quote. She has a statuesque beauty . . .

With the move to Simla, Trix's nickname changed to 'the Ice Maiden'; it is possible that she had an unhappy love affair in 1884 - the poem, *A Lost Love,* may be autobiographical. This is only surmise but it is true that she refused several offers of marriage in the ensuing years - two from the Viceroy's son and heir, Lord Clandeboye.

Looking back in old age on the Season of 1886, Trix, in a letter dated August 1942 to one of her Simla dancing partners, General Sir Ian Hamilton, wrote:

Photograph, taken in Bombay, 1879, of an unknown friend. Perhaps 'Maurice', who wouldn't take 'No' for an answer, and was killed fighting in Burma in 1886. It might also be Ralli, Robinson, Hodgson, or Smith - all of whom proposed and were turned down.

I don't think anyone guessed there might have been a third 'romance of the peerage' that season, [Sir Ian and Lord Herbrand Russell being the other two] if I had been less of a critical little prig. Funnily enough though Lord D [Dufferin] loved me for my good sense, Lady D never forgave me, and she had been so nice to me before. Of course a penniless daughter-in-law was the last thing she wished for, but she said openly that she had always thought me a sweet and charming girl - but - if her 'splendid Arch' was not good enough for me - she gave me up. What could I expect? He was not fickle, for the next year after Lord D. became a Marquess he suggested that though I didn't think him up to much it might amuse me to be a countess. 'Too expensive', I said and he explained at length in his stodgy schoolboy way that though of course I should have to be 'presented on my marriage', my wedding dress with a train of family lace would be A.1. and a small tiara that belonged to his beautiful Granny would suit me far more than 'the fender full of shamrocks Mother sports'. His profile was an abiding joy to me and I've always liked Irishmen, but I drew the line at marrying them somehow - four times I drew it - though they were very nice.

Trix in Grecian costume, 1887, aged 19.

Rudyard's fears, expressed in a letter to his cousin, seem to have been groundless:

You being a mere woman can't understand my intense anxiety about the maiden and my jealous care lest she should show signs of being 'touched in the heart'.

It is difficult to understand why he should have been so afraid of marriage for Trix -

I trust her strong sense of humour to keep her on the straight and easy course of unmarried life,

he commented in 1884. Was it jealousy? He admitted,

. . . I promise that unless he is a most superior man, I'll make it desperately uncomfortable for the coming man. . . .

[a promise he fully kept].

I think it more likely that he was thinking of his own comfort, and that, without Trix, life in what would be the family triangle would be insupportable. Under the brilliant, idyllic surface there were considerable stresses.

Life with Alice Kipling could not have been easy. She was witty, quick and lively but also self-willed and volatile. Rudyard says in one of his letters that the main thing is, 'not to flutter the Mother', and Lockwood was unable to stand up against her determination. Other indications of tension can be found in Rudyard's poem, *My Rival* (claimed by Trix to be a joint effort and ostensibly **not** about Trix and her mother), and *Kim*, which is Rudyard's experience of India, 'recollected in tranquillity'. Kim himself is an idealised self-portrait (Ruddy's nickname in early childhood in Bombay was 'little friend of all the world'), the Lama is his much revered father, and the shrill, bustling generous but interfering and exhausting 'woman from Kulu' is a sufficiently disguised portrait of his mother. Kim turns to her for succour of physical needs, food and nursing, but escapes from her constant demands and talk whenever he can. It is also significant that, almost as soon as Rudyard had left the family home to work in Allahabad in the autumn of 1887, he wrote, and published, *Baa, Baa, Black Sheep*.

1887 - 1889

The underlying strains of life in the square may explain why Trix, with so many suitors to choose from, became engaged in the summer of 1887 to John Murchison Fleming, a tall handsome but dour Scot, ten years her senior, an officer in the King's Own Scottish

John Fleming, wearing his Afghan campaign medal.

Borderers, but seconded to the Survey of India. She must have realised how volatile her temperament was, and hoped that marriage with a calm man who adored her would provide a haven from the tensions of being a Kipling. It was an attraction of opposites, and 'Jack' was thought so unsuitable by Lockwood and Rudyard that, by the autumn, the engagement was broken off.

Trix was now the one left behind in the family triangle, and she was extremely miserable. However, by the summer of 1888, with her mother's support, but against the better judgement of Lockwood, Trix and Fleming were engaged again, and were married on her 21st birthday, June 11th 1889 at Simla.

Rudyard, the beloved brother, was in San Francisco. He had written to Margaret, now Mackail, the favourite cousin, in the February:

> . . . *tell me some day what you think of Fleming. He's an unresponsive sort of animal but appears an honest man,*

and to Edmonia Hill, at about the same time (he was planning to leave for America with Prof. and Mrs Hill in March):

> *Trix has been showing me her photo books . . . I daren't tell her that, so far as I can see, when she wasn't taking 'Jack', Jack was taking her and so I breathe it in your private ear. Her fianceé has hung her about with jewelry from pearl necklaces to curb-chain bangles and one - two - three engagement rings . . . I perceive now there is a steady undercurrent of Jack flowing through the house and I gather that the mail is an event. He comes to India on the 22nd of next month. I fancy that I shall begin to see the good points of his nature when the Bay of Bengal and the Straights of Malacca . . . lie between us.*

Undercurrents like these could not have been lost on the hyper-sensitive Trix.

1889 - 1898

Married life in India, and leaves at home with their families.

In 1890, Trix found Rudyard ill from overwork and the stresses of his meteoric success in London, and 'The Family Square' was briefly together again as the parents came back on leave to enjoy his fame.

Trix was still writing, of course, and there are clues to the state of her marriage in the novel, *The Heart of a Maid*, published in 1891 under the pseudonym, Beatrice Grange. (It is No. 8 in A.H. Wheeler's *Indian Railway Library* series. The first six are stories by Rudyard). It is a slight, rather romantic piece about various young women in India, and

Labelled 'Blanefield' 1891. 'Jack' and Trix standing respectively extreme left and right. According to the signatures on the fan, they were at Blanefield on 3rd October 1891, and the signatories are John Coulborough, E.W. Coulborough, and Edith M. Morrison. The man standing in the doorway must be a Fleming brother - the family resemblance is more than just the 'Roberts' moustache - but there is no indication which one (see obituary press cutting) - could Edith Morrison be his 'intended', one of the women in the doorway? And is E.W. Coulborough a married Fleming sister, and John C. the chap in the natty bowler sitting on the step? Pure conjecture about these four, of course!

the men they marry and their motives for doing so. The chief figure, May, who marries to please her parents, has this to say to her husband:

> *Percy, if you were another man and I another woman and neither of us were so perverse, we should get on beautifully.*

The descriptions of the petty irritations of daily life ring so true that they must be autobiographical (although the main plot is not); Percy wants to rub out her pencil annotations in her books because they make them look so untidy, and:

> *He was naturally self-contained and undemonstrative. May would have liked him to be passionate. She had married him not for her own sake, but for his and she wanted assurances from him that his happiness was now perfect, but it seemed to her that his marriage had made very little difference to him . . . Sometimes the very sound of her husband's slow monotonous voice made her clasp her hands together in silent, intense irritation. Half this was purely physical, but it was none the less very real and hard to bear.*

No wonder she had used a nom de plume!

In 1892, Rudyard also married someone his family did not like, Caroline Balestier, the 'good man spoiled' of Lockwood's words and, according to Henry James, who gave the bride away, 'a hard, devoted capable little person'. She was the elder sister of Wolcott Balestier, the rather enigmatic young man with whom Kipling wrote *The Naulahka*, and to whom he was devoted.

Wolcott died shortly before the very hastily arranged wedding. Much has been written about Carrie's personality; all that needs to be noted here is that Lockwood visited the couple frequently, Trix when she could (although usually without her husband), and Alice only occasionally.

After his parents had settled in Tisbury, Wiltshire, in 1893, and once Rudyard and Carrie were back in England after the Vermont interlude (their plan to settle close to Carrie's family having ended in tragi-comic disaster), Rudyard visited his parents alone. Christmas 1897 seems to have been an exception; Trix, Alice and Lockwood were expected at Rottingdean in Sussex, where Rudyard and Carrie were living across the green from the Burne-Jones', Rudyard's favourite aunt and uncle. Carrie, as usual, was making heavy weather of it. 'I am full of labour and preparations', she recorded in her diary.

1897 was also the year that Trix's second novel, *A Pinchbeck Goddess*, appeared. It was published in February by Heinneman (the firm with which Wolcott Balestier had been associated), in their 'Popular 3/6d Novels' series, and reprinted in March. This time she wrote under her own name, and made no attempt to curb her passion for quotation. There are four lines from Shakespeare on the title page, a dedication to Rudyard with six lines of Ben Johnson, slightly adapted, and each of the nineteen chapters is headed by a quotation from authors as diverse as Coleridge, Browning, and Meredith. She is aware of her predilection, however, as one of her characters says,

> *. . . there are eight deadly sins, quotation being the last and worst, especially when one alters the poet's holy writ to suit one's own base ends.*

The main plot is not credible. Madeline, a repressed, sulky woman, past her first youth, is travelling back to England after what her friends had hoped would be a 'fishing trip' for a husband in India. At Suez, she is greeted by the news that her martinet guardian Aunt has died. End of chapter one.

The rest of the book is an account of life in Simla, and the descriptions of parties, gossip, amateur theatricals, picnics, and various successful and unsuccessful love affairs are written in a very lively and entertaining style. The central figure, Winnie, the 'pinchbeck goddess', is a spritely, painted widow with a secret past and dyed hair who, nevertheless, has a kind heart and wins the love of a good man at the end. It then transpires that her red hair is a wig (which even her maid does not suspect!), and that she is in fact Madeline, returned to take revenge on the society which had ignored her in the past.

Apart from this totally implausible plot and a certain amount of whimsy from Winnie, the picture of Indian life rings very true, and there are clues too, I think, to Trix's state of mind. One of the women, Lilian, is married to a silent control freak who feels he has to 'punish' his wife by refusing to speak to her for days on end. When she breaks down on Winnie's sofa, she says:

> *Who is there for an unhappy woman to confide in if she breaks down and has not strength enough to keep her troubles to herself? . . . It wouldn't be fair to tell my own people, for they really love me and it would make them unhappy; besides, they would be prejudiced against Gilbert, and that would hurt me, and my husband's family would say it was all my own fault. . . I would not mind if our quarrels were about serious matters but they are about such silly things, and mere trifles lead to terrible consequences. We don't speak the same language, he and I.*

This passage and almost the whole of chapter 10, 'Black's the life I lead wi' you', are a moving description of two people, fond of each other yet quite incapable of understanding or helping the other. In the book, harmony is restored when Lilian finds herself pregnant, but in real life things were very different.

General Sir Ian Hamilton, signed 1892, was one of Trix's dancing partners during the Simla Season of 1886.

1898 - 1902

Trix's first bout of mental illness (a nervous breakdown in modern parlance?) began in the autumn of 1898. Writing in April 1910 to his brother-in-law, Dr Theodore Dunham, whose wife was suffering in the same way at that time, Rudyard says:

> *. . . some years ago, my sister went through a couple of years of the deepest melancolia and depression, brought on by the gradual wearing out of nerve resistance . . . The silence and the brooding, the stone rigidity, the obsession of the fixed idea, recurring when one begins to hope that the mind has cleared, is not a thing to speak of save to one who has had to watch it in his dearest.*
>
> *You of course know the pathology of the trouble and how to deal with it. We did not, and so time was lost while we let it cure itself. The thing passed, like an evil dream, and left no more trace behind than any other trouble of flesh and bone . . .*

[Ironically, it was to recur in the November of that year].

Trix returned in her distress to her parents at Tisbury, and Rudyard, in spite of what he says in the letter above, **did** attempt to get treatment for his sister. That Alice was the stumbling block to prompt care for Trix is made clear in Rudyard's letter of November 18th 1898 to his uncle Alfred Baldwin:

> *Dear Uncle Alfred,*
>
> *You've been married to a Macdonald for some time and I've been the son of one for a few years. They do not strike ME as a very pliable breed. However - this is what we arrived at. On the 22nd inst. (not before) my mother comes up to town and with Trix goes into retreat at the Royal Palace Hotel for three weeks while Colenso and a masseuse work over her and she is dosed and dieted and generally looked after. I tried to forestall the date but found that it didn't suit mother's arrangements*
> *. . . If she does not kill herself before the 22nd we shall at least have the satisfaction of knowing that she will then seriously enter upon the care of herself. I shall take steps then to introduce a specialist, because though I do not know precisely what kind of ass Colenso may be, I incline to think he is many varieties . . . The main point is not to flutter the mother . . . This gives you the situation up to date; and bless you for setting the machinery in motion.*

Four interesting points emerge from this letter:

(a)   Trix was obviously in deep depression. (Her maternal grandmother also suffered from it, although probably triggered in her case by constant child-bearing, too little money and the demands made on the wife of a peripatetic Methodist minister).

(b)   Nothing and no one could move Alice Kipling.

(c)   Rudyard's reaction to R.F.Colenso. He was presumably the doctor consulted by Fleming, as there are letters from him dated December 1898 among the Macdonald papers. Trix seems to have been in a clinic in London by this time, but being uncooperative, refusing to eat or be examined etc. At this time, Colenso was making two daily visits but only charging for one - a fee of half a guinea a day.

(d)   Rudyard turned for practical help to Alfred Baldwin, married to his mother's younger sister, Louisa. After the birth of their only child, Stanley, she was an invalid, suffering from back trouble for many years. She took frequent cures, at home and abroad, and seemed to improve considerably when staying with her sister Georgie in London. The Baldwins were knowledgeable about doctors.

It is not known exactly how long Trix stayed in London, but by March 1899 she was back in Tisbury, and by July her father reports her back to normal in a letter to an American friend.

This report, however, was premature, and a letter to Fleming from Dr N.R.Gowers (presumably called in after Colenso), dated November 15th 1899, reports his lack of success. He says he had arranged for an experienced lady companion for Trix (Miss Ross, who stayed for two months), and:

> *. . . I was very anxious that the two should have gone away together and tried various ways to secure this, but to no purpose. Mrs. Kipling was on the verge of frenzy at any suggestion of such a thing and Mr. Kipling, though ready to be firm when he was with me, yielded before his wife's excitement at once . . .*
> *PS. I have delayed posting this until I had seen Miss Ross who has called on me on her way back from Tisbury . . . Mrs. Kipling is exercising constant restraint on her nervous manner and your wife is maintaining her stability and is, I should think, now in her normal state . . . with such companionship for cycling as can be secured for her.*

Trix's condition continued to fluctuate for the next eighteen months, but, in May 1901, Rudyard reported her quite well again, and, in September 1902, she returned to Calcutta and normal life with her husband.

It was probably at this period, before her return to India but while she was recovering, that she wrote the monologues included in this book. They are not dated, but they are labelled Tisbury, and she was certainly writing during these years. Her third novel, *Her Brother's Keeper*, was published by Longman in 1901 (although I have not been able to trace a copy), and the joint book of poems with her mother, *Hand in Hand*, appeared in 1902.

At this point, it seems appropriate to discuss the question of Trix's psychic powers and her lifelong interest in the occult. Her husband and Rudyard (for once in agreement) thought it contributed to her illnesses and disapproved very strongly. Rudyard, sharing the descent from the Macdonalds of the Isles, was not a sceptic (one has only to read, *They*), but was terrified of introspection and too frightened to dabble.

Fleming seems to have regarded it as noxious rubbish, but Trix enjoyed her 'gift' and for many years was in contact with the Society for Psychical Research in London and, in later life, was a member of the Edinburgh Psychic College. She kept her correspondence with the S.P.R. secret from her family, writing under the name of Mrs Holland until everyone who objected to her activities was dead, when she allowed her own name to be published. *The Journal and Proceedings of the Society* contain a large number of examples of her automatic scripts and cross-correspondence with other Automatists (she usually in India, and they in the British Isles), a lengthy paper on the subject by Alice Johnson, and critical replies by other Society members. Her work was taken very seriously by the experts, and she was active in the production of scripts between 1903 and 1910.

A letter to Alice Johnson, dated September 14th 1903, explains how she began and what the process entailed:

> *. . . Ten years ago I first tried automatic writing, having seen a reference to it in, I think, the 'Review of Reviews'. My hand began to form words almost immediately, but only short sentences of an uninteresting kind, and the questions I asked were not answered.*
>
> *The next time I tried (these attempts were always made when I was alone), verses were written and since then, though I have often discontinued the practice for months and years, and tried to give it up altogether, and automatic writing that comes to me is nearly always in verse, headed:*
>
> *'Believe in what thou canst not see,*
> *Until the vision come to thee.'*

The verses, though often childishly simple in wording and jingling in rhyme, are rarely trivial in subject. Their striking feature is the rapidity with which they come. I once wrote down fourteen poems in little over an hour, another time ten, and seven or eight are quite a common number to come at one time. When I write original verse I do so slowly and carefully with frequent erasures; automatic verse is always as if swiftly dictated and there are never any erasures. I am always fully conscious, but my hand moves so rapidly that I seldom know what words it is forming.

Unfortunately, none of these verses seems to have survived and the sceptic may say that to produce ten or so childish jingles in an hour is not very remarkable for someone so steeped in language and literature, but it is clear that she was not in any way frightened by the phenomenon.

However, later in the same letter she discusses automatic letters, and here the picture is rather different:

I have said that automatic verses do not deal much with facts, but once, when I was sensitive after illness I experienced a new form of automatic writing, in the shape of letters which my hand insisted on writing to a newly-made acquaintance.

The first of these letters began with a pet name I did not know, and was signed with the full name of some one I had never heard of, and who I afterwards learnt had been dead for some years. It was clearly impressed upon me for whom the letter was intended, but thinking it due to some unhealthy fancy of my own, I destroyed it. Having done so I was punished by an agonising headache, and the letter was repeated, till in self defence I sent it and the succeeding ones to their destination.

They generally came when I was trying to write ordinary letters; I never 'sat for them' or encouraged them in any way. I never read them over, feeling they were not meant for me . . .

As I regained perfect health I tried to free myself of this influence, for it used to give me cruel headaches and was very exhausting. I have often left my writing table and taken up needlework or knitting until the force had spent itself. If my hand was not actively employed at these times it would clench itself, and make the motion of writing in the air.

Since then I have felt on three other occasions that some unseen but very present personality was striving to transmit a message through me to a well-beloved. In every case the communication was utterly unsought by me, and came as a complete surprise to the recipient, who was always a recent acquaintance, never one of my friends. My attention was always enforced, as it were, by a severe pain in the head, which vanished when I had delivered the message . . .

Since I have spoken of illness, perhaps I ought to say that I have only twice been ill in the last twenty years, and am now a healthy cheerful woman, thirty five years of age. I prize my health and strength exceedingly, and it puzzles me a little that with it, and with no desire to consider myself exceptional, I do sometimes see, hear, feel, or otherwise become conscious of beings and influences that are not patent to all. Is this a frame of mind to be checked, or permitted, or encouraged? I should like so much to know. My own people hate what they call 'uncanniness', so I am obliged to hide from them the keen interest I cannot help feeling in psychic matters.

I have never been in surroundings that encourage this interest, I have never been mesmerised, I have never attended a seance, for the idea of anything connected with paid mediumship is peculiarly disagreeable to me. I only discovered by accident, five years ago, that I have the clairvoyant faculty.

This letter has been quoted at length because it not only shows Trix's own feelings, but gives clues to what was going on around her. If what she says is true, it suggests that the family had not been involved, in India or at home, with the fashionable interest in the supernatural - Lockwood, who had met Madame Blavatsky in India, was openly sceptical, and Rudyard firmly against dabbling - and this letter suggests that Alice too was against it. Trix may not have kept her activities as secret as she thought, and anything which caused her daughter pain would not have had Alice's support.

It is interesting that the automatic letters were only for acquaintances. Throughout her life, Trix seems to have had the gift of inspiring friendship; was this an unconscious way of getting to know new people? It would be interesting to know who these three recipients were.

The letter also points to another cause of stress and friction in her personal life; she longs to be reassured that there is nothing harmful in the activities which she finds interesting but which those around her condemn. Contrary to what her family thought, it does not seem that her interest in the supernatural contributed to her breakdowns, except insofar as it produced tension between her and those she loved.

In later life, when she had completely recovered from her illness and was living happily with her husband in Edinburgh, she was still pursuing her interest with, apparently, no ill effects.

1902 - 1910

These years were spent in India with her husband, based mainly in Calcutta, and in England, Scotland, and Europe on home leaves. In September 1903, they were in Scotland, planning a trip to Italy; in March 1905, she was at Tisbury, preparing to go to Spain with Fleming; and in 1908, Trix left India for the last time, as her husband's army service was coming to an end, although he didn't reach England until 1910.

Letters from Alice Kipling, written to various friends and relations throughout these years, reiterate how much she still missed her daughter, even after 21 years of separation. In October 1909, Alice was diagnosed as having Graves Disease (hyperthyroidism) and parting from her daughter in the following year must have been particularly hard. Trix and her husband were in Edinburgh by August 1910.

Trix and Lieut. Col. Fleming, as he now was, lived at 8 Napier Road, probably the family home as it was leased until 1916 by Mrs Catherine Fleming (presumably his mother), and thereafter belonged to him until sold in 1919. The Fleming family seems to have been in Edinburgh and the Borders, and Trix may have found domestic harmony hard to maintain with her husband's disapproving relatives so close at hand. This period of her life did not last long. In November 1910, a few months after Rudyard had written to his American brother-in-law that Trix had been fit and well for years, she was knocked completely off balance by the death of her mother.

1910 - 1919

(The information on this period is based largely on a record in Col. Fleming's handwriting. It seems to have been written at one time, after the events it describes, perhaps transcribed from diaries, as an aide-memoire and perhaps to refute the entries in Trix's own notebook - of which more below).

Trix left Edinburgh on November 19th and was at Tisbury when her mother died on November 23rd. Fleming came down for the funeral on the 25th and called in the first of many doctors, Dr Lang, on the following day. From November 28th until December 5th, the Flemings seem to have been in Salisbury although no reason is given. Perhaps Fleming thought his wife would be better away from the cramped conditions and depressing circumstances of 'The Gables', or he may have taken her to see Dr R.C. Monnington at Laverstock.

He returned her to Tisbury on December 5th and went to London himself but was recalled on December 12th as Trix had completely collapsed. What followed was a pattern that was to be repeated over the next ten years or so of her fluctuating illness. Her husband and her family disagreed over the care she should have, and Fleming, naturally wanting to look after his wife, found himself more and more sidelined as

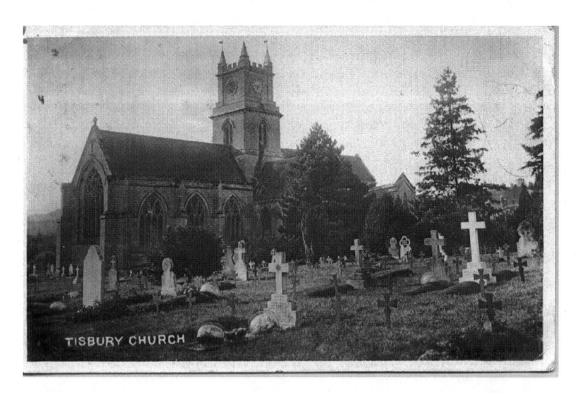

TISBURY CHURCH

Postcard of Tisbury Church, sent by Alice Kipling to her daughter Trix on 22nd November 1906.
It arrived in Calcutta on 9th December. Notice that no message was allowed on overseas mail.

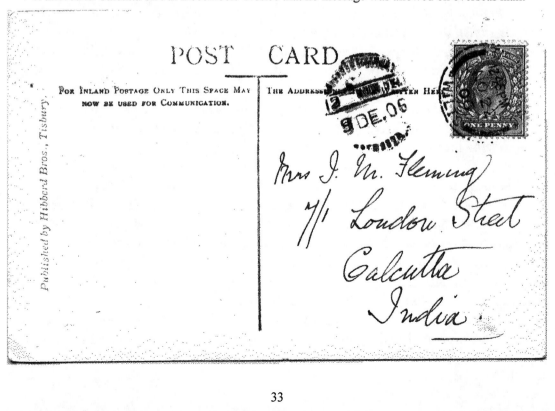

POST CARD

FOR INLAND POSTAGE ONLY THIS SPACE MAY NOW BE USED FOR COMMUNICATION.

THE ADDRESS

Published by Hibberd Bros., Tisbury.

9 DE. 06

ONE PENNY

Mrs J. M. Fleming
7/1 London Street
Calcutta
India

doctors suggested by Macdonalds and their friends were called in. (In December 1913, he complains that he has been inveigled into meeting a Dr Munro at the home of Burne-Jones' daughter). By December 20th, it had been decided that Trix should stay with her father, and Fleming left unwillingly, hoping that a nurse would be brought in. With hindsight, this arrangement seems to have been more for Lockwood's comfort than Trix. An undated letter from Dr J.P. Williams-Freeman of Weyhill House, Andover, to Fleming was probably written about this time; in it he suggests replacing the existing nurse with a more educated woman, sympathises with Fleming's wish to have Trix with him, and promises to make room for her if in the future she needs a quiet place to recuperate. Letters from Rudyard to Lockwood in January 1911 show how little sympathy the Kipling men had for her husband:

> *Your last two in - notably the second with the news about the Nurse, who seems to be satisfactory; and the still more satisfactory news that there seems to be reasonable hope of a good place for T. to meditate in at Andover . . . (since 'tis not I who have to bear the brunt of carking Jack!) make me more cheered. But I can imagine the desolation of daily letters (such men leak daily) from that sleeplessly cantankerous invalid. Blowed if I see though what can be done. There's no law to forbid a man writing, or advising, about his wife: all one can be thankful for is that he don't assert all his rights. But I conceive that a reasoned plan, such as T. going to Andover, plainly set forth, ought to ease him and for a while keep him quiet. He must have some sort of idea that he ought to do something - and since worrying comes easiest, why he worries the nearest thing in sight! When T. is away he might be led, by medical advice, to look after his own precious health in the south of Europe for 3 or 4 months. . . As you say, there's no restraint needed. It's change and firm sympathy the poor child wants but above all change, and - low be it spoken - the assurance that J. will not descend on her and tell her to 'pull herself together.' Here's hoping and praying that the new nurse will secure her confidence.*

Trix did move to Andover, on January 13th 1911, but Lockwood's death at the end of the month set her back again, and when her husband went to visit her on February 1st, the day after her father's funeral, he found her 'shrunk and wandering'. This was probably the absolute low point of her breakdown as, at the beginning of March, Fleming was making out papers for the Lunacy Board, presumably because she was too ill to manage her own affairs. The pattern of the next few years, whereby he was only allowed to visit her briefly every few months, had been established.

There are no contemporary records of what Trix felt then, but a later notebook records that she felt orphaned and deserted by both Fleming and Rudyard, and that death would have been preferable. Letters in 1944 and 1945 to J.H.C.Brooking, moving spirit and founder member of the Kipling Society, return to this theme; she finds it inexplicable that her husband should have left her - she was only 42 and they had been on normal, affectionate terms, and even more inexplicable that her brother, with a daughter of his own, should allow insanity to be imputed to a member of his family. She also accuses Rudyard of destroying some of her papers when he was destroying Alice's papers, and also of destroying, after Lockwood's death, a will that left everything to Trix, deliberately drawn up to prevent anything falling into Carrie's hands. There is no way of telling if this is true. Rudyard's propensity for destroying papers is well known, and there was little love lost between Carrie and Alice and Trix. Some of Trix's later memories are certainly inaccurate but, while her brother and husband still lived, she may have been inhibited from expressing her true feelings, although Fleming's record may have been compiled to justify himself against her accusations.

Throughout 1911, Trix remained at Weyhill, near Andover in Hampshire, and her husband visited her on average once a month. There is no indication of how he passed his time, but he refers to returning from Plymouth in July. Letters to him at the beginning of July from Dr G.A.Savage of 26 Devonshire Place, refer to having seen Trix ten years earlier and holding out hope that this time too, patience and restful conditions will eventually effect a cure. He suggests periodic short visits by Fleming and cautious handling for the next year or two, when she returns to normal life, because of her critical age. By November, Trix seemed much improved, and, by mid-December, Fleming is in contact with a Lady Paget (perhaps wife of Sir James Paget who treated Louisa Baldwin). That he was hoping to transfer his wife to Scotland - into his own sphere of influence, perhaps - is suggested by entries for January and April 1912 when he looked at asylums at Craighouse and Dumfries, and 'places' at Dollar and Kingussie.

He visited Trix twice in January, when she seemed to be still improving, but by February the Paget-Kipling-Macdonald faction was pressing for her to be transferred to the care of a Dr Munro in London. In April, Rudyard and Carrie motored over to Weyhill, but after Fleming's May visit he reports her worse again, and after consulting Clouston (another mental specialist?), it was decided that Trix should stay at Weyhill for the summer. In June, she was well enough to go for a four week visit to Sir James and Lady Walker at Worplesdon. She was accompanied by a nurse/companion, Miss Stickles or Stickler (Fleming's writing is small and difficult to decipher). Back at Weyhill, Fleming found her unchanged at the beginning of September; a fortnight at Lyme Regis, in Dorset, brought little improvement. Trix finally left Weyhill on October 10th to stay again with the Walkers. Fleming joined her there on the 25th, and two days later she was examined by yet another doctor, Robertson, with, as Fleming says, 'little result'.

November 1912 saw the beginning of what was to be the pattern of Trix's life for the next seven years; constant moving from place to place for shorter or longer periods, always with a nurse, sometimes with her husband, sometimes with friends, in hotels, lodgings or private houses, and with fluctuating mental state.

In November, Trix and Miss Stickles sailed for Jersey, and when Fleming arrived in February 1913, Trix had put on weight and seemed better. (I have been unable to find out why Jersey was chosen. There might have been a family connection - her uncle, Frederic Macdonald was at school there for a year in 1856 - but this is conjecture).

On February 19th, Miss Stickles was replaced as nurse/companion by Mrs Postle (who may have been a native of Jersey), who remained with Trix at least until 1919 and perhaps until she had no further need of such an attendant in the 1920s. The rest of this year saw Trix at York in June, and at Scarborough in July, where Rudyard visited her. They walked on the beach together and he found her so much better that he planned to take a house in Norfolk in the autumn where she could visit. This plan came to nothing because his son John contracted mumps at that time.

In September, Trix was at Harrow, in October, Fleming visited her at Sudbury, and families called Kemp, King, and Divers, and a Miss Holt are mentioned.

In 1914, Trix was at Hazelmere and Sudbury in February and March, returned to Jersey at the end of March and, when her husband saw her again in June, had relapsed and was most unpleasant to him when they were alone. (If, as her notebook suggests, she felt she had been exiled, this is not surprising). In October, Trix and Mrs Postle returned to London, and a Dr Bartlett was called in; a week later, she saw Dr Maurice Craig of 87 Harley Street. He must have recommended stout to increase her weight and fitness because a note exists from Craig to Fleming, agreeing that Trix could have burgundy instead if she does not care for stout!

By November, the outbreak of the Great War was altering circumstances, and Fleming was considering re-joining the army. Two letters from Rudyard to him explain the situation. (Rudyard's letters begin, 'Dear Fleming', and end, 'Sincerely yours, Rudyard Kipling.'!) He wrote on November 11th 1914

> *. . . I quite understand that at the present crisis . . . you should be anxious to make arrangements which will enable you to serve.*

He then goes on to suggest that Dr Craig should suggest somewhere for Trix within motoring distance of 'Bateman's'.

> *It seems to me a somewhat better arrangement than your suggestion of an asylum . . .*

Then on December 3rd

> *I have been away from home almost constantly since your letter of 13th. Nov. came . . . I have made several trips to town to see Trix and the last time I saw her she went for a drive with me and seemed much brighter.*
>
> *I am anxious to hear what Dr. Craig thinks of her when he sees her next and greatly hope he will be able to assure you that there is no necessity for taking so extreme a step as putting her in an asylum - the more so since you realize that she herself would resent it.*
>
> *I feel that sending her to an asylum would definitely close all hope of her recovery. I should like to say that my offer to look after Trix is always open.*
>
> *It never occurred to me that you would return to field soldiering. I suppose that your Survey experience would be of the greatest value to the W.O. and I take it that it is only a matter of time when the W.O. will realize this.*

Either the good sense of this letter prevailed, or the War Office refused his services; there is no further mention of asylum or war service. In December, Fleming records Trix as unchanged but pleased to see him.

Trix seems to have been staying at the Hereford Hotel all this time, but March 1915 appears to have been some sort of turning point. Fleming, having lost confidence in Craig (he reports 'the usual drivel' on March 8th) moved Trix to 21 Portman Street on March 22nd, and on the 24th took her to the Public Trustee who passed her (presumably as fit to look after her own affairs again, although this is not specifically stated).

In May, Trix was first at Worplesdon, then Carlisle and Keswick, where she had rooms at 24 Alexandra Street. Mrs Postle took a month off in Jersey in July, and in October Trix and Mrs Postle removed to 11 Derby Road, Blackpool. Fleming took charge of the later moves, and in each case found his wife thin, peevish and distant.

In November, there is a reference to Mary being with them at Blackpool, and this was probably Mary Sinclair, one of the 'prickly pear' (sic), Mary and Mina, the servants who stayed with Trix for over twenty years.

There are fewer entries in the record for 1916. In February, Fleming visited Blackpool and found his wife much more human.

In June, she returned to Edinburgh for a week, and then Fleming installed the ménage at 10 Alexandra Place, St Andrews.

In September, she cut off her hair in a fit of temper, and was very obstreperous. A few days later, a Dr Huntingdon considered her to be normal. She was also gaining weight at the end of this year.

By February 1917, Trix appeared to be on an even enough keel to return to her husband at 8 Napier Road, Edinburgh (the family home which he had inherited on his mother's death in 1916), but it was a false dawn. There are no entries in the record until the end of August, but they must have been a very difficult six months for everyone. The thyroid treatment she had been having (it is not made clear who first prescribed it), had been stopped, and there was talk again of a home for Trix. The situation was serious enough to stir Rudyard and Carrie to go to Edinburgh for a family conference, and it was decided that Trix should go for an extended visit to Bateman's, staying in Dudwell Farm, up the lane.

On September 19th, Fleming saw Trix, Mrs Postle, and Louise (another servant?) off to Dudwell.

The tale is picked up in Carrie's diary and letters. She wrote to her mother:

Trix . . . and her nurse are to come for three months and occupy the farmhouse. . . to see what the change and contact with fresh scenes and people will do. She is better but still so very far from well that I dread the visit and the extra work involved but must put it through.

Three days after Trix's arrival, she writes again:

It was thought that a milder climate and different scenes might help her and R. has more influence with her than anyone else. Her trouble now, whatever else it has been, seems to be simple hysteria and hope is at this critical year of her life when the change is finishing she may just pull round and get the better of it.

Some days later, writing again to her mother, her view has changed somewhat:

Rud and I go daily to see Trix who has settled down and enjoyed her first week . . . She is not interested in much except her self but we hope to improve that.

By September 30th, disenchantment has set in:

Trix Fleming is going to be a heavy additional burden. There is nothing in the world the matter with her except selfishness and self centredness carried to the Nth, and she does not, poor thing, see where that will lead.

Jealousy probably inspired this bitter comment; Rudyard and Trix enjoyed daily walks together while Carrie laboured. At the end of November, Fleming received a letter from Rudyard saying that he needed the house for other guests after Christmas and, after further prompting in February 1918, the ménage moved to 11 Rutland Gate, Blackpool, on March 12th. A month later, they returned to 8 Napier Street in a snowstorm! Mrs Postle and the servant are reported as performing wonders in spite of burst pipes etc.

Trix's passport, renewed on 23rd September 1919.

Nothing more is reported until July, but domestic life was not running smoothly. Trix appears to have fluctuated between fractious screaming fits and spending all day asleep. In November, she was smashing glass and hurling hatpins. The next entry is for the end of May 1919, when Fleming saw them off to stay with a Mrs Calderhead at 'Carradale', Pitlochrie. They returned on June 26th, and on July 12th, Trix smashed up her rings (presumably the ones Fleming had given her during their courtship). This seems to have been the last straw, for by August he had sold the Napier Street house, and was en route for Jersey. Trix and Mrs Postle went back to St Andrews.

The record ends at this point, and the only indication of where Trix was until 1925 (when Fleming is listed as the owner of 6 West Coates, Edinburgh), are brief entries in her notebook claiming exile in 1920 and 1921. For 1924, the entry is:

> *T'is but the shadow of a wife you see,*
> *The name but not the thing.*

which suggests that she was back from St Andrews (or Jersey) by 1923, but still living apart from her husband. Still the peripatetic life, perhaps, until she was well enough to join him. For she did recover, and they lived amicably together until his death in 1942.

On May 25th 1932, when they lunched at Bateman's, Carrie noted 'Trix quite herself' while Rudyard found her 'unmarked by Time, fresh and witty as ever.' The relationship between brother and sister was resumed as before; he asked her for ideas for plots, warned her against putting on weight, swapped quotations, suggested books she would enjoy and, also in 1932, warned her of the miseries of dentures, as he had had all his teeth out eleven years before.

1925 - 1948

In the pre-war years, records are sparse. She seems to have settled into a domestic routine of family, friends, gardening, the Edinburgh Psychic College, and the animals at the zoo. In December 1935, there were worries about Fleming's health, and Rudyard wrote (he seems to have mellowed with time):

> *I'm grieved to hear about Jack, but the habit of keeping fit helps a man to get over much even when he's elderly. Only - somehow or other - men never realise how their natural strength is abated. Bed's the only palliative I know for an obstructed (?) heart.*

After Rudyard's death in 1936, she talked and wrote enthusiastically about their early life together, and wholeheartedly supported the formation of the Kipling Society.

Rudyard and his wife Carrie at St Margaret's, Westminster, for the wedding
of their daughter, Elsie, in October 1924.

A letter, dated March 1945, to her cousin Stanley Baldwin shows how determined she was that the record should be accurate:

> . . . *I'm so glad to hear from Elsie that you are 'doing' Rud in the D.N.B. [Dictionary of National Biography] . . . Please mention and destroy the 'black blood' and the 'below the salt' legends which still lift Hydra heads at times. It's ugly lying and should be done away with, not ignored.*
>
> *Quite lately, some one, grubbing among old Indian newspapers proclaimed as a discovery that, as R.K. and his sister both acted in Simla they must have been members of the exclusive Amateur Dramatic Co. there and therefore must have moved in the upper circles. Of course we did - of course we went everywhere.*

She goes on to describe how full their Simla 'seasons' were, and interjects some personal details:

> *I annoy my doctor by weighing 101 lbs. and losing about a stone yearly - but I feel so well and walk 5 miles with pleasure and 'eat like an augur' so what does it matter if I do look like an écorchée? I'm so lucky to be able to keep my house and the same servants - 21 years - but it's very poor fun to be a widow - 77 years is an over large helping of life . . .*

and then returns to her main theme:

> *Please emphasise that it would be difficult to find two families more free from any link or connection with India than the Macdonalds or the Kiplings . . . the 4 annas in the rupee legend of duskiness or the black blood slander of later years - Rud used to laugh at this - but a strange American woman gripped me in an opera box once and rubbed my bare neck so hard with her black gloved hand that red streaks followed it - 'Oh, it doesn't come off!' she said in a disappointed voice, looking at her glove. 'You see everyone said your brother had black blood, so when I saw you sitting there looking so white, I thought I must just see!' I have never been so angry. And in 1914 a woman in a London hotel where I was staying trumpeted abroad that R.K. was an 'old Eurasian', and Mrs Fleming's complexion meant nothing for 'lots of Afghans had blue eyes and there was always liquid powder.'*
>
> *It's an ugly legend but in spite of the Kipling Society it still crops up . . . Jealousy started it . . .*

Trix and Jack Fleming in June 1932

The outbreak of the Second World War brought changes, and a letter to Rudyard's surviving child, Elsie Bambridge (then living at Wimpole Hall in Cambridgeshire), shows Trix at her liveliest and best:

. . . as a 'woman citizen' I've been helping to write names and addresses and figures on Ration Books - and though we (1500 of us, and a few men) did our job in half the time expected, one day was spoilt by alarms and excursions - down 89 steps to the basement - and a long wait, cheered only by tea. We are in Minto House - university building in Chambers St. - opposite the now closed Museum. Having led a sheltered life in Jersey and St. Andrews last time, it was my first glimpse of an air raid and I was glad to find I had no 'Eek-a-reeka-ree' feeling. It's so trying when one's body plays one false. One woman only fainted - and two in the street. Monday's real raid on the Forth was unrecognised -

> *'When war guns thundered in the hills,*
> *We said "It's not a raid*
> *For listen - not one siren trills*
> *We need not be afraid.*
> *Our trusty wardens never nod,*
> *Come risk, they'll warn us soon."*
> *And this was odd, because it was*
> *A sunny afternoon.'*

I was sitting with Jack after lunch - seeing that he 'rested' till 3.30 - and thought the big guns were a railway accident, and he (knowing well what they were) tactfully agreed with me. Meanwhile Mary and Meena bringing in the washing from the back green were fascinated by 3 small planes fighting a big one - 'some of the shells burst into figures of 3 some just like lyres.'

They only knew after that the 'splendid practice' was real. We had some kind offers of country quarters from both relatives and friends but what's the good of a detached old fashioned stone built house if you can't stay quietly in it. Tweeny sleeps downstairs now instead of up at the top - and we have sand and water and shovels on each floor - and the servants ask nothing better than to stay on - and have put me to shame by the amount of khaki knitting they have already done . . . We should be very tired of the black out if being tired did any good. Ten days ago I was given a dog - a dear little cocker - the colour of autumn bracken. Her name is Ryan, I don't know why. Praps it was one of the titles of her princely pa. Her own missis died five months ago and the poor little beast's joy at being owned and petted again is touching to see. For the first 3 nights she

Street photograph of Jack and Trix Fleming, undated but probably 1930s. It is likely that it was taken in Edinburgh, and that it is a good likeness of each of them.

used to wake with a start and leave her rug and cushion by the window to pad softly to my bedside and assure herself, by deep sniffs, that she had not been deserted again. Now I hang an old coat within reach and that does just as well. She has perfect house manners and at present eats dog biscuit and green vegs. with avidity. She takes me country walks - the ones Jack and I used to go before he had one lame knee and two bad feet. He can only manage a mile in to Club or shops now - and that very slowly. I used to think 10 years younger was a perfect difference - now I would we were both 76. [They were 71 and 81].

You are in lovely country, are you not? Father used to talk of it - and exquisite old houses I remember.

All my love,

Your Trix

In June 1940, writing to Elsie again, after Carrie's death, she is surprisingly critical of her brother, worried about her husband's health and still interested in everyone's doings (see also the Appendix for a copy of a letter to Florence Macdonald about Carrie):

How wonderful to see that black MS book again! I think Mother gave it to him when she went back to India in 1881 - he had it at the U.S.Col. and it was known and loved by me when I was 13 or 14. I'm so glad it has escaped the frenzy of burning any letters and papers connected with his youth - (and mine too, alas!) which possessed him directly after Mother's death - perhaps your Mother kept it hidden away . . .

'Ungkel Jack' has been having a miserable time with eyes - in spite of obeying all the best eye doctor and oculist here tell him. He hates his new glasses and complains of constant 'jitterbugs' that curl from pages when he reads. It's partly, I think, the result of long depression and anxiety and the misery of feeling 'like a log in a backwater', but at 82 one must be content to take things quietly . . .

Of her great nephews now in the Forces, she writes:

And one used to tuck them up in bed and take them to the pantomime and gently suggest a ginger snap instead of a fifth or sixth cream bun!

and on the vexed question of billeting:

your stately halls could I think take in a regt. without inconvenience - but do you find it upsets your household? I hope you still have that charming old butler who lent me a fountain pen . . . I hope you and George are as well as can be expected in these terrible days.

By October 1942, Jack is clearly very ill (he died later that year) but she writes as wittily as ever about her family and domestic problems:

Dearest Elsie,

. . . I forget if I wrote to you of my good fortune in finding a nice little Nurse Attendant who comes nightly about 9.30 and is alert and kind and helpful . . . she lives out, so does not clash with that prickly pear Mina and Mary, and paralysed old gentlemen are her strong suit. I have had her since August and my weight has gone up . . . and I feel twenty years younger. Jack is suffering from a heavy cold - the gift of his sister who 'does not believe in infection' and therefore scatters it freely . . . She is a handsome, headstrong 85 and her last illness was mumps in 1868.

[Moona Richardson, who lived just round the corner in Eglinton Crescent.]

In 1943, perhaps finding time hanging heavily after her husband's death, she took on the lease of a shop in Kelso, on the corner of Roxburgh Street and Union Street, which she held until her death in 1948. The shop was called 'Gifts and Gratitude', and was intended to raise funds for army charities. She had a shop manager, but enjoyed working in it herself.

At an age when many women would have been content to slow down, she seems to have been ever more active and involved with the world around her. Perhaps she felt she should make up for the lost years.

Looking back, with the benefit of our improved knowledge of hormone therapy and the damage done by the 'dysfunctional family', it seems tragic that so many people were made so miserable for so long; Trix's deep-seated resentment of her perceived treatment by husband and brother is very clear. Most women have felt the need to throw things, and nearly everyone has been told to 'snap out of it' at one time or another, but the hyper-sensitive Trix also had to contend with being torn apart by her affection for her husband and his relatives, and her love for her own family, none of whom made any secret of their mutual dislike. Her childlessness was a deep source of sorrow, and being passed from hand to hand, from pillar to post, from doctor to doctor, while her loved ones quarrelled over her treatment, were additional burdens. It seems clear that the primary cause of her condition was hormonal (a fact grasped by some of the doctors) as,

6 West Coates, Edinburgh, bought by John Fleming in 1925. He and Trix lived happily together after her recovery until his death in 1942. She then remained there, with her loyal Mary and Meena, until her death in 1948.

The shop in Roxburgh Street, Kelso, which Trix leased from 1943 until 1948 for her 'Gifts and Gratitude' fund-raising business.

by her mid-fifties, she had quite recovered, but it seems to have been aggravated by insensitive handling.

She died at home at 6 West Coates, Edinburgh, on October 25th 1948. One has only to read Gwladys Cox's memoir to realise that the family and friends who survived her all remembered her with deep love and affection.

It is typical of her love for living things, and her essentially joyous and hopeful personality, that for her funeral service, in St. Mary's Cathedral, on October 28th, she stipulated, 'No flowers, no mourning.'

Undated photograph by Edinburgh Picture News, captioned in Trix's handwriting -
"Loretto 'wolf cubs' at Carberry Towers - all under 11. Oh are you really R.K.'s sister?
How topping! Do be photoed with us -"
(Photograph shows how petite she was.)

Trix.
Gattonside
Melrose
1892

Photograph glued on to the first page of the red folder. See note opposite.

"AUNT TRIX"

MRS. ALICE MACDONALD FLEMING

Some Recollections[1]

by

GWLADYS COX

---

[1] The original document is 78 pages of carbon copy typescript, punched with three holes and bound with red cord into a red folder. The poor quality of the carbon copies meant it was unsuitable for facsimile reproduction, but we have laid out the pages roughly as the document, together with the punctuation, underlining, and spelling etc. of the original typescript prepared by Gwladys Cox.

I grudge the time that I must spend
   On things that do not matter.
Visiting and the notes I send.
   Shopping and dress and chatter.
Could I lie on the grass all day
   For one long perfect season
I might learn what the linnets say
   And how the roses reason.

               A.M. Fleming
          A Daughter to her Mother
            Hand - in - Hand

I

The fine, open-work, iron bell-pull of the old house, The Grange,
Fulham, one day quietly pealed.   A visitor had called to enquire,
not for its one-time owner, Samuel Richardson of Pamela, Clarissa
and Grandison fame, but for a baby girl, who was born there in
1868. A remarkable baby girl. She was Alice Macdonald, the
daughter of Alice and John Lockwood Kipling, who with their
three year old son, Rudyard, home on leave from India, were
staying with Alice Kipling's sister, Georgiana Burne-Jones.

The Burne-Jones family had moved into The Grange the
year before, and from then on, a loving welcome awaited all
visitors, particularly children.   In years to come, when the
house passed out of the possession of the family, Rudyard
Kipling, on acquiring a home of his own begged for, and was
given, that bell-pull, for his entrance, "in the hope that other
children, also, might feel happy when they rang it".   It hangs
today in the porch of his home, Bateman's, Burwash.

So the little girl, soon to be called "Trix", "because she was
such a tricksy little thing", although fated to bear full measure
of sorrow, and, early, at that, was born into a happy home.

Alice and John Lockwood Kipling, with the two children,
then, returned to India, and when Rudyard was six and Trix
three, they were brought back to England and remained some
years in Southsea.   It was usual, in those days, for young
children to be sent home from the tropics but the experience
proved a very unhappy episode in the lives of both of them.

Many years later, towards the end of her life, Trix,
broadcasting some memories of her brother, referred to that

unhappy time at Southsea. She and her brother, she said, "were left to face a <u>very</u> cold world without one familiar face, with strangers who were very unkind to us. I think child psychology is better understood now. No kind, loving parents would leave their children for years without giving them any preparation or explanation. As it was, we felt deserted - everything had gone at once. Mama, Papa, our home in a garden full of sunshine and birds.....'Aunty', as we called the woman we were left with, because she was no relation, used to tell us we had been left behind because we were so tiresome and she had taken us out of pity. I was rather spoilt before I saw through 'Aunty', but Ruddy was systematically bullied day and night. She took the line I was always right and Ruddy always in the wrong, but he never loved me the less for her mischief-making. There could hardly have been a more miserable childhood. However, we amused ourselves together - we had a sort of play that ran on and on for months in which we played all the parts .... I was the reader in those days, funnily enough, because I had more time, as I didn't go to school. When Ruddy was thirteen and I was eleven, he went to school at Westward Ho, and I lived with mother in London. I remember now, at that time, we had a lovely holiday at a farm in Epping Forest. Our cousin, Stanley Baldwin, came for a six weeks visit and we infected him with our lawlessness, too - even to donkey-riding... I really believe the happiest time of Ruddy's life - and mine - was when we all lived together after we came out to Lahore. I was then fifteen, and although we were always devoted comrades, there was never any Charles and Mary Lamb, or Dorothy and William Wordsworth nonsense about us."

Trix's good looks, quick intelligence and great vivacity made her exceedingly popular and she was soon drawn into the social whirl, then at its peak in British India - "visiting and notes, shopping and dress and chatter", when, at whiles, maybe, her spirit yearned for "the perfect season" listening to the speech of birds and thoughts of flowers.

Rudyard says of their home life in Lahore "we delighted more in each other's society than in that of strangers, and when my sister came out a little later our cup was filled to the brim. Not only were we happy, but we knew it... My mother and sister would go up to the Hills for the hot weather and in due course my father too. My own holiday came when I could be spared."*

"In the early Indian days, Ruddy and Trix worked closely together" writes Hilton Brown.** "It would be interesting to know how much of Departmental Ditties was first strung together by Trix, or how much of the recondite femininity of Plain Tales sprung from that shrewd judgement and delicate observation which were afterwards to blossom in The Pinchbeck Goddess. 'The best dancer in the Punjab' too, should have known something about it. The call would sound 'Ho, Infant! give me pen and paper, genius is burning!' But when the final casting had dropped from the forge of genius, the acetylene flame of the Infant's criticism came into play."

As to Departmental Ditties, Trix's niece, Mrs. Ethel Hector, assures me that Trix was responsible for, at least one "ditty",

*Something of Myself Rudyard Kipling **Rudyard Kipling A New Appreciation

"Seventeen Forty Nine"[2]; of Trix's collaboration with her mother in a volume of verse, Hand-in-Hand, of which she contributed sixty-three of the poems, I have something to say later.

She had several offers of marriage. Late in her life she told her old friend, Sir Ian Hamilton, she had four times refused Irishmen, "although they were very nice"; and she might have married into the Peerage.

In 1889, on her 21st birthday, she married, in India, John Murchison Fleming of the Indian Army and continued to live in India, returning to England for leaves.

Colonel Fleming's eldest sister, Moona, some ten years[3] older than Trix, married my husband's uncle, Ralph Richardson, W.S. of Edinburgh, generally called "R.R." by the family, grandson of Adam Black, the Publisher. Owing to this marriage connection, Trix had herself [been] called "Aunt Trix" by all the younger members of the family, including the in-laws, like myself.

Ralph, my very tall husband, well remembers her when he was a small boy staying at R.R.'s fine place, Gattonside House, Melrose, while she, also, retained a lively recollection of Ralph, when they met in London after a lapse of some 40 years, and talked to me about "little Raffie" in a sailor suit.

From all accounts, there were great doings at Gattonside in the old days. R.R. was well-to-do, and, with his large staff of servants, house parties and theatricals were the order of the day, Aunt Moona, a very beautiful woman, being the life and soul of the parties. The attractive portrait of Trix I have used for the

---

[2] Hilton Brown, Hamish Hamilton 1945. "Seventeen Forty-nine" - real title *My Rival*
[3] Moona was born in 1857, making her 11 years older than Trix.

frontispiece of this Memoir was taken at Gattonside during a visit to England in 1892.

Spiritualism was fashionable at the time, so spiritualism, table-turning, planchette and seances were included in the amusements of the guests. Trix possessed the peculiar gift, common among Highlanders, of "The Sight", and falling in with Sir Oliver Lodge, acted as his medium on more than one occasion, he having a great opinion of her remarkable faculty.

Not so my mother-in-law, a Lowland Scot, who regarded such goings-on with great suspicion, and always had a lot to say about the "strange" doings at the Gattonside House parties.

On Colonel Fleming's retirement during the First World War,[4] he and Trix settled in Edinburgh, and, eventually, bought the house, 6 West Coates, which was to be their home for the rest of their lives.

Trix had spent many leaves in Scotland and longed, like other exiles when abroad, for a settled home in the Old Country. When in India, she had sighed:-

> "Where Hugli flows our English eyes are weary
> Our hearts are sometimes very far away
> Needs must that exile should be long and dreary"

The exile over, however, she found that leaves-home, and living permanently at home are very different things, and, before long, realized that, as in long ago Southsea days, she had, again, to face a very cold world. Gone, for good, was the warm, golden Indian sunshine; the life, movement and colour of the East; easy Anglo-Indian friendships; the busy social round, empty though she

---

[4] For details, see "Biographical Notes".

had sometimes found it. Without the children she had longed for, she felt frustrated, and looked back

"Perhaps through tears that burned

Where Hugli flows"*

She found herself, as well, out of tune with many of her dour, stiff, Scots-in-laws, who, narrow and conventional in outlook, and in their dull, dark, everyday tweeds, criticized her pretty clothes and classed her as a vain Bohemian scribbling stuff they did not understand.

Trix wilted. Added to this, she had been fretting over the deaths of both her parents within a short time of each other and to whom she had been devoted. A serious breakdown followed, and, for several years she was in poor health. For the sake of the warmer climate, she spent some time in Jersey, and on returning to Edinburgh, lived for years very quietly. Two good maids, Mina and Mary, came to her at this time and remained at West Coates until her death. Only very gradually did she win back her health, but, in the end, made a remarkable recovery, when her mind and memory became as clear and keen as before her illness, and she was again able to lead a happy, busy and useful life.

During the Second World War, Aunt Moona gave us news of Trix from time to time, as in her Christmas letter to me, 1941, when owing to the impossibility of getting servants for her large Edinburgh house, 29 Eglinton Crescent,[5] she wrote that she was on a visit to her brother, not long before his death, and Trix.

*Hand-in-Hand   A.M. Fleming

[5] Eglinton Crescent is just around the corner from the Flemings' last house in Edinburgh, 6 West Coates.

6, West Coates,

Edinburgh

Christmas 1941

"I am leading a very quiet life now" she said "and have hardly been anywhere and the days have been so dark. Trix and I were invited to a luncheon at the N.B. Hotel some little time ago given by the R.L.S. Club. There were about 150 present and the new Lord Provost and his wife Dr. and Mrs. Darling. We sat near them at the High Table and the after-dinner speeches were very good. Among other remarks on the Lord Provost of Edinburgh, they said that two of them were commemorated by statues, Chambers and Adam Black, and that the latter has laid out the new town of Edinburgh."

The Kipling family always had great admiration for Robert Louis Stevenson, and, according to The Scotsman, Trix paid a visit about this time to the R.L.S. Club, Overseas House, Edinburgh, and, in a talk, described how they all first came to read Treasure Island. The family, she said, were on holiday in August 1884 in "a little hired house" at Dalhousie, continuous rain kept them indoors and her brother and father were reduced to drawing enormous designs and decorations on the walls. Then, Treasure Island arrived. Her father seized it and neither spoke nor moved till dinner-time, when he reluctantly came to table bringing the book. Rudyard and she waited greedily for the last page to be turned and by 10 p.m., it was her turn - then, Rudyard read Treasure Island.

The family hailed the romance as an inspiration and a delight, but Trix added, she had lived long enough to see it set as a holiday task at a big Scottish school and to hear a mother lamenting that it was too old and dull for her boy.

She went on to reminisce about Andrew Lang. At a dinner party, she said, Lang told her that he and Stevenson had once planned to write a novel together, chapter by chapter. There was one huge difficulty - who was to undertake the heroine? At that time, R.L.S. had not charmed the world with Catriona and Lang had not written The World's Desire. They decided that they would introduce their heroine in the first chapter, then lose her until the last. R.L.S. booked a chapter in which a meal was to take place in a diving bell. The plot was to contain a murder by means of poisoned fruit, and Trix described how Lang stabbed the tangerines with a fork until the hostess enquired whether he were doing a conjuring trick and swept them all into the drawing-room. It was Lang, she added, who was the first English critic to notice her brother's Departmental Ditties, quoting from it in the monthly notice he contributed to Longman's Magazine.

Colonel Fleming died during the Second World War in his 85th year, almost up to the last a familiar figure in the streets of Edinburgh, tall, erect and handsome.

From The Scotsman, I have gathered a few facts about his life and interest. He served with the KOSB during the Afghan War of 1880-81, excelled as a draughtsman, and was, also a student of military history. Among his more ambitious M.S.S. was a work entitled "The A.B.C. of the More Important Battles of the Eighteenth and Nineteenth Centuries". Publication of this work, however, was held up by the outbreak of War, but the M.S was highly commended by the late Lord Tweedsmuir. Colonel Fleming came of fighting stock, one of the members of the family winning the V.C. during the Indian Mutiny, while during the Boer War, another was a posthumous V.C. Keen soldier as he was, however, Col. Fleming often expressed regret that he had not gone into the Navy.

Aunt Moona had two nieces, Ethel Craigie, who married Thomas Walker Hector, and Katharine ("Kit") Johnstone, who married Harry Crossley. Ethel lived at Banchory until the death of her husband in 1951, when she moved to Eastbourne to be near her married daughter, Irene Elmslie, the wife of a well-known doctor there. Katharine married after the First World War, and settling in London, Ralph and I frequently met her and her family down the years.

It was not until after the death of her husband, and after the war, that Trix was able to visit London and take a greater interest in the Kipling Society (founded in 1927), and it was with Katharine, at the latter's house in Streatham, that she generally stayed.

We ourselves joined the Kipling Society in the autumn of 1945, attending our first Meeting at the Society's temporary Headquarters at 105, Gower Street, and making, (for me, re-making), the acquaintance of the Hon. Secretary, Sir Christopher Robinson. (He, later, changed his surname to Lynch-Robinson by deed poll.)

Many years before, in 1909, I had met Mr. Christopher Robinson, as he then was, when I was living with my parents in

Halfway Tree, Jamaica, my old home. He was, at that time, Private Secretary to the Governor, Sir Sidney Olivier, afterwards Lord Olivier, and I well remember dining at King's House, the residence of the Governor, which had been considerably damaged in the earthquake of 1907 and not as yet rebuilt. Tall and slim, resplendent in his white tropical uniform, I remember Mr. Robinson very active, in spite of the warmth of the evening, in looking after his Excellency's guests.

It occurred to me at the Meeting that Jamaicans might be interested in the Kipling Society, so I took away copies of their Kipling brochure to send to the West Indian Review, published in Jamaica.

I still have the letter from Sir Christopher welcoming us as members.

The letter-head of the Society's note-paper of that date gives the name of the Founder, J.H.C. Brooking M.I.E.E.; President, Major-General L.C. Dunsterville C.B., K.C.B.I., D.S.O.; Hon. Secretary Sir Christopher Robinson, Bart.; Hon. Editor of the Kipling Journal, E.D.W. Chaplin; Hon. Librarian D.G.B. Maitland.

October 24th 1945

Dear Mr. Cox:-

I am indeed delighted to learn that you and your wife have joined our little Society and I will look forward very much to seeing you at future Meetings. You will find that these will get much better as time goes on, and every summer we have a Kipling Luncheon which is really great fun ..."

The Membership Card is a gay affair, the decoration in red and blue showing maps of the world, British possessions in red, of course, flanked by shelves of red and blue books - Verse to the left, Prose to the right.

It was during the summer of 1945 that I met Trix for the first time, at Katharine's house, Streatham Common.

It so happens that Ralph's boot-maker, Coggins, "the best boot-maker in England" according to Ralph, lives in a small house in Streatham Vale, not far from Katharine's, and Ralph having occasion to visit him, suggested that, as the afternoon was fine, I might accompany him for an outing. Our business with Coggins over, we went on to Katharine's and spent an extremely interesting afternoon, I being introduced to "Aunt Trix" and all of us enjoying the fine tea Katharine provided. Trix chatted away nineteen to the dozen, stopping only to help herself to another buttered Scone - it _was_ butter, and I wondered, at the time, how Katharine had come by it, fearing it might be the family's weekly ration.

Trix recalled old days in Edinburgh with Ralph and seemed delighted to meet him again. She talked a lot about a gift-shop she was Godmothering in Kelso, and lamented that one could not buy Christmas wrapping-paper and tinsel etc., as before the war.

When we said "goodbye", she looked at me carefully - "That's a very pretty hat you are wearing!" she exclaimed and was duly impressed when I told her it was several years old and I had just retrimmed it. I remember it, now, as a Victorian affair with a brim, and swathed in navy and purple ribbon.

That evening, Harry Crossley put her on the train for the

night journey to Edinburgh. The carriages were crowded with soldiers and not a vacant seat was to be had. Finally, Harry shouted down the corridor:- "Anyone willing to give a seat to Rudyard Kipling's sister?"

So Trix got her seat, and I have no doubt the passengers in the carriage spent an interesting time, with such lively conversation as they never thought to hear, or will ever forget.

Returning to our flat, Sandwell Mansions, West Hampstead, I found letters awaiting me from old Jamaican friends, Mrs. Ellis Wolfe and her sister May Lopez, who had been living in New York for thirty years and whom I had not seen all that time. During the war, May had sent me gift-parcels of food, haberdashery, notepaper etc., and, now, she begged me to tell her what she could send for Christmas. I remembered Trix's longing for festive wrapping-paper, so wrote, at once, asking May to send what she could of it, together with Christmas labels and other "glitters", unknown luxuries in England by that Christmas.

I, also, told my old friends about the Kipling Society and my re-meeting Sir Sidney Olivier's former Private Secretary and asked if Mrs. Ellis Wolfe, who, as the wife of the then Post Master for Jamaica, and was often at King's House remembered him.

Trix had, unfortunately, to shorten her visit to town this summer and hurry back to Scotland because Aunt Moona had had an accident in the Edinburgh house, falling and breaking her thigh. In September, she wrote to tell me how she was getting on. Her handwriting is firm, even, sloping and very clear, with my Welsh Christian name correctly spelt.

September 23rd 1945.   6 West Coates,

                                   Edinburgh 12.

My dear Gwladys,

I spent this afternoon with Aunt Moona. I generally go there every other day but, this time, I had not seen her for three days and I was really surprised at the advance she has made. She is able now to sit up in an armchair for more than two hours daily and is answering her own letters.

The doctors can hardly believe that she was born before the Mutiny, 1857! She is even able to bend the joint which has the "silver pin", as big as one's little finger in it, and is quite free from pain. She enjoys her massage and radiant heat and looks both well and handsome with her white hair in two long plaits. Her patience and cheerfulness under such trying conditions is really beautiful. Not one word of complaint or self-pity, and always gratitude for the Nurses. It is certainly an unusually nice "Home", and her room is always full of the flowers she loves. The recent gales have so battered my poor little "back-green" that even the Michaelmas daisies were spoilt and I had to take her a little jar of home-made lemon marmalade for her breakfast, instead. Her appetite is quite satisfactory.

"Next month she is hoping to see Peter Johnstone" (Katharine's nephew) "back on leave from Germany and his brother, Bobby before he goes abroad. Their mother is coming to me for a few days to try and rent a flat, but I fear she is not likely to find one.

When Aunt Moona is able to be in her own house again,

Ethel Hector is coming to me for, I hope, a fortnight to help her in re-arranging house. Her bed-room must, of course, be on the ground floor to begin with. Its a dreadfully tall house for stairs - does Ralph remember it? Her nurse companion, Miss Bostock, who has been with her for two years is living alone in 29 Eglinton Crescent and having it as much cleared as she can manage, with the help of a charwoman. Before she returns we are to try and find a cook-housekeeper and a house table-maid. May we be lucky! Its many years since she had anyone satisfactory in the kitchen.

My hands are full, now, of string bags and dolls to be made for Christmas. Small dolls especially which are fussy to make, but the bairns love them. I also, have several orders for berets. The difficulty is to find non-coupon material for them. Mothers say:- 'I'll give you anything for a beret like the one you made so-and-so'. 'Then give me a skein of wool and I'll only charge 2/6 for making it!' 'But that would take a coupon!' 'Exactly, and I can't spare a coupon, if you gave me 10/- for it!'

We have to make Christmas stockings this year, instead of trees. No tinsel, no glass balls!

With love to you both, if I may, even though "little Raffie" is no longer in a sailor suit.

Very sincerely,

Trix Fleming.

Towards the end of the year, Mrs. Ellis Wolfe writing from New York, said she did indeed remember Sir Christopher Robinson, and recalled a wet and tiring adventure, Sir Sidney Olivier, her husband and he had once had inspecting up-country flood damage.

Sir Christopher, also, remembered the floods in Jamaica, as he wrote me in December 1945:-

> The Kipling Society,
> 105 Gower Street,
> W.C.1.
> December 17th 1945.

Dear Mrs. Cox,

Many thanks for your letter of December 15th, together with the Flat Earth Map which I return. It was most interesting.

(At a previous Meeting of the Kipling Society, reference was made to Kipling's story, "Village that voted the earth was flat", so I sent Sir Christopher a print of Middleton's Eclipse and Sunrise Plan of the Flat Earth, which had been given me many years before by a visitor to the Tourist Office, Jamaica. The earth is shown flat, pear-shaped, surrounded by sea, the whole enclosed by barriers of ice and high mountains).

"Thank you so much for your efforts to rope in the Daughters of the British Empire" (an Anglo-American Society, of which May Lopez was a devoted member). "I certainly remember the Post Master for Jamaica. I don't remember the particular incident to which you refer, but we were always having floods and hurricanes in Jamaica and I was always being dragged out with the Governor and various other officials to visit the scenes of destruction. I used to loathe these visits, as I hate getting wet in the tropics! How interesting it is to cast one's mind back like this when life held something more than Fish Queues and increases of Income Tax!"

A week or so before Christmas, May Lopez' parcel of Christmas wrapping-paper arrived and was sent off at once to Trix in Edinburgh. Early in the New Year she wrote:-

6 West Coates,
Edinburgh 12.
January 10th 1946.

My dear Gwladys,

I am badly ashamed of myself to think that my prompt p.c. to thank you for that wonderful parcel of pretties and glitters and dainty wrappings - such as we never see here - was never followed by the thank-you letter it promised!

Do forgive me, though I haven't even a cold to offer as an excuse; we, the maids and I, have kept wonderfully well all through the mild moist weather, which is supposed to be trying.

Aunt Moona "(who was on a visit with a nurse, hence Trix's preoccupation)" kept wonderfully well, too, and enjoyed a good helping of turkey and mince pies. Our turkey had been ordered long before, and as it lasted 5 people for 6 days, it was a thrifty bird and well worth the 33/- we paid for its tender 10 pounds. Meat is really a difficulty now. For the past 3 weeks, our choice has been between pork and frozen mutton of a very coarse kind.

Irene Elmslie and her school-boy son, who is doing very well at Glenalmond, came on Monday for a few days. She is Ethel Hector's daughter - perhaps Ralph remembers her at Gattonside, when she was Ethel Craigie, a fair girl with a lot of yellow hair. Her son, a Major in the R.A.M.C., is out in India now, and so is Bobby Johnstone, whom we miss very much.

My Brother's official biographer, Lord Birkenhead, is still sending me long letters crammed with questions about our early days. I have a good memory, luckily.

I spent a few days at Kelso and my shop looked fascinating with large Christmas Tree in one corner with a doll's bungalow in the other, both to be raffled for, and the dear little sisters, who won the Dolls House are my favourite customers.

Auntie Moona has a cold - they hope not 'flu - and I have not been allowed to see her for two days. She had a good night and the Nurses, kind experienced women hope it is passing.

I made funny hearts to hang on Christmas Trees and one comes with my love and many many apologies.

Love to you both,

          Yours affectly

          Aunt Trix.

The "funny-heart" is four paper hearts cut out of the New York Christmas wrapping paper, pasted together, ornamented with a tinsel star and slung on a loop of Christmas paper ribbon. It remains one of my treasures.

In April 1946, the <u>West Indian Review</u> came out with my account of the Kipling Society and Trix, together with an Editorial on Kipling. This write-up was reproduced in the <u>Kipling Journal</u> July 1946.

Fashions in Authors

A note from Kingston, Jamaica.

"A letter from a member of the Kipling Society indicates that there are still those who reverence him. Like many writers before him who have attained recognition little short of idolatry in their life-time, Kipling suffered an immediate eclipse of his popularity soon after his death. What has been termed imperial jingoism became most distasteful to many enthusiastic admirers. It became almost a hall mark of the Philistine to admit to finding any pleasure in his works. Tennyson suffered almost precisely the same fate and like that great Victorian, Kipling is now climbing back to that recognition his writing and particularly his lyrics and ballads justly entitled him. His place in English letters is as assured as that of Dickens. It is curious that there are these fashions in writers as much as there are fashions in masters of painting.

"Here is an extract from the letter to the Editor of the West Indian Review which appears in the same issue of that publication. It is written by Mrs. Gwladys Cox, 16, Sandwell Mansions, West Hampstead, London, N.W.6. :-

'I am enclosing for your acceptance a couple of copies of the Kipling Brochure recently issued by the Kipling Society, which I feel sure will interest you.

After the manifold upsets of the War, we are now picking up the threads of life again and the Kipling Society is trying to push ahead with its aims, chiefly, "to honour and extend the influence of a writer, who was, in our time, most patriotic, virile and imaginative in upholding the ideals of the English-speaking world."

In my day, Jamaicans of the best type were highly patriotic, and I imagine that in these particular times a study of Kipling would be all to the good. If you agree, perhaps you would like to call attention to the aims of the Society in your paper.

It will, I am sure, interest you to know that the Hon. Secretary, Sir Christopher Robinson, was Private Secretary to Sir Sidney Olivier (afterwards Lord Olivier) in 1909, and when we attended a recent meeting of the Kipling Society, we had a very pleasant chat with Sir Christopher about the old days in Jamaica, he remembering old mutual friends. He introduced another member, Colonel Wood-Hill, D.S.O., who had been in Jamaica at the same time, and recalled his friends the Lucie-Smiths, Cargills, Captain Nicholson and others.

"As a personal note, perhaps you would be interested to know that Kipling's sister, Mrs. A.M. Fleming, is a marriage-connection of my husband's. Now a widower of 77, she lives in Edinburgh, but comes up to town now and again. Small and slight with a perfectly chiselled, small, aquiline nose and deep, sapphire-blue eyes, she is extraordinarily energetic for her years, with amazing powers of conversation. Among the many interesting things she told me was the following:-

The Curator of "The Wonder House" in Kim was really her father; once he gave his own spectacles to an Indian Priest, receiving, in return, an iron pen-holder, which is, today, one of the exhibits at "Batemans", Kipling's old home in Sussex."

Trix was in town again in June 1946 and sent a note from Bailey's Hotel, Gloucester Road, June 19th:-

"I am here again for a few days and it would be so nice if you and Ralph would come in for a crack and tea on Tuesday or Wednesday of next week, 4 o'clock.   We still have little hotel-made cakes!"

So, donning our best, we presented ourselves at Bailey's on the afternoon arranged by telephone.   But there was, alas, no sign of Trix!   We waited for some time, and, at last, went sorrowfully away, leaving a message with the Porter.

Then, came a hasty, hurried note:-

> Bailey's Hotel,
>
> Gloucester Road, W.2.
>
> June 26th 1946.

My dear Gwladys,

Some man has blundered!

Twice, I tried to get you on the phone and the bell seemed to ring in an empty house.   Kit said she fancied you must be away.   And, then, this morn. the Porter handed me, <u>just arrived</u>, your note, post-marked 24th inst. together with a severe:- 'Where was you yesterday, Madam?   A very tall gentleman and lady came to tea with you, they did!'

I was aghast - I had spent a blameless afternoon at Broadcasting House, having a rehearsal - record of "My Brother - Rudyard Kipling"   I go again today to <u>hear</u> <u>my</u> <u>own</u> <u>voice</u> - nervous work - and make the final record.   Don't know when it will appear - if it does - but doing it has been fun.

Tomorrow, I am going to stay with Kit at Streatham for a few days and I <u>do</u> so hope we may meet then and that all may be forgiven and forgotten. It was the post - not me.

Aunt Moona has gone to Wemys near Aberfeldy in an ambulance for a month's change. She is <u>very</u> thin and frail-looking now.

Love to you both,

affectly

Aunt Trix.

Shortly after this, Trix's long-promised visit materialized and she and Katherine came to tea with us at West Hampstead.

At first, there were more explanations about her missing us at Bailey's - "she had had to go to the B.B.C., at short notice, to make a recording for "<u>In Town Tonight</u>," and amused us by recounting how the youthful announcer, thinking to put her at ease - she who could unflinchingly have faced the Great Panjandrum - addressed her as "Trix". I remember how tickled she was when I reminded her he might have called her "<u>Ducks</u>"!

Then, a tour of the flat to inspect, carefully, my collection of pictures and embroideries; next, her formal introduction to "Bob", our very beautiful, nine-year-old Tabby, who had shared all our war-time adventures, and now, gazed at our lively visitor with round, wondering honey-coloured eyes. Then, tea - what an afternoon it was! High spirits from Trix and a ceaseless flow of entertaining, witty conversation, quotations from the classics, and, withal, a simplicity, humility and appreciation of the smallest attention. Katharine, Ralph and myself sat silent, while this one small, elderly lady with flashing, intelligent, deep-blue eyes talked and talked - for two solid hours. We listened spell-bound, and when she left, the place seemed empty and silent - such was the spirit of her.

I saw her again after this at a Meeting of the Kipling Society, the occasion I think, when her old friend Rachel Ferguson was present. Trix was a great swell in a black evening dress with diamonds in her hair and at her neck, and she gave us a lively talk largely on her early years with "Ruddy" in England.

Aunt Moona, who had been gradually failing after her serious accident, died in June 1947.

Ralph's sister, Ailie, was in Edinburgh at the time of the sale of her effects at 29, Eglinton Crescent. Here, she came across Trix, who embraced her warmly. It was many years since they had met, so getting together in a quiet corner, they had a great "crack". Trix was jubilant at having bought some plush curtains at the house - alas, she did not live long to enjoy them for she herself died in October the following year.

But before this, a large scrap-book compiled over many years by R.R. was sent to Ralph, and among the papers and cuttings we set aside to keep were a couple relating to Trix, one, a note in her own handwriting accompanying a birthday gift she had made to R.R.,

> 6 West Coates,
> Edinburgh.

A small addition to your library,
a pocket volume of
Good Matches
by Dickens Howitt Burns

To wish you Many Happy Returns of your
Birthday... from
Trix Fleming.

the other, a cutting from The Scotsman 17th September 1932,
inscribed in R.R.'s, then, somewhat shaky handwriting (he died
the following year), "Trix's Poem" :-

Dearth of Butterflies

6 West Coates,

Edinburgh 12.

September 15th 1932.

Sir:-

A correspondent enquired some weeks ago if there was any
known reason for the curious dearth of butterflies in Scotland
this fine summer. As no scientific explanation seems
forthcoming, I send you a child's suggestion on the subject:-

[The poem is reproduced in full in Part Two of this book]

I sent a copy of the poem to Trix's cousin, Miss Florence
Macdonald, whom we had met at Kipling Society Meetings and
she wrote to thank me:-

11 Murray House

Buckingham Gate

S.W.1.   15:9:48.

Dear Mrs Cox,

It was kind of you to think of me and send me that poem

of Trix's, I had not seen it and I am so glad to have it. Thank you very much for sending it. As you say it is really charming.

Trix wrote and asked me to pay her a visit this month, but unfortunately, I can't do so, but one of my brothers and his wife hope to spend a few days with her early in October, so I shall be able to get some first-hand news. She very seldom writes letters now.

How beautifully you have printed the poem; it certainly enhances the value of it.

With renewed thanks and kind greetings to you and your husband.

Yours sincerely,

Florence Macdonald.

On the afternoon of July 14th, 1948, Ralph and I attended a reception at the Dorchester Hotel given by the Kipling Society when Lord Wavell was introduced as President to members by the Hon.Treasurer, Lt.Gen. Sir George MacMunn K.C.B., K.C.S.I., D.S.O. Sir George MacMunn paid an eloquent tribute to Lord Wavell's service to the country and assured him of the Members great appreciation of the honour he had done the Society of becoming its President. There was a large turn-out of members, many of whom came from various parts of the country to attend the reception.

Among the guests, we saw Florence Macdonald, and for the first time, Mrs Elsie Bambridge, Kipling's daughter. Photographs were taken of the assembly, which were reproduced in the Kipling Journal, incidentally very good pictures.

It is sad to recall that Lord Wavell was destined to be President for such a short time, for he died in 1950.

In the autumn of 1948, we subscribed to the appeal made by Mr C.W. Parish (who has lived at Bateman's, Kipling's old home at Burwash since it was left to the National Trust) for the Burwash Church Restoration Fund.

With our subscriptions, I sent Mr. Parish a copy of Trix's poem "Dearth of Butterflies". In return, he sent me a booklet he had written, "Mrs Fleming's Visit", and wrote:-

Batemans,

Burwash,

Sussex.

7 : X : 48.

Dear Mrs Cox,

This is to thank you for your kind letter and the two cheques to our fund.

I am delighted to have Mrs. Fleming's poem "Dearth of Butterflies". She is a most wonderful old lady and I have had lovely letters from her.

She was so pleased when I asked her if a copy of her letter to our Rector could go out with my appeal. She wrote:- 'I can only say I am honoured you think my silly letter can earn a stray 5/- or so'

Please accept a copy of what I wrote about her in 1945.

Again thanking you both

Sincerely,

C.W. Parish

"It was not long after our arrival in 1940 as tenants of Bateman's" writes Mr. Parish in his booklet "that we learnt that Mr. Kipling had a sister and we wondered what manner of lady she might be, little expecting ever to meet her.

Judge then our pleasure, five years later, when a letter arrived from Mr. Brooking, founder of the Kipling Society saying that Mrs. Fleming, whose home is in Edinburgh, was on a visit to London and had expressed a wish to see Bateman's again and that he would escort her. The date was fixed for July 10th, and at midday I met them at Etchingham station. Now how better can I describe this most charming little lady than by saying that she was exactly what you would wish a sister of Mr. Kipling to be.

Her effect on us would have been described in other eras as "overwhelming", or "devastating"; the adjective today is "atomic". Seated by my side, with her escort Mr. Brooking seated behind us, we drove gaily away from the station and, to "open the ball," I said "So you live in Edinburgh? "yes" she replied, "Edinburgh is like a beautiful woman with a bad temper", and I realized, at once, that this was no ordinary visitor to Bateman's. As we passed it, she admired Etchingham Church, and said she had never been inside, and as it so well repays a visit - rebuilt in 1388 with its original richly carved choir stalls - we entered for a few minutes.

Bateman's looked very lovely in the sunshine as we walked across the lawn, happily newly sown, to the front door, and Mrs. Fleming eagerly pointed out an old friend in the fine open-work iron bell-pull from her uncle Sir Edward Burne-Jones' house at

Fulham.   Of this R.K. wrote:

'When I had a house of my own and the Grange was emptied of meaning, I begged for and was given that bell-pull for my entrance, in the hope that other children also might feel happy when they rang it.'

At our next meeting Mrs. Fleming told me that she was born at The Grange, and also that, in earlier days, it had been the home of Samuel Richardson.   If Defoe (1661-1731) be taken as our first, or earliest, English novelist, then Richardson (1681-1761) may be placed second and it was in the garden of The Grange that we know his Pamela, Clarissa and Grandison received their birth.   To what interesting visitors must our old bell-pull have responded!   Callers first on Richardson, a century later on Burne-Jones and finally to ask "Is Mr. Kipling at home?"

Entering the hall Mrs. Fleming told me that the first picture on the right was of the Burne-Jones' dining room at The Grange, painted by Rook, a pupil of Burne-Jones.

This was indeed to be a chance to learn something of the history of the treasures of Bateman's.

The two fine water-colour sketches of the south side of the house that, also, hang in the hall were painted by the uncle Sir Edward ; "Uncle Edward Poynter", I was told, was for many years President of the Royal Academy and was buried in the crypt of St. Paul's.   This honour was, also, offered when "Uncle Edward Burne-Jones" died in 1898 but his widow knew he would prefer his ashes to lie in the little green churchyard of St. Margaret's Rottingdean.

I showed the grand "Sussex edition" of Kipling's works that

Macmillans so kindly gave me for Bateman's in 1940, and opening Volume I, "Plain Tales from the Hills", I pointed to the dedication "To the wittiest woman in India I dedicate this book." Proudly smiling, the little lady exclaimed "My Mother".

These 35 beautiful volumes exactly fill one shelf of the bookcase by the front door and in front of them stands a fine painted chest which Mrs. Fleming said had belonged to the King of Oudh. This sovereign she described as "a mutiny gent", and explained that he was deposed by the British Government and his possessions - which included "some mangy lions and tigers" - were sold. Lockwood Kipling recognised this chest as a museum piece of period about 1620, Chinese design, Indian workmanship, so bought it, and, in due course, it found its way to Bateman's. On the right on leaving the hall, is the large brass tray of fine Benares workmanship. This, Mrs. Fleming said, was her wedding present to R.K. and that it was always used for tea on the hall table at Bateman's.

Ascending the stairs we paused at the half-landing where the long low window gives on to the garden with its pleached avenue of limes and background of yew hedges, the lily pool and rose beds with the immense willow tree rising as sentinel over all - a view unsurpassed in England - and Mrs. Fleming pointing to the cushioned window-seat said "I have seen my three aunts sitting together in that window." These were Lady Poynter, Lady Burne-Jones and Mrs. Baldwin. One can picture Burne-Jones feeling for his sketch book!

We had hardly entered the study when I was called away, but Mrs Fleming was deeply moved to see it all unaltered and exactly as her brother had left it on the last day he used it. She said the round painted ruler on his desk was given him when he was eight years old.

All too quickly the visit ended, but not without a promise to come again next summer and then to tell us more about this dear old house and its precious belongings which give such dignity and importance to my proud title - self bestowed - "Custos Batemani."

....

"Little had we done that summer day to earn the reward of the following letter which arrived from Edinburgh some two months later:-

> 6 West Coates,
> > Edinburgh 12.
> > 17 September 1945.

My dear Mr. Parish,

At last, at long last, I have the chance of thanking you for that Golden Day at Bateman's. A joy at the time, a jewel in memory.

I have been tiresomely busy and an accident to my husband's eldest sister shortened my holiday. Her nursing home is quite the other side of Edinburgh. "It takes a watch to steer her and a week to shorten sail;" and when I return I spend the rest of the day writing letters to her numerous relations.

I often thought of sending you a hasty note, but like a greedy child I saved the plums of your letter till I had really time to write.

Of course the first thing that struck me that Golden Day was that I had never seen Bateman's gardens looking so beautiful. In Rudyard's time they were never up to "Hampton Court standard" as they are now. I hope he sees them; I feel sure he does.

"For a loving Shadow that brings no gloom
Broods in the dead man's favourite room,
O'er his well-loved books the spirit lingers
With wistful eyes and caressing fingers."

I had an almost overwhelming sense of his being there and even more in the house than in the garden. It was all I could do not to tell you of him, very especially in his study.

Yet, though C.K. died there I was not at all conscious of her except for a moment in the dining room when I looked at your wife's sweet face in Carrie's chair. Strangely enough during my last visit to Bateman's after his death, I could not feel him at all. I felt lost and lonely; now, you have, as it were, given him back to me and I am unspeakably grateful. How have you brought back the very essence I wonder; I suppose by those master magicians Love and Sympathy. It was not only that the things were there in their old places, but the old spell was there too. I thought it had died with him, even Mick, his old Aberdeen, lying on my feet could not bring back any shadow of Master in that last sad visit. But now you and yours have swept those mists away and how can I thank you enough.

I am so glad your girl is making a beautiful young marriage. "New prows that seek the old Hesperides". I am making bold to send her a small gift (an Egyptian Scarf, white and silver, the kind that never tarnishes, I think they don't make them now) as a luck bringer. The pattern will show her how large and prosperous a household I wish her, so many camels and attendants.

Kindest regards,

Yours very sincerely,

ALICE FLEMING

....

"Come again, Alice Fleming, Come to Bateman's. Here in his loved land of "Oak and Ash and Thorn ;" here in sight of Pook's Hill you will find us keeping watch and ward over this his home; the home for thirty-three years of one of England's greatest sons - prophet, patriot, seer."

II

Alice Macdonald Fleming - "Trix", to all who knew and loved her - died in Edinburgh 25th October 1948.

Although 80 years of age, she never impressed one as an elderly person, so bright and youthful was her mind and spirit. With most of her contemporaries gone, new and younger friends were scarcely made aware of a difference in age, so fully alive, almost up to the last, was she, and many were sad at her passing.

Tributes were paid to her memory in the Kipling Journal by her cousin Florence Macdonald and by Hilton Brown, who, when he published his book, Rudyard Kipling, A New Appreciation, in 1945, dedicated it to Alice Macdonald Fleming ("Trix"), whose help has been invaluable and whose kindness to an importunate intruder angelic."

[Both these tributes are shown in full at the end of Part One].

Florence Macdonald mentions Trix's gift of "The Sight". Not only did my mother-in-law disapprove of dabbling in the occult, but, so, apparently did Colonel Fleming and Rudyard Kipling.

In the Kipling Journal of October 1945, Trix gives some of her interesting experiences in Psychometry. "Now that my brother and husband are both dead" she writes "I talk openly of "The Sight" - they loathed any reference to it, though, a few years ago, my husband twice saw 'the appearance' that had been haunting me for months, and helped me to lay it. Remember, my mother was the eldest of seven sisters and a Macdonald of

Skye, so her only daughter had a right to 'The Sight'. I'm so glad it never frightens me; she was afraid of it. I have always found it helpful. For instance, a message a dead child gave me one sunny morning in the College Chapel at St. Andrews saved his mother's sanity. I had only met her once and I never saw the child living, but the few words and the caress that came with them drew her out of the melancholia and enabled her to be a happy handsome woman leading a normal life.

For the last two years I have had some interesting experiences in psychometry (the measurement of mental processes) helped out by crystal gazing. A Polish Unit at Hilso[6] gave me the name of "the lady who knows everything". I began by mending a pair of socks for a lance-corporal and I begged his Chaplain to tell him not to worry so about his mother's health, for he would soon hear of her recovery, and to reprove him for his mistrust of his sweetheart, who was as good as she was pretty. He came to see me with Father Obertynski as interpreter and showed me a photo of the girl and I was able to describe her surroundings, friends and present employment in a way that he recognized at once! A few months later, every detail was confirmed. My best triumph was when a crusty old Bishop, who had escaped from Warsaw in disguise, reproved Father Obertynski for believing in the 'trances', utterances of a lady who does not even belong to the True Church. "She is never in a trance" - no matter, if she does not read it all from your thoughts, she is undoubtedly prompted by the Devil.

---

[6] "Hilso" - probably a misreading of Kelso; her writing is not always clear.

However, he tested me by sending me a large iron key saying that no one knew what it opened except himself, and if the "lady who knows everything" could give even one correct fact from it, he would believe in her.

I slept with the key under my pillow and had a vivid dream in which the Bishop, dressed as a peasant, buried the oldest and most valuable of the golden altar vessels in a dummy grave in the monks' burial ground. At the last moment, he took from his neck a case like a small camera holding the most sacred relic in the monastery, a Pectoral cross. This was sunk a little to the left of the gold plate. I noted the order of the jewels and that the emeralds were cabuchon while the rubies, topaz and diamond were table-cut. Date about twelfth century. I wrote it all down and the Bishop reluctantly owned it was all true. I had seen through the steelcase, hide-covered, that held the cross, and as no Devil (he seemed to have a great belief in devils) would dare even to glance at so holy a relic, he owned that "the lady's wisdom comes from on high". He would have sent me his blessing, only I was a heretic, but he sent me an Easter card with flowers from Jerusalem and a tiny rosary of pebbles from Gethsemane. I hope his treasures are safe still. Three of the most striking instances of 'The Sight' have come to me in church on sunny mornings. But I am babbling on at too great length."

A letter of Trix's to General Sir Ian Hamilton, quoted by him in his autobiography, Listening For The Drums, gives some idea of her youth in India, with its references to Simla 1886, when she was 17 and 18 years old, and to Calcutta in 1903.

"My very dear Sir Ian,

How more than good of you to give me that precious "Book of Remembrance" of the beautiful lady who fascinated me 57 years ago, when she was the loveliest girl I had ever seen. She has always lived in my thoughts as the one fair beauty, and Pamela Grey (who used to be Wyndham) as the one dark beauty, I have been privileged to see. And now they are:-

> "That City's shining spires
>
> We travel to"

All the early pages - and the Simla photos - give me my 17 and 18 year old memories again. How I used to watch for "Miss Muir" on the Mall or at dances and note in my diary if I had seen her.

Of course in 1886, we were all on the alert, hoping that the dull-faced Prince Louis would not be the favoured one. I knew it would be all right for I had seen the difference in her expression when she rode with you and with him. Her eyes were delightfully tell-tale - you might have said with Bassanio:-

> "From her eyes, I did receive fair
>
> speechless messages."

You both looked so happy together. I used to think the phrase; "gallant and gay" might have been invented for you. No wonder Simla found your romance so much more attractive than the one of 'The Lost Tribe and our Hat band' as Lord Clandeboye would call them. I don't think anyone guessed there might have been a third "romance of the peerage" that Season, if I had been less of a critical little prig. Funnily enough, though Lord D.

loved me for my good sense, Lady D. never forgave me and she had always been so nice to me before. Of course a penniless daughter-in-law was the last thing she wished for, but, she said, openly, that she had always thought me a really sweet and charming girl - but - if her "splendid Arch" was not good enough for me - she gave me up. What could I expect? He was not fickle, for, next year, after Lord D. became Marquess he suggested that though I didn't think him up to much, it might amuse me to be a Countess. "Too expensive" I said, and he explained at length in his stodgy school boy way, that though, of course, I should have to be "presented on my marriage" my wedding dress with a train of family lace would be A.1., and a small tiara that had belonged to his beautiful Granny would suit me far better than "the fender full of shamrocks mother sports". His profile was an abiding joy to me and I've always liked Irishmen, but I drew the line at marrying them, somehow - four times I drew it - though they were very nice.

Oh, the photo of your Stirling Castle drawing room. I can identify some of the framed photos. I still have that one of Lord D.

I love her poems, especially the last Romance. I should like to illuminate it on vellum if I could do it well enough and the last two lines are as enchanting as one of her own pastels.

This is a terribly long letter, but I've not begun yet - there are so many things I want to tell you and ask you. The peaceful end of your good old Simla Khansamah, who came to us in Calcutta in 1903, stipulating that when General Hamilton Sahib returned to India as Jungilat [War Lord, ie Commander-in-Chief], he must return to him at once to order his noble household befittingly.. He had <u>chits</u> from you both.

General Grant's version of the pin-curl you innocently kissed out of place - "Ian, you know, is often un peu malin". She took it beautifully, but we all wanted to hit him". I said it didn't sound like you at all - this was in 1892 and <u>now</u> I know I was right. The man I mean was Inspector of Cavalry that year and rather amusing.

It would be a real joy to see you again; when you come to Edinburgh, do ring me up and I will come and sit on your door step, if necessary.

I am very thin and grey now, distinctly witch-like, but a recent Valentine from a boy cousin informed me he

> "Knew a lady who's past three score
>
> Yet eyes, smile, heart are sunshine to the core
>
> Yes, she's a child, while I at 24" etc.

I congratulated him on the truth of his first line. Seriously, dear old Friend, it would do my heart good to hear you talk - try and fit me in..........."

Besides dances, parties, riding, when Simla was at the peak of its social life, circa 1887, there were amateur theatricals, in which, of course, the Kiplings played a leading part. Sixty years on, <u>The</u> <u>Times</u> of March 7th 1949 says:- "The curtain went down on more than this century of Social life of British exiles in India, when pictures and other souvenirs of the Simla Amateur Dramatic Club were handed over to safe keeping in London."

Captain E.W. Martindell recalls in the <u>Kipling</u> <u>Journal</u> July

1949, a theatrical performance at the Gaiety Theatre, Simla:-

"In the Pioneer (Allahabad) of August 1st 1887," he writes "there appeared an account of a theatrical performance at the Gaiety Theatre at Simla in aid of Summer Homes for Nursing Sisters who were, under Lady Roberts' scheme, to be brought to military hospitals in India. The performance was a great success. There was a very large attendance including the Viceroy and Lady Dufferin."

The prologue, reproduced in the Kipling Journal in full, consists of some 100 lines and was composed by Rudyard Kipling, then in his 22nd year. It began:-

> "So please you, Gentlefolk, a drama slight
> Awaits your verdict on our opening night
> But e'er the call-bell rings we pray you take
> In all good part the humble plea we make
> For mercy at the hands of those who know
> Exactly how a comedy should go ...."

Being an appeal for Nursing Sisters, reference is made to the ministering angels:-

> "Fight Death with money, money that can buy
> The soft cool soothing touch, the sleepless eye
> The woman's art that coaxes and commands
> The fevered mouth and weak and trembling hands ..."

The prologue was recited by Trix Kipling; and, continues Captain Martindell:-

"When in August 1945, I had the privilege of meeting Mrs. Fleming, I recalled this prologue spoken by her at Simla and asked her if she remembered the incident. "Quite well" she replied "and what is more, I can recite that whole Prologue", and, straightaway she recited the opening lines. She was gifted with a marvellous memory and wonderful vitality, added to most winning ways."

Some time after Trix's death, Katharine Crossley allowed me to look through a packet of old letters, papers and photographs of Trix's that had come into her possession. There was a short story by Trix, <u>At A Christmas Ball</u>, published in <u>Black and White</u> Christmas number 1892, a tale about a girl who meets the shade of her dead lover at a Simla Ball; original pen-and-ink flower designs by John Lockwood Kipling; a letter to Trix from Rudyard written at Bateman's; a faded birthday letter dated 1864, exquisitely hand-printed by Trix's future mother-in-law (the wife of Surgeon General Fleming, then at Berampore), written to "little Johnnie" (Trix's future husband) in England with Moona and the other children; an account by Trix in <u>The Pioneer</u> of Feb., 21st 1897 of 'A Journey in the Jungle', the north west Provinces and the Kingdom of Oudh; and a copy of the book of verses by Trix and her mother entitled:-

<u>Hand in Hand</u>

Verses

by

A Mother

and

Daughter.

This dainty volume, $6\frac{1}{2}$" x $4\frac{1}{2}$", bound in light saxe-blue cloth with a scroll design and title in white on the cover, was published 1902 in London by Elkin Matthews, Vigo Street, W.; in New York by Doubleday Page and Company, and printed by R. Folkard & Son, Devonshire Street, Queen Square, Bloomsbury, W.C. The first part of the book contains verses by the Mother dedicated to the Daughter, the second part, the Daughter to the Mother. The frontispiece is a picture in relief, signed J.L.K. (John Lockwood Kipling) showing the Mother with her arm round the Daughter's shoulder both in stylized costume, literally portraits of Mrs. Lockwood Kipling and Trix, sitting beside some Indian sea shore with Arab dhows on the water, and, in the distance, a lighthouse.

The two poems I quote are India-haunted:-

By the Mother,

Summer in the Indian Plains

The fiery feet of Summer march in haste
Across the fields swept bare of ripened grain
And all the garden lies a barren waste
Beneath her scorching steps athirst for rain.

The red rose blossom and the white rose lie
In one pale scentless ruin side by side
Poor faded queens, that erst in rivalry
For beauty's crown each with the other vied.

With perfume honey-sweet from blossoming trees
The heavy air turns faint before the noon,
And stagnant odours load the evening breeze
Which 'neath their weight dies ere the day be done;

While languidly, with long stems fresh and cool
The lotus lilies lie upon the pool.

By the Daughter,

Where Hugli Flows

Where Hugli flows, her city's banks beside,
White domes and towers rise on glittering plain
The strong, bright sailing-ships at anchor ride,
Waiting to float their cargoes to the main,
     Where Hugli flows.

Brown waters, treacherous currents, whirling by
The painted fishing-boats haste to and fro,
Brown sails, brown sailors, crimsoned curiously
Under the all-transfiguring sunset glow
     Where Hugli flows.

Where Hugli flows, our English eyes are weary,
Our hearts are sometimes very far away,
Needs must that exile should be long and dreary;
How slow the hours, how lagging long the day,
     Where Hugli flows.

Yet, years hence, when the steamer's screw shall beat
The homeward track, for us without return,
Our bitter bread, by custom almost sweet,
We shall look back, perhaps through tears that burn
     Where Hugli flows.

Calcutta.

Katharine Cossley saw more of Trix in her later years than other members of the family, a close friendship following upon Katharine's visit to Trix in Jersey when she and Harry were on their honeymoon. Eventually, Trix appointed Katharine one of her Executors, the other being Julius Macdonald, the brother of Florence Macdonald.

In sending me her impressions of Trix, Katharine writes:-

"I would like you to show her as very beautiful, charming (beyond the modern easy use of the word) and fascinating with her interest in things psychic and out of this world. Her very real love of children and her sorrow in never having any of her own is important. She could charm the heart out of any child and was full of amusing little tricks with handkerchiefs and finger magic to hold them by her. Her love of the Zoo, her tit-bits for James the aloof camel, her love for the macaws all made a trip to the Edinburgh Zoo with her a real joy. Her facility for turning out light verse (on A.P.H.[7] lines) without any effort - a paragraph in the papers, and odd sentence overhead, and off she would go, improvising and rhyming. She had a wonderful memory for quotations, Shakespeare and so on, which was a mine of rich ore for any cross-word fan. Her needlework was beautiful, I have a wool picture you'd like to see and during the last war her shop at Kelso, a sort of charitable continuous sale-of-work was her main interest. It was run by a manageress Dorothy Braidwood, but nothing delighted Aunt Trix more than to have a week or two in Kelso serving behind the counter! She was very much interested in the Poles who were in the Borders in the war years, and had a special crony in an old priest, to whom she divulged some secret treasures hid in Poland, so that the Nazis would not find them. She certainly had psychic gifts, but little chance to practise them as Uncle Jack (Colonel Fleming) looked on them as the blackest magic, saying grimly, "you'd have been drowned, or burned as a witch a year or two earlier and deserved it!" He blamed her friendship with the Wyndhams and

---

[7] "A.P.H." A.P. Herbert, barrister, M.P., and humorous writer.

those who called themselves "The Souls", and dabbled in esoteric matters, for her breakdown, and was really obdurate in breaking up any attempts to crystal gaze or "telepath" while she was with him.

The breakdown was explained to me as the result of losing Father and Mother within a matter of months. The Father was supposed to be ill - heart - but the Mother died quite unexpectedly and, then, he followed her while dressing for dinner one night with a heart attack, and the double shock unnerved Aunt Trix completely.

She and Uncle Jack, though deeply attached, scarcely shared one thought or pleasure. He was Army to the toe-tips and looked on all writing or painting as rather riff-raff stuff. I believe when they married, our family looked down on the marriage as a very Bohemian alliance, an opinion they had to modify later when all her relations, Baldwins, Poynters, Burne-Jones, not to say Kipling himself achieved a good measure of fame and couldn't be dismissed as penny-a-liner journalists or daubers, but, by then, the harm was done, and relations were never cordial between the two sets of in-laws. I think the split in her affections, real love for her husband and real yearning for her own relations and all the fun they had in the world of life and letters was too much for her. She could have married many times during her early days in India. My own people persisted through life in regarding her as a light-weight, vain and frivolous. Admittedly, she never passed a glass without a long glance therein, but why not? She was well worth looking at, and if her tastes ran to pretty colours and floating draperies, when theirs were wedded to useful blacks and good-wearing tweeds that is just a difference of taste, and no crime.

After Uncle Jack's death, she took on a new lease of life, coming up to town for a few weeks each year, seeing and charming everyone and picking up the threads after so long. Angela Thirkell (her cousin) and her son, Colin,[8] Rachel Ferguson (Aunt Trix had been at Notting Hill High School with Rachel's mother), Hilton Brown, the Secretary of the Kipling Society and all the Macdonald cousins used to rally round and fête her. She was very fond of Stanley Baldwin as a child and told me he taught her to read the clock when she was very small. Oh - there's lots more - but just say she was made of "spirit, fire and dew", and at 80 died young."

In 1951, Rachel Ferguson's book <u>The Royal Borough of Kensington</u> was published. As I had spent several years of my school days in Kensington, I immediately borrowed the book from The Times Book Club and great was my surprise and delight to come across references to Trix whom Rachel Ferguson, herself interested in psychic phenomena, referred to as "Seppy".

"In Phillimore Terrace" writes Miss Ferguson "our friend, Mrs. Fleming, (sister of Rudyard Kipling) has seen an elderly man of the late Georgian period standing upon the steps of a house a few doors from our own. The house at that time was bomb-damaged and unoccupied. Our own house, number 2, has been intermittently haunted for many years. The latest apparition to

---

[8] "Colin" - Colin McInnes, another writer descended from Rudyard's favourite cousin, Margaret Burne-Jones, who was so castigated by him in their youth for not being a writer herself.

join the procession is a black cat. My sister has seen it several times, my mother once, I never. But we have all heard the "impersonating voice" many times.

In Kensington Square, There are one or two types of phenomena, which, following the classifications of Mr. O'Donnell, one must list as "Phantasm of the dead" and a reputed case of poltergeists in a well-know and historic house opposite.

It was again Mrs. Fleming, who, one winter morning, experienced a 'flash-back' in time in Hereford Square, South Kensington. She was passing a derelict garden, the house of which had been demolished by a bomb. Sitting in the garden in deck chairs were two girls in summer dresses, and the whole garden was summer-like. And I was once sitting with her in one of the lounges of a large hotel after dinner, and, knowing her almost overpowering psychic gifts, I said to her, 'Is there a ghost in this room?' to which she placidly responded, 'One has just gone out of the door.' Alice Fleming also had command of what the late Harry Price terms telekinesis - the ability to transpose the position of inanimate objects without touching them, a curious business, of which the poltergeists of Borley Rectory were such masters. For it was upon the same evening that "Seppy" pointed to a pencil on the table near her and said: 'I could make that pencil come to me if I concentrated'.

When Rudyard Kipling died, it was only to be expected that he, who, also, possessed a strong psychic streak, though it never apparently approached the strength of his sister's, should come back and talk to her. She was pondering what type of wreath to take to the funeral, and the well known voice of "Ruddy" said:-

'For God's sake, don't send me one of those awful old life-buoys!'

Seppy was the only clairvoyant of whom I have ever even heard who could project herself into the scene she is seeing in the crystal. She once told me that when gazing at a street scene in some Eastern City she almost at once found herself walking down that street. And, unlike all the gazers I have ever heard of, she needed no conventional glass ball. Any colourless ornament would do, and I have sometimes sat by her as she reeled off a description of some event as pictured in a nut crystal pendant that she was wearing.

I first met Seppy at 6 Pembroke Gardens, the house of her cousin Mrs. Margaret Mackail "(daughter of Burne-Jones and mother of Angela Thirkell)" and the reason I called her "Seppy" arose from her own appreciative amusement at her psychic gifts (which she calls Fish, one of my readers Fish-cake and I, Chiswick), a word Seppy swore she couldn't spell. One day a letter came from Mrs. Fleming signed 'Madame Septuajessamine' and she has been called 'Seppy' ever since. She was easily the most remarkable woman I ever expect to meet, and to listen to her stories (Chiswick or social) was well-nigh to expire of assorted excitements and interest."

I wrote to tell Rachel Ferguson of the great pleasure her book had given me, recalling, as it did, so many haunts and memories of my girl-hood; of my father's friendship at a house in Hereford Square, Kensington with George Borrow (he lived at 22, Hereford Square 1860 - 1874); of my own friendship, many years later, with Dicken's daughter, Mrs Kate Perugini, who, for long, lived in Victoria Road, Kensington; of how from the shoulders of a stalwart policeman, as a schoolgirl, I had watched Queen Victoria, in 1897, drive up Kensington High Street - then exactly as portrayed on her book jacket - to attend a service at St. Mary Abbots during her Diamond Jubilee celebrations; then of our connection with "Seppy", and asked how she came to know about witch-craft in Jamaica, and lastly, as she was a cat-lover about my beautiful Tabby, "Bob" - a long letter, I am afraid.

Rachel Ferguson replied:-

2, Phillimore Terrace,
Kensington W.8.

March 1st/51.

"So very many thanks for your most interesting letter. It is indeed delightful to have one more link with dear Seppy. She was at school with my mother, but in spite of this, there was no age between Seppy and myself.

She had but one flaw; a tendency to interminable poetic quotation. At times, it really was Half Hours with the Best Authors! She once wrote an extremely good poem in which various jungle beasts argued as to how she should enter heaven and the great King-elephant said, "She shall ride on me!"

I take it you know her first [2nd actually] published novel "A Pinchbeck Goddess?"* Long years before I met her, that book was one of our family Bibles. It was Kipling at his very best, but with more warmth. I have actually been lent by her the

*No, I have never, so far, been able to find a copy. G.C.

typescript of her unfinished novel, but it wasn't a patch on the other. She published, also, an intermediate one that I have never read, or been able to get hold of.

I miss her badly. She ought to have done tremendous things, but was ridiculously humble, and acquiescent in being over shadowed. She isn't, of course, really dead; even in life she had at least one foot in the other world and I shouldn't wonder if she is in my room at this moment, if I could see and sense her. Two little tricks of speech I remember so well: 'Aaaaand dear one', and 'But - but .....'

I was on my way to an afternoon outing with Seppy, when I was knocked down by a car in the Cromwell Road, so the outing ended in my lying on her bed at Bailey's, while she regaled me with stories of Lord Curzon!

The only Perugini whom I knew was Mark E. who married the dance teacher.* She used to hold classes in Philbeach Gardens Hall.

The chairman of the General Purposes Committee of our Borough Council is a grandson of Dickens and father of Monica.

I have no knowledge of Jamaica, but my great friend, Winifrede Berlyn, lived there when her husband Sir Fiennes Barrett-Lennard, was Chief Justice. She had a lot to say about "duppies" and one curiously haunted house.

---

*Irene Mawer, who taught Grecian Ballet. When I sent the late Mark E Perugini my "Chelsea Memories of Mrs Perugini", his aunt, published in Chamber's Journal, he sent me a copy of his book "<u>Victorian Days and Ways</u>", and we went to tea with him and his wife in Bayswater.

No, you would be surprised, but I have had at least one far longer letter than yours, from an old Kensington lady.

Cats: I wonder if you would care to become members of our Kensington Cat and Kittens Club, of which I am president?........"

It was not until May 1954, that we were able, at last, to visit Bateman's, Kipling's home for 33 years.

During a holiday in Bexhill, Ralph and I, on Wednesday May 19th, drove the twenty odd miles inland by car to Burwash. It was a beautiful late spring afternoon, the countryside, "Oak and Ash and Thorn" golden in the sunshine, the narrow winding ways a joy in fresh green foliage, the hedges blue with hyacinths, or yellow with late primroses, the hawthorne just whitening the trees.

Bateman's is far from the madding crowd, just as Kipling wished it; and, there we came upon it slumbering peacefully in the sunshine, set high, but sheltered by higher encircling hills; a 400 year old house of warm, pale brown stone and tall chimneys. Fortunately, few visitors were about, so we had the place more or less to ourselves.

The house and its interesting contents have often been described; it was the garden, that appealed to me most, a garden of perfect peace - a green garden* - acres of smooth well-kept lawns, the whole surrounded by tall yew hedges, an indigo-green wall, while the grass-green of the lawns was relieved by the two

*"the wonderful English foliage which is the only living green in the world" The Brushwood Boy, Rudyard Kipling.

rows of lemon-green lime trees down the centre of the main lawn. Standing with one's back to the house, to the right towards the bottom of the garden, there was the square pond fed by the Dudwell; flower-beds there were, but these were to one side, and did not interrupt the quiet of the lawns. Three gardeners were busy weeding the flag-stone rockery behind the house. We complimented them on the trimness of the yew hedges. These had just been clipped, they said, and using electric clippers, it had take them six weeks.

When we left, like Trix nine years before, I carried away the memory of "A Golden Afternoon".

The following Sunday, we drove across the marshes and through Pevensey to Eastbourne to have tea with Ethel Hector at the Hydro Hotel, and sitting in the lounge while the Hotel band played, we had a great family chat. Presently, Ethel went up to her room and brought down a packet of papers connected with Trix, after whose death she had helped to clear up the effects at 6 West Coates, Edinburgh. There was an interesting photograph of Trix taken with Maj.Gen. L.G. Dunsterville, and his wife; a couple of letters to Trix from Rudyard at Bateman's and a letter to Trix from Lord Birkenhead, who at the date of writing, July 1944, was engaged on the official biography of her brother and sending her letters "crammed with questions".

Lord Birkenhead writes from:-

Political Intelligence Department

of the Foreign Office,

Centre Block,

Bush House, Aldwych,W.C.2.

Dear Mrs Fleming,

Thank you so much for your last letter. I continue to be lost in amazement and admiration at your marvellous memory.

I can't remember whether there are any more answers coming from you, but I feel I must give you a rest for a time from further questions. You have responded most magnificently." (nevertheless he asks a few more questions and ends) "Please forgive this filthy piece of paper. We have been bombed out in this office and everything is in chaos."

Since that afternoon, Ethel, who had spoken about Trix's strange gift of "The Sight" has sent me further recollections of her:-

"I well remember Aunt Trix telling me about that vision of the child she had in church. She saw quite a lot of Father Obertynski during the war and I remember her telling me of how she had described the exact spot where the treasures were hidden. She used to visit the Edinburgh Zoo every week, I think. I was with her once, when she took a lump of rock salt for a camel, who licked it. She talked to the animals, and the Indian elephant used to salaam as she spoke in Hindustani. When we approached the large cage of Parrots and Macaws, they would fly from the furthermost corner to greet her, making a great noise, as they knew her well, and she always had something for them. I could not help sometimes feeling a little self-conscious of the crowd of people that used to collect behind us.

Another story she told me, once, was about a girl who fell from a yacht and was drowned. Aunt Trix was at one of her Psychic meetings, and suddenly, a call came asking if Mrs. Fleming was there, because the medium had contacted someone who wanted to send a message - 'would Aunt Trix tell the drowned girl's parents she had not suffered at all and her grandmother had been waiting to greet her on the other side.' Aunt Trix wrote to the family and they seemed very glad to hear from her.

"One of her chief interests latterly was a little shop she opened in Kelso called "Gifts and Gratitude", to help some fund for soldiers. A woman ran it for her and she made and collected all sorts of things for it.

"You may know Kipling's Departmental Ditties. Aunt Trix wrote one of the "ditties", I think it is called "Seventeen Forty Nine".[9] It was her own experience at Balls in India. So many women came out 'for the season' and there was one, who though no longer in her first youth, got a lot of attention."

The three letters written by Rudyard to Trix, which were lent me by her nieces, I have kept for the last. One is typed by Rudyard himself, the other two are in his own handwriting, which is small and neat but, not bold and clear like his sister's. It is noticeable that no telephone is included in the Bateman's address.

The letters show the same camaraderie of the far away Indian days; touch on old mutual literary interests - he is, even

[9] Hilton Brown, Hamish Hamilton 1945. *Seventeen Forty-nine* - real title *My Rival*.

then, struggling with one of her poems "to get it into ballad shape"; his deep affection for children wells up with its wistful reference to "my Josephine", the chief love of his life; his joy in animals, in his dog's, Michael's puppies, "adorable", but who have "no manners". He is in his last illness, spending much of his time in bed, and in pain; he is coming to the end of the Road on which he saw so much, of which told so much; the Road he trod with gusto, though the sharp stones sometimes cut his feet; in weariness of the Road, at last, he cries "it is enough!".

> Bateman's,
>> Burwash,
>>> Sussex.
>>>> May 21st.

Oh Delightful Daughter of my Mother,

Your acceptance duly followed your wire; and I'm delighted, only I fear it will be a hard day for you my dear. C. will be confirming the trains etc. Unluckily we haven't got a car now, but an hireling will be sent to meet" (you) "at station - and I do pray the weather will be fine for that Day!

Re Tempest - "put your head in a bag" as William would have said had the expression been current in his day. <u>Remember</u> that first and foremost he was a working dramatist - hampered by the limitations of his stage and age. He never put in more nuances than were needed. What worried him most were the boys that had to take the girls' parts. Hence when he had a good-looking boy for a part his insistence on such details as "this <u>little</u> hand" in Macbeth; hence his Violas, Rosalinds and so on in doublets and breeches. What William in the <u>Tempest</u> was worrying about was his incidental Masques, and the boy who played Miranda probably looked best from in front when posed for sleep. Think <u>that</u> over!

Moreover when P. talks to Miranda of her birth etc he needed the whole stage plus expectancy in his audience who had the figure of the drowsy Miranda (I'm writing with one hand - 'tother in the <u>Tempest</u>, to concentrate on.) If you're good I'll lend you a book about Shakespeare's stage-craft the odds are that the boy who played Miranda was also Olivia (This is me not anyone else) anyway there wasn't any hypnosis or sich. (Haven't been in the S.K.[10] for 200,000 years, but there was the old smell still)

To go back to William for an instant, I had a joyous time writing "The Coiner" in Limits and Renewals. Now, would you believe it ? the reviewers wanted (such as read it) to know what on earth it meant ?

Now I will take my Mike out for a walk.

Ever your lovingest

Rud.

P.S. I've done a William tale - a short one - called "Proof of Holy Writ". Him and Ben in the garden at Stratford looking over the proofs of the Authorized Version. One of the Bishops has asked for W's help over Isaiah!! It was fun to do but there's no intention of turning it loose on a cross-word public.

---

[10] "the S.K." South Kensington Museum.

Bateman's,

Burwash,

Sussex.

Jan. 22nd/33.

Daughter of my Mother!

The ginger was hot in the mouth and was most gratefully received. So was the Northern equivalent of Toroni - the stuff we used to eat in our extreme youth at the Grange - 'memberest?

In return (and I am no mean expert on child-tales) I send you a Perfect Pearl - listen.

It is a small friend of mine, aged about seven. Fair with blue eyes and a shadow of a look of my Josephine about her.

She has been suffering from some small ailment, which involved pain - in tum and so forth. Her mother and she discussed the matter and symptoms, and by that way, generally the mysteries of the human body. Then, she, reflectively:-
"Mummy, I cant see whats the use of the little hole in my tummy. What<u>ever</u> good is it ? Do we all have one ?"
Here I suppose Mummy said that the navel was common to all humanity. There was a little thought and then the child of the Dominant Race - I suppose it is to show that we are British.

You cant - the Gods themselves can't - defeat a breed like this!

The conception of the God-given Trademark ....but your imagination can fill in at leisure. Isn't it perfect ?

It is dour and cold here and we are cleaning up books and

such ere we go away South. It is good exercise on a frosty morning.

That dam poem of yours worries me. I want to get it into simple ballad shape, but it insists on squirming into Morris or Christina. What am I to do ?

Your lovingest

Brother.

Bateman's,

Burwash,

Sussex.

July 13th 1934.

Dearest Trix,

I think you're right in respect to most photos, but that one of the Blessed Aunt* is an exception. Its the loveliest that ever was and I'm deeply grateful. She was as near perfection as the angels make them.

No! I didnt know that James had "trokings" (with respect to witches) with his revising Bishops. I put nothing, nothing beyond the power or scope of W's activities when idle. I'd like to believe that the whole of the O.S. was sent him in proof and that he just went through it gloriously at his ease! The raising of the widow's son (the "only son of his mother") I've always tried to believe and hope was touched up by him.

*Lady Burne-Jones

This goes to you to St. Andrews, hoping it finds you a heap better than it leaves me. I've had a set-back since I returned from Paris and spend most of my time in bed cherishing my tum. It is said to be nothing more than long-standing gastritis - But it is enough!

Michael has sons (two were given me - Hom and Mikey) of three weeks old. Most adorable. They live in a baby kennel and run of their own. Mike rejoices in playing with them! They have <u>no</u> manners.

Ever your own
Brother.

Rudyard Kipling died two years after this. Trix survived him twelve years.

I like to think he was waiting for her on the other side, and that she rode to meet him on the great King-elephant.

Photograph is in a home-made blue folder, signed
"Trix Kipling March 1885. For Grandmama with Trixie's love."

MY MEMORIES

OF

TRIX KIPLING

by

Margaret E. Macdonald

Trix's christening mug and address book.

A N EARLY memory of Trix Kipling was when Helen and I spent an evening with her and her other guests, Angela Thirkell and Rachel Ferguson, at Bailey's Hotel in June 1946. She decided we should do some 'table turning' in the lounge. We sat round a small table on which we placed our hands, each touching her next door neighbour's, except for Miss Ferguson who was sitting nearby holding pencil and paper in readiness to take down messages. In spite of Aunt Trix's efforts, the table refused to co-operate but we certainly gave pleasure and amusement to other people in the lounge who were pretending to be engrossed in their books and papers - indeed one man nearby appeared to be reading his paper upside-down.

I spent a very happy holiday in Edinburgh with Trix and her two maids, Mina, the housekeeper/cook and 'Sheet Anchor' Mary, the housemaid. I had not been to Edinburgh before, and very much enjoyed being show round by Aunt Trix. One of our outings was to the Zoo. Before leaving home, Aunt Trix did her best to persuade Mary to give her some food with which to feed the animals, but Mary was adamant - 'No, Mrs Fleming, feeding the animals is not allowed.' When we got to the Zoo, the first thing we did was to go to the restaurant where she asked for coffee, cakes and biscuits. We enjoyed the coffee, but the food went into a bag which she had thoughtfully brought with her! Whether it was allowed or not, the animals and birds were fed.

Maggie, the hippopotamus, was a particular friend of hers, but she was nowhere in sight when we got to her enclosure. However, when Aunt Trix called to her, she appeared out of the house at the end of the run and came trotting up to her. They 'chatted' together for some time, much to the amazement of the crowd which had gathered round. I have no idea what they said to each other - maybe it was 'Hippo' language they spoke, but, whatever it was, they both seemed to enjoy it and, when the conversation was over, Maggie trotted back

Trix feeding the pygmy hippo at Edinburgh Zoo.

to her house at the end of the run, taking absolutely no notice of anyone else.

In earlier days, Aunt Trix had become very attached to an Indian elephant at the Zoo, and used to talk to it in elephant language. She could make it do anything she asked it to do, whether it was standing on its hind legs, or kneeling down, or just waving its trunk about, much to the keeper's dismay because <u>he</u> couldn't make it do anything it did not want to do. When the elephant died, Aunt Trix was given one of its tusks.

I have a little notebook of hers, and on the front page, under the heading 'ELEPHANT TALK', she has written:-

MAIL	- Go on	BIRI	- Don't do it
BAITH	- Sit down	BIRI CHUT	- Drop it
CHAI	- Turn	BILLAI	- Lift fore leg
DHAT	- Stop	TUL	- Lift hind leg
DHUT PECHE	- Step back	PHULAI BAITH	- Lower hind quarters
DHIR	- Take	and many more words.	

Another strange incident was when Aunt Trix was walking through a large cemetery in Edinburgh, and heard some music. She stopped, listened and looked to see where it was coming from, but there was no house or building of any kind near enough for her to hear any music. She knew the music well, and then realised that the last time she had heard it was at a dance in India many years previously. She remembered exactly with whom she was dancing at the time and, to her surprise, when she looked down at a nearby grave, she found it was that of her dancing partner all those years ago. She had completely lost touch with him, and had no idea he was dead or that he had any connection with Edinburgh.

Just one more personal memory - and this proved to me, beyond all doubt, that Aunt Trix truly had second sight - was when we were sitting at the table having our supper one evening. Aunt Trix was talking about a lot of people I didn't know, and my mind began to wander. It went back to my office in Town where I quite frequently had a little 'flutter' on the horses. Just a bob or two to win, or perhaps a 5/- accumulator - handed to the man on the door as I reported for work. Suddenly, she interrupted her 'talk' to say, 'You know, backing horses is not a very sensible thing to do; the majority of people only lose their money. The bookmakers are the winners nearly every time' - and then went on talking where she left off!

That Aunt Trix had second sight, there is no doubt, and I think it probably crops up in other members of the family to a lesser degree. I have Aunt Trix's crystal ball and her black wooden box with gold relief, made by her father, John Lockwood Kipling, in which she kept her fortune telling cards. I have never seen anything at all in the crystal ball, but I have for a long time, been interested in Spiritualism, and have been to meetings and healing circles, but I do think in some instances that it could lead to dangerous situations. It is more than possible that Trix's mental illness was caused by her body being possessed by an evil spirit. Be that as it may, there was certainly no trace of it during the later years when I knew her.

She was a delightful person, extremely kind, very entertaining, talked nineteen to the dozen, a character, an eccentric perhaps, but she was a dear and I loved her very much.

Betty Macdonald

Trix's black wooden box with gold relief, decorated by John Lockwood Kipling and referred to by Betty Macdonald, containing her fortune-telling cards, her crystal ball, a newspaper cutting about fortune telling, entitled *Your Fortune in the Cards*, and the signs she used when telling fortunes for charities - 'Fate 2/6' - etc. The significance of the feathers and the identity of the young soldier are unknown.

MY MEMORIES

OF

TRIX KIPLING

by

Helen M. Macdonald

Trix's copy of *The Kipling Birthday Book*, open at the entries for Josephine and Rudyard - December 29/30th.

THE first I heard of Trix Fleming (Kipling) was early in the second world war after we had an oil bomb on our house at Hampton. It caused a lot of damage, and many of our belongings were burnt. Aunt Trix, for that is what she told us to call her though we were actually first cousins, once removed, wrote and sent two warm nightdresses for our Mother, made by her maid 'Sheet Anchor' Mary. In the days of coupons, these were indeed a blessing, and shows how kind and thoughtful she was.

Aunt Trix was a most generous person. She had a habit of showing you something and asking how you liked it. When you replied and said how nice it was, she would then say, 'then you must have it', so you had to be careful when replying or she would have given you anything you admired. I have an Indian mosaic necklace acquired in this way before I knew her little habit.

When my father and mother stayed with her in Edinburgh, she asked Mother how she liked the teaset she was using. When Mother said she thought it was lovely, Aunt Trix said, 'It is yours, I will give it to you now but I will borrow it for as long as I live.' After she died, the teaset duly arrived, so presumably she had left instructions to that effect.

Helen Macdonald with Trix on a London visit in the 1940s.

I didn't meet Aunt Trix until she was in her seventies. She lived in Edinburgh, and periodically came up to London to stay at Bailey's Hotel in Gloucester Road. At that time we lived at West Kensington Court (very near the Grange where she was born) and quite near her hotel, and she visited us there. On one occasion, my sister and I went with her to the London Zoo. She loved all animals, and frequently visited the Edinburgh Zoo.

When in London, she enjoyed seeing her family and friends, and loved to tell of her psychic experiences. She was a great chatterbox, as if to make up for the time when she suffered several mental breakdowns and withdrew into herself, refusing to speak.

She told us of one occasion when she attended a reception, and the Chinese Ambassador, Wellington Koo, was the speaker. She went to speak to him, and, to her amazement, found she was talking to him in his own language of which she had no knowledge. She had no idea what she said to him but he appeared pleased, and said he would like to see her again.

Aunt Trix told us how her spirit used to leave her body at night and travel around. She had one special friend she used to visit and, then to prove she had been to her home, would write and tell her what book she was reading and what flowers she had in her room. One night, when she returned, she saw her Mother waiting for her. She was very cross with her and told her never to do it again. In the morning when she woke up, she was tucked up so tightly she could hardly move. She believed her Mother had done it as a warning.

Aunt Trix was in Edinburgh when Rudyard Kipling was suddenly taken ill, and was in the Middlesex Hospital; she could see him quite plainly with their Mother on one side of the bed and herself on the other. She described the room, and the young doctor and the two nurses, one elderly and the other young, and found out afterwards that her description was quite correct. The older doctor, who had been in attendance, had left for a short time to have a rest, and it was while he was gone that Rudyard died. When she was writing a quotation from Shakespeare on the card to put on his flowers, to be sent to the Abbey, she heard Rudyard say, 'Infant' (he always called her that) 'can't I even die without a Shakespearean quotation?' So she said, 'All right Ruddy, I'll give you one of your own.'

Another time, Aunt Trix thought she would like to go round York Minster as she had never been and knew nothing about it. Her Great Uncle James Macdonald had been so impressed by the beauty of the Minster that he had wanted to enter the Church of England. As soon as Aunt Trix got inside, she felt as though she had been before as it was all quite familiar. Then she asked one of the vergers where a certain window was, and he told her it had been removed years before. Later on, she came to a place where she expected to find a certain tomb, and again asked the verger. He looked at her very strangely and said it had been moved to the vaults about 70 years before, adding, 'You must have been reading a very old guide book.' After that, she dare not ask about anything else as she was afraid he would think her quite mad. As she had never been to the Minster before, or read any guide books, it seemed to her that the only explanation was that she was seeing everything through the eyes of her Great Uncle James as he had seen it years before.

Aunt Trix lived to be 80, and was looked after by her two devoted maids.

She was a dear and had a wonderful memory, and frequently quoted long passages from Shakespeare. She was known to her young relative, Colin Thirkell, as 'Auntcestress' Trix.

Helen M. Macdonald.

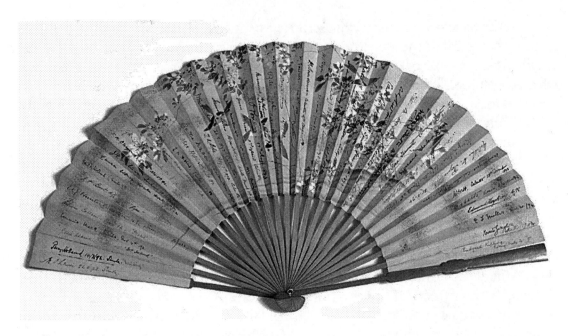

The large paper fan used by Trix as an autograph album, between 1891 and 1895. See the following page for a complete list of the signatures, dates, and places written on each section of the fan.

The signatures, places and dates on the fan provide a rough outline of Trix's movements from the autumn of 1891 until September 1895. September 1891 finds her in London with parents, uncles, aunts, and cousins, followed by a few days with the Baldwins at Wilden, in Worcestershire. In October and November, she is in Scotland; was this her first visit home with her husband since their marriage two years before, and the first meeting with the in-laws? She was in Edinburgh, briefly at Blanefield, north of Glasgow, at St. Andrews for a month or so, and then back to Edinburgh. January 1892 finds her returning to Calcutta; in April, she is in Lahore, and from May to November, in Simla - perhaps involved with the Dramatic Society again and meeting old friends, among them Lord Roberts and Sir Ian Hamilton.

In 1893, she is in Calcutta from February to May, during August, and from November to December. In 1894, she is in Calcutta from January to March. Most of the spaces on the fan were filled by now, but she might have spent time travelling with Colonel Fleming in the course of his surveying duties (the details in the story, *The Joys of Camp*, ring very true), which would account for the long gaps. The autographs resume in June 1895, en route for England on the *SS Simla*, and in July she is in London, and at Tisbury with Rudyard and Carrie, who were escaping the irritations of living near Carrie's family in Vermont. The last signatures are those of her parents-in-law in September in Edinburgh.

Trix's Fan

(Some of the signatures are difficult to decipher!)

Front

N.O. Lewis	22.06.92	Simla	
Percy Holland	14.07.92	Simla	"Wilding"
Jessie Deane	15.07.92	Miss Seabrook	
Emmie Merk	04.11.92	Simla	
Lilian Collen(?)	15.07.92		"Mabel"
A.P. Hunter-Weston	16.07.92	Simla	(Harry)
H.P. Burt	16.07.92		"Ryan"
Ethel M. Holland	92	Simla	
Laura Stoney	02.09.92	Simla	
J.P. Dalison	18.10.92	Simla	
G.B. Greenwood	05.11.92	Simla	
G.R. Elsmire	06.11.92	Simla	
A.M. Elsmire	06.11.92	Simla	"The Park"
F.B. Hebbert	11.11.92	Simla	
Alice Hebbert	11.11.92		
Nettie Webb	02.02.93	Calcutta	
T.A. Pope	05.02.93	Calcutta	
M.?. Wilkins	08.02.92	Calcutta	
James Lewis Walker	08.03.93	Calcutta	
Nellie Mackenzie	18.03.93	Calcutta	
Maisie O'Brien	03.04.	Calcutta	
J. O'Brien	17.08.93		
Miriam M. Scott	04.05.93	Calcutta	
Rita Repton	14.08.93	Calcutta	
C.I. Martins	15.11.93	Calcutta	
M. Fawcus	21.11.93	Calcutta	
J.E. Sanderson	15.08.93	Calcutta	
H.S. Leger	24.06.95	S.S.Simla	
Edward J. Poynter	08.07.95	London	
Andrew Fleming	09.09.95	Edinburgh	
Katie F. Walker	10.07.95	London	
C.L. Fleming	11.09.95	Edinburgh	
Edith Carter	24.06.95	S.S.Simla	
A.M.?. Miller	30.03.94		
Stella M. Morgan	21.01.94	Calcutta	
Freda Smith	24.06.95	S.S.Simla	
Sarah Jeannette (Duncan) Cotes	13.11.		
Everard Charles Cotes			
Caroline Kipling	25.07.95	Tisbury	
Mary L. Pope	25.03.94	Calcutta	
Malcolm W. Rogers RE	25.03.94		
Mary Rogers	25.03.94	Calcutta	
A.E. Webb	28.12.93	Calcutta	
Roberts	05.09.92	Simla	
Edmund Heyking	16.10.92		
E.F. Miller	30.03.94		
Terrie Gordon	17.11.94	Calcutta	
Rudyard Kipling	20.07.95		

Reverse

Ed. Burne-Jones	27.09.91	
John Fleming	20.10.91	St Andrew's
John Lockwood Kipling	14.09.91	London
Louie Baldwin	24.09.91	Wilden
Alice Kipling	14.09.91	London
Georgiana Burne-Jones	17.09.91	
Edith Macdonald	14.09.91	London
Stanley Baldwin	30.09.91	Wilden
Ambrose Macdonald Poynter	14.09.91	London
Margaret Mackail	30.11.91	
William Emerson	14.09.91	London
Josephine Mary McKenzie	04.03.92	Sealdah House
Agnes Poynter	15.09.91	
Caroline E. Macdonald	24.09.91	
Editha Plowden	16.09.	London
Ada M. Reynolds	17.09.91	
Isabella K. Napier	16.09.	
Sibylla Healey	11.01.92	Sealdah House
		Calcutta
Lucy Clifford	17.09.91	
H.L. Fleming	11.10.91	St. Andrew's
Geo. W. Allen	19.09.91	
? Mc. ? Graham	13.10.91	St. Andrew's
Aimée Fleming	02.10.91	Edinburgh
John Coulborough	03.10.91	Blanefield
Edith M. Morrison	03.10.91	Blanefield
William Ferdinand Wratislaw	03.10.91	
E. W. Coulborough	03.10.91	Blanefield
J.E.M. Aitken	09.10.91	St. Andrew's
Lilian Latham	21.10.91	St. Andrew's
Murdo D. Macfarlane	07.92	S.S. Mombasa River
		on R. Hooghly
Isabella J. Lindsay		St. Andrew's
Howard M. Collinson		Hooghly
Georgina M. May	29.10.91	St. Andrew's
Alan Walter May		
Evelyn Pemberton		S.S. Mombasa River
Edward J. Corbould	03.11.91	St. Andrew's
Mary A. Craigie	26.11.91	Edinburgh
G. Sinclair Farqharson		Hooghly
M.E. Richardson		
F. Warren Markham		Hooghly
C. Lyon Sidery (?)	07.01.92	Garden Reach Beach
Laura Violet Marshall	02.04.92	Lahore
H. Bower, Capt. 17th R.C.	01.05.92	Simla
Ian Hamilton	05.06.92	Simla
H.I. Grant	11.06.92	Simla
Mary R.D. Gloag	27.09.92	Simla

In Memoriam
Mrs Alice Macdonald Fleming

By Florence Macdonald M.B.E.

Reproduced from the April 1949 issue of The Kipling Journal, *with the kind permission of the present Hon. Secretary of The Kipling Society.*

BY THE death of Mrs. Fleming, only sister of Rudyard Kipling, the Society has lost a valuable and keenly interested member. She was a woman of rare gifts and accomplishments. She and Rudyard were lucky in their parents, for both Mr. and Mrs. Lockwood Kipling were highly gifted, and their two children inherited their qualities. Their mother, Alice Macdonald, had a strong literary turn and wrote poems, stories and articles from her girlhood. She was, also, a witty conversationalist, with a swift insight and vision that could only be compared to flashes of lightning.

John Lockwood Kipling was an artist and sculptor, with a knack of acquiring and retaining knowledge that was extraordinary. He had a phenomenal memory and seemed to know something about everything. With such a heritage, it is hardly to be wondered that their children were remarkable.

LITERARY GIFTS

Alice, or Trix – which was a pet name given by her brother, because as a baby she was "such a tricksy little thing" – had marked literary gifts, and stories and verse were a natural outlet from her child-hood. As an infant, she literally "lisped in numbers," and picked up Hindustani as quickly as English. She was never idle and her mother writes of her at that time as showing "constant industry and unremitting application, with an amazing gift for quotation," a characteristic she never lost.

I remember when as children we shared a night nursery, one of my amusements as we lay in bed, was to suggest a subject for a poem, and almost instantly the verse was forthcoming. Doubtless if she hadn't had a genius for a brother she would have made a name for herself in literature. She published one novel,[11] "The Pinchbeck Goddess", long out of print, and numberless stories and articles in the Indian and English Press. She also contributed a story to a unique publication, "The Quartette" published in India,

---

[11] "one novel". In fact, she published three:- *The Heart of a Maid*, pub. by A.H.Wheeler, 1891; *A Pinchbeck Goddess*, pub. by Heinemann, 1897; and *Her Brother's Keeper*, pub. by Longman, 1901.

and containing stories, poems and articles by the four Kiplings. She and her mother published a volume of verse called "Hand-in-Hand, Verses by a mother and daughter," and Trix contributed sixty three of them.

Her memory was extraordinary, and everything she read was retained, pigeon-holed and produced at will. One family amusement was to give a quotation from Shakespeare, and she would immediately continue it till the scene or play was finished.

IN INDIA

When her education in England was finished and she rejoined her family in India, she, at once became a real asset in the English society there. She was a beautiful girl, and her amiability of character, as well as her brilliant conversational powers made her quite a sensation. Even that misogynist, Lord Kitchener, paid tribute to her beauty, and remarked that she had "the whitest shoulders and arms in Calcutta, and she didn't need to powder them", adding "I have seen her across the dinner table, and she was actually luminous and would have shone in a dark room."

She was an excellent dancer and a fearless rider, and often rode with Lord Roberts who was a close friend of the family. Lord Curzon spoke of her as follows: "Mrs. Fleming was the one lady in India with whom I could really converse," and he added, "she was also distinguished by beauty and personal charm, which rarely go together, and are almost irresistible when the twain meet." The Kipling quartet were a happy family with similar interests and vocations, and if one was writing, and was short of a word or phrase, and asked for help, it could always be supplied by one or the other, and the brother and sister with their quick wits often mutually supplemented the other's need.

A LETTER-WRITER

Trix was a superb letter writer as her numerous correspondents can testify. In Sir Ian Hamilton's autobiography, "The Following of the Drums,"[12] two good specimens of her letters are given. Strangely enough, music was entirely lacking in her mental equipment. She had no ear for tune, and couldn't distinguish between "God Save the King" and "Home Sweet Home." As a child I tried in vain to teach her nursery rhymes, with lamentable results.

SECOND SIGHT

Another gift Trix possessed, and this was a doubtful blessing. She inherited from her Highland forbears, the gift of second sight - her mother possessed it also in a lesser degree. From early girlhood she saw ghosts or spirits, and in her later years the gift

---

[12] *Listening for the Drums*, pub by Faber & Faber, 1944.

developed considerably, so that she was able to converse with many who had passed into the spirit world. These experiences had no terror for her, but were only of intense interest, and she wondered why others couldn't see what she saw. She had a swift intuitive knowledge of the characters of those she came into contact with, and with the use of a crystal globe[13] foretold many interesting events. Once at a house-party, where she met the late Lord Balfour and Sir Oliver Lodge – both keenly interested in psychic matters, she gave a lengthy proof of her skill as a crystal-gazer, while the two sat spell-bound or taking notes of what she said.

She was a member of the Edinburgh Psychic College, and her knowledge of Yoga acquired in India, was of great interest and benefit to the members. For some years she was a regular contributor – under a pseudonym – to the Psychic Press. Of her life in India after her marriage to Colonel Fleming I know little, but I have heard much from friends in Calcutta and Simla of her brilliant career and also of her kind generous heart and sympathetic understanding, equally ready to help anyone in need, either nursing the sick or packing boxes for tired mothers returning to England. She had a passion for children and animals, and could control both. In the Edinburgh Zoo she had many friends among the wild animals, and one Indian elephant always salaamed at her approach because she spoke to him in Hindustani – the language he was used to in his early days.

Naturally, a highly strung and delicately balanced nature such as hers, was over-sensitive, and when she lost both parents within two months of each other, the result was a bad nervous breakdown; for some years her brilliance seemed eclipsed, and her facile pen and felicitous speech were in abeyance.

IN EDINBURGH

After her husband's retirement they settled in Edinburgh, and we resumed the friendship of our earlier days, which continued intimate and close to the end of her life.

And now she has passed out of this life, but she lives still in the hearts of those who knew and loved her.

---

[13] The crystal globe is only about the size of a hen's egg. It is shown in a photograph with other items of her fortune-telling paraphanalia, on page 114.

Trix on the left, with Mr J.H.C. Brooking, first Hon. Secretary of the Kipling Society, and Florence Macdonald, at a Kipling Society Luncheon, probably in the late 1930s.

"Trix"

By Hilton Brown, author of Rudyard Kipling: A New Appreciation

Reproduced from the April 1949 issue of The Kipling Journal, *with the kind permission of the present Hon. Secretary of The Kipling Society.*

IT MAY seem absurd that one should try to write of "Trix", who knew her only during the last three years of her life. On the other hand, I perhaps worked more closely with her in those years than had anyone else for some time past – first over my book about her brother, next over her proposed London broadcast in 1946 and lastly over her highly successful broadcast from Edinburgh in 1947, a transcript of which has appeared in this Journal. (The cold print gives but a poor idea of how good she was). I have heard it suggested that in her last years she had lost something of her keenness and vitality; that the flame of her intellect – if it had not exactly dimmed – had perhaps flickered. Nothing – in my experience could be wider of the fact. It is true she was not an altogether easy person to work with; to pin her down to the exigencies of a broadcast script, for instance, which must be compassed within an exactitude of minutes and almost of seconds, was not the simplest of tasks. But this was so, not from any deficiency on her part but from the very richness of her mental store; you could not say a word to her without firing a train of recollection, a mine of associations; and her own delight and interest in these must be communicated immediately to *you*.

I have never met a finer or more exact memory;[14] she was minute on detail and particular on substance; under test, she never contradicted herself. I do not think she could ever, of herself, have written a book of her memories; but it seems to me a lamentable pity that no one ever took the trouble to sit down with her and – by a process, I admit, of elimination – evolve what would have been a shining record of two interwoven and outstanding lives, her own and her brother's.

Of her personal charm I need say nothing; it is sufficiently known to many readers of these words. Like her gaiety and her common sense, it did not flag. How, then, was she not better known? Perhaps the combination of physical attractions and brilliance of mind was – as it has been to so many women – fatal to her success; perhaps she was overshadowed always by her brother; one feels at any rate that her contemporaries did

---

[14] "...a finer or more exact memory." This is not supported by checkable facts; her memory for dates is often inaccurate, and her description of the Southsea days is more concerned with supporting Rudyard than with factual accuracy.

not make all of her that should have been made. To the last – or the last I saw of her – she was stimulating and delightful; she captivated everyone at both Broadcasting Houses, Edinburgh and London. I am rejoiced to learn that up to within a short time of her death, she was still storming the heights of the Edinburgh Zoo on Corstorphine Hill – this at a pace which would test an able-bodied man – and discoursing with her old vivacity on all her friends in the paddocks and caves and cages.

As I have said, I knew her only in the very last years of her life and I must therefore have missed a great deal; but at least I have the consolation – and it is a solid one – that I did not miss her altogether.

Trix at Gattonside House, her sister-in-law Moona Richardson's house near Melrose, in 1892.

Part Two

Poetry
of
Trix Kipling

Introduction

Verse and Worse

This is a collection of poems, hand-written in a blue exercise book and dated 1931. Verse and poems written over the years and collected by Trix, plus new work written after 1931.

She delights in lists - plants in *Weeding*, jewels in *Sorrow Island*, eastern riches in *Quest of the Magi*, lepidopterae in *Butterflies*.

The influence of R.L. Stevenson is very strong in *Tramp's Testament* - compare it with *Give to me the life I love,* and *I would like to rise and go* . . . He was always a favourite, and Trix recalled how the entire family fell avidly on *Treasure Island*, newly arrived during a very wet spell at Dalhousie. As late as 1932, Trix and Ruddy were swapping quotations from him, and Rudyard was wagering a box of Edinburgh Rock, cinnamon flavour, that she had misquoted.

The contents of the exercise book are reproduced on the following pages, completely unedited, and laid out roughly as Trix wrote them, including her own corrections and margin notes.

[title page of blue exercise book]

Trix Fleming
6 West Coates
Edinburgh -

September 1931

Verse and Worse

[page 2]

Folly and Fun are sisters twain,
  One holding her sides:
The other testing how much inane
  In Wisdom bides.

———————————

Tales are easy enough to tell
  In words of glamour & glory:
But to write them down - & to write down well,
  Is — quite another story.

———————————

Philosophy is rare: – & most bewildren'-
Philosophy is rare: – by its great aid we bear
The ills we do not share – & bury neighbour's children?
Philosophy is rare: – & most bewildren!

To me Metaphysics appear,
(But alas! I can't phrase it aright.)
The attraction the Infinites bear,
To a man's mind finite.

For a Pussy Willow Calendar -
Who will tell us the day of the week?
As the year swings round with a will - oh -
We may trust her words though she does not speak -
       Pussy Willow!

Who will tell us the age of the moon,
Ruling over the billow:
Keeping the seas & the tides in tune?
       Pussy Will - oh!

Who'll remind you a faithful friend,
Or ever she seeks her pillow,
Has always a loving thought to send?
       Pussy Will - oh!

(With a moonstone)

"One end of me is flawed & grey,
　And one is heavenly blue,
To teach when Earth mists fade away,
　Love maketh all things new."

———————————

(Ditto)

So far apart our orbits beat,
　While planets hold their tune:
It seems that you & I may meet
　But once – in a blue moon -
We needs must bow to Fate's decree,
　So far our lives are thrown -
So Friend with Birthday love from me -
　Accept a Blue Moonstone!

———————————

With a cairngorm brooch -

To Sibyl of the heart of gold
　I send a little heart of stone;
With memories of dear days flown,
　And much more love than can be told;
"For Oh I shall be dead and cold,
　Ere I forget you - Heart of Gold."

———————————

Pleasure comes to play with me, a rosy laughing guest -
But Sorrow spends all day with me, & Sorrow is the best.

———————————

For a Birthday - January 14th.

> One violet is more than verses,
>   No lyric yet was worth a rose:
> But till Spring comes with loving mercies,
>   Only the scarce seen snowdrop blows.
> My birthday posey is but verses,
>   Dear Pamela, your spirit knows,
> That though I only send you verses -
>   My love for you is like a rose.

> Raising his little crozier green,
>   A fairy bishop's crook,
> Beloved Bishop Bracken's seen,
>   In every shady nook;
> The self same staff he carried,
>   That very merry tide,
> When Oberon was married
>   And Titania his bride.

Motto for a Book Plate.

> I am my master's treasure,
> He lends me for your pleasure,
> Do not keep me beyond measure,
> Prithee use me, not abuse me,
> Enjoy me - not destroy me.
> So read me & heed me –
> And home again speed me.

Ditto –)

> *This book is my treasure,*
> *And sent for your pleasure,*
> *Pray read and enjoy it,*
> *Take heed - not destroy it -*
> *Not lend it - or rend it.*
> *But home again send it!*

———————————

> *Bunches of buds that cannot ope*
> *In my October garden sway:*
> *Each with a sure and certain hope*
> *Of bloom and length of day.*

> *So many buds that cannot blossom,*
> *Within my autumn garden grow:*
> *Each bearing in its close shut bosom*
> *Firm hope of bloom, no fear of snow!*

23/10/31.

———————————

> *Next of Kin - or Weeding -*
> *I stubbed up nettle, burdock,*
> *Sow - thistles' milky stems,*
> *The honey-scented charlock,*
> *The hyssop's diadems -*
> *Light tip-toe growing groundsel,*
> *And firm tap-rooted dock,*   *(With plantain leaf most excellent!)*
> *With homely sturdy waybread*   *(healthy)*
> *Established like a rock.*

Bad bishopsweed's spread wings,
    The bindweed's strangle-hold,   Ring-all-men's
The purple bee-buzzed spires   (bee-loved)
    That keeps our fays from cold -   (That save fay's fists from cold)
The lions tooth in splendour
    The day's eye, star of light,
With stitchwort elfin-slender
    And giltcups closed at night-
Red pimpernel, the prophet,
    Dark nightshade's clinging curse,   (serpent)
The friendly, fragrant fennel   (fish sauce)
    And well-filled shepherd's purse.

When garth had changed to charnel,
    And I was tired indeed,
The torn stems of the darnel,
    Squeaked bravely: − Sister, heed!
Art sure, that in God's Garden
    Thou also, art not weed?   (too, art not a weed?)
Then did I kneel for pardon,
    And all my soul did plead.
That ruth I had not given   (grace)
    Might help me in my need -
When - weed - or flower shriven,
    I face my every deed -
Ah - none can give me rede;
    Would God I knew indeed.   23/10/31.

———————————————

Faith is child of soul & spirit, God's good gift and God's great due;
Belief is born of mind & reason, offer it Thy Maker too.

———————————————

For daily bread, & each good gift,
Our hearts to thee in thanks we lift:
May we look from the gift to the Giver,
And turn from the stream to the River.

Lord, by Thy Hand we have been fed,
We thank Thee for our daily bread.
Grant us, we pray, of Thy great love,
Eternal Bread in Heaven above.

A Nursery Grace - (At Teatime)

We thank Thee Lord, for milk and bread,
    And that Thy bees make honey,
That apples grow so ripe & red,
    And summer days are sunny.

The Martyr –

They beat me down, but as I fall
With lightening sureness I recall,
    That in some life gone by,
It was my hand that flung the stone,
My tongue that mocked the dying moan;
Praise God, who lets me thus atone
    Ere the last death I die.

Upon the ramparts of Man's Pride,
A warrior thrust a priest aside,
"The world of deeds awaiteth me,
I have no time to sing" quoth he -
   "Miserere Domine!"

'Mid shattered walls, that were Man's Strength,
A captive writhed his anguished length,
"The bruized reed wilt break?" moaned he,
The smoking flax quench utterly?"
   "Miserere Domine."

Before the altar of Man's Soul,   *Within the minster of*
His wounds all healed, his heart made whole;
A strong man knelt, from self set free,
And his new song rose joyfully, –
   "Gloria tibi. Domine."

_____

    The Messengers[15] *–*   *(Oct 11th. 1931)*
In grey St Andrews, by the sea,   *"Yet speaketh (?)"*
Labrador, Redbreast, Admiral,
Dog, bird and fly brought word to me,
   And thus it did befall.

Grey ruins weather-mumbled dull,   *(graved and)*
Ranges of graves surrounded me;
Beyond and very beautiful
   Terrible crystal sea.

---

[15] *The Messengers* - a memory of St Andrews in 1919, when she was still suffering from mental illness.

Here lay a twelve year parted friend,
Frank, simple-hearted, no renown,
Whose face beamed kindness without end,
*   Through small keen eyes, bright brown.*

While I remembered something hooked
About my arm, and glancing down,
A big dog fawned, & kindness looked
*   Through small keen eyes - bright brown.*

Another grave - Ah Little Thing,
Loved, lost, lamented! Did the Choir
Invisible touch that sweet string?
*   A cithern's throbbing wire?   (thrilling)*

No - Robin, throwing breast knot gay,
Yet beads on me, who brought no crumb,
Sang "Sweet, sweet, sweet! Sweet, sweet to-day!
*   Sweet! Sweeter still to come!"*

Blessing his faith, I made my way
To flowers on a name graved new:
So dear, that when he went away,
*   Joy of three lives went too.*

St Michael's daisies, purple, gold
Is that a withered leaf that clings?
Watching, I saw the leaf unfold
*   Red Admiral's undreamed wings -*

Emblem of immortality,
A little honeyed pollen found,
Then, measures more than I could see,
*   He took the blue profound.*

I thank my Angel for the three
Dear Messengers that came to me,
In grey St Andrews, by the sea,
Making the graves proclaim to me
The three great words of grammary
For which my heart gives grammercy   (The words I hold in memory)
"Love. Hope. Eternity."

———————————

A Lost Love[16] *(Written in 1884.)*

"We have lost Love, you & I."
*   "Seek him in the roses."*
Nay, but summer roses die,
*   Every blossom closes;*
Only thorns remain, in the wind & rain."

"Love is swallow swift they say,
*   Seek him with the swallow."*
"Summer's heralds will not stay
*   When the winds blow hollow -*
Only robins sing, other birds take wing."

[16] *A Lost Love*, 1884. Perhaps written after her first season at Dalhousie and a brief hill-station romance. There are no other clues.

"Nightingale is Love's own bird,
    Seek him in the forest."
Philomel is never heard
    When our need is sorest.
Nightingales are still, silent wood and hill."

We have lost Love, you and I
    Lost him past regaining
For a Summer Love will fly
    When the woods are waning."
"Love too weak for pain, seek him not again."

———————————————

Roses.   (Words for music.)

In Springtime, when the lark rose high,   soared, sprang
    And days were glad, in sooth,
We plucked together, he & I,
    The sweet pink rose of Youth.

When Summer wove her witchery
    And skies were blue above
We plucked together, he & I,
    The deep red rose of Love.

And now, 'mid Autumn's harvest shown,
    I walk, with sobbing breath,
For my dear love has plucked alone,
    The wan white rose of Death.

Though Winter's woeful, spent apart,
*   Each pulse beat proves through strife -*
He waits to meet me, in the heart -
*   The Great Gold Rose of Life.*

I cannot follow, Jeremy, where you have gone away;
And so you should send word to me, for you know where I stay;
But you, - O give me your address, are you with flowers or stars?
Shall I write care of Rose trees, or Vesper, Neptune, Mars?

He.   "Your genuine indifference has taken me in thrall,
*   And so I must lay siege to you, till you surrender all."*

She "But afterwards what would it be? Forever and Forever?
*   Or the serene satiety of carried-out endeavour?"[17]*

In Hospital - A Xmas Carol -

(Tune - "O little town of Bethlehem") D.C.M.

"O! Little town of Bethlehem"
The kindly nurses sing:
Nor dream that near and even here
We find Our Heavenly King.
Last night, before the bells rang out
To herald Xmas morn,
A wanderer came, in pity's name,
And her young son was born.

---

[17] These lines have the cynicism of some of the *Plain Tales*. Undated, they could also be Simla echoes.

A Magdalene - maybe,
Let none ask, or despise -
His purity of infancy
Makes Gabriel wing his eyes.   (veil)
A tinsel star, from Woolworth -
Shines at his cradle side,
But all the worth, of all the earth
Could not more truly guide.

A Babe too young for playthings,
But Magian gifts are bright:
Fruit of the vine is hers for sign,
For Him a Lamb snow-white.
Rich gold of Christmas crackers
Is scattered there indeed,
Sweet frankincense to soothe the sense,
Kind myrrh, in case of need.

They sing God's Loving Mercies,
To human hearts that sin:
"Where meek souls will receive Him still,
The dear Christ enters in."
They sing that "Christmas Angels,
The great glad Tidings tell."
Can they not see, that this is He,
Our Lord Immanuel!

Xmas 1931 -

———————————————

Sorrow Island[18] [crossed out and replaced with] *"Tossed with Tempest"*

I thought I braved an unknown sea,
Yet all was charted plain for me:
Flung shipwrecked on a barren land,
I found guide - footsteps on the sand.
Made deaf by sobs, & blind with tears,
I turned the kindest hopes to fears.
The rustle of my Angel's wings,
Set me a-search for fangs & stings;
My signal smoke implored the sea,
Though bannered Love protected me.
With bleeding hands I scooped a cave,
Though His Pavilion there did wave;
Stooped for my thirst to tainted pools,
And gathered sloes, & rank toadstools.
Yet, those I falsely thought were dead,
Had left me store of wine & bread.

Too sunk to hear my Angel's words
She spoke to me through mice & birds,
The furry folk, the feathered things
Brought healing in their paws & wings.
How could I rail at all to come?
It drove the shrew-mouse from her crumb:
And birds, good friends when I was still,
Flew from me when my voice was shrill.
Each morning brought me - thankless one -
The benediction of the sun.
Noumenon of the noonday hush,

---

[18] *Sorrow Island* - looking back on her years of mental instability from the calm of 1931.

The favour of the flowerset bush:
At night - to soothe mind out of tune,
The lavish silver of the moon:
Or skies so clear they took my breath,
Showed stars whose light unterrored death.

The waves that rippled round my bay
Washed sourness of soul away:
Streams swept aside the dust of grief,
Leaving me gold of true belief   *the gold for my relief*
The birds grew silent now from choice,
That I might hear my Angel's voice.
The branches lost their flowers fair   *shed*
But O! his face and wings were there.
Emerald & beryl, amethyst,
Such sapphires as I never wist,
Chalcedony and chrysolite,
Glories by day & flames by night,   *Jewels*
More than my narrow heart could hold,
He gave, with pearls & Heavens gold.
Teaching, that even tears may be,
As diamonds in the Crystal Sea.

When my novitiate was spent
A rescue sail to me was sent:
And now my wistful heart looks back
With longing to that desert track,
Where - in a magic circle's spell -
I learnt - what words can never tell -
And Island Sorrow gave me strength
To face whatever comes at length.   *1931.*

Glory Trailer or Gate-crasher?

Next flat's first baby, wet, distressed,
　　Yelling with bad pain in his tummy;
When soothed upon an alien breast,
　　Smiled, hiccoughed, took her for his mummy!
His tears, trials, tininess <u>should</u> move
　　A woman's heart to make him happy:
His mother says she "cannot love
<u>It</u>, while it pukes, & soils its nappy"!

The wind is wild to-night,
　　The trees are crying:
And hither, thither - gusty light
　　Are spirits flying.
I hear a voice I love.
　　Cry once - & not again
While many a voice that has no power to move -
　　Howls at my window pane.

　　　　　　　　　　　　　　　　1905.

You did not come to me last night,
　　I think your spirit knew,
That I should tremble in affright -
　　But not because of you -
Only because of night.

I did not hear your footfall press
　　The stairs you know so well,

But O the wind was pitiless
    On down and dell -
Howling and merciless!

You loved the lovely ways of life,
    And all things good:
I know your nature shrank from strife.
    Come now! Your wood
With tender songs of birds is rife
    Your English wood.

Come now! The sun sheds morning gold
The branches gleam -
The yellow aconites unfold
Beside the little stream:
And now - my spirit - morning bold,
Will know you are no dream!

                                        Stockton - 1902. G.B.

_____

Answer to a child's question -

"I do not think that Robin
    Covered the Babes with leaves,
But when he heard them sobbing,
    He flew to ask "What grieves?"

And then I'm sure he stayed with them,
    Sharing their last least crumb,
And if they had but understood
    He would have led them home.

Not to their own home maybe,
  Where bad men plotted harm:
But to a pleasant barn he knew
  Beside a friendly farm.

He would have called the farmer's wife
  To give them milk & bread,
She would have kissed their sleepy eyes
  And tucked them up in bed.

While Robin sang "Dear silly things,
  More helpless than a mouse:
With foolish paws instead of wings -
  You're welcome to my house.

––––––––––––––––––

1890 - 1932

I passed through the town on the Borderside -
  A way grown strange to my feet,
And the ghost of a bright haired, laughing bride
  Came merrily down the street.
She looked at me - with blue eyes of my own,
  Then vanished - before we could meet:
And a grey-haired grim faced, serious crone[19]
  Went heavily down the street!

                              July 29th. 1932.

––––––––––––––––––

[19] "Grim-faced, serious crone" is belied by the street photographs taken of her at this time!

The Story of Piccaninny, Pekinese, and Six Foot Three in Blue[20]

One fine day, a little Piccaninny,
*   Playing in the Park, met a Pekinese:*
Both were brown, and one was skinny,
*   Each made friends with the greatest ease.*
Little brown Dog he danced - chin-chinny,
*   Little brown Boy flopped on his knees.*
"How you? how? asked little Piccaninny.
*   Yow? How yow? asked pretty Pekinese.*

"My name Sam," said simple Piccaninny,
*   "Pearl of Champion Chu-Ching-Chang," said high-born Pekinese.*
"What for short?" asked puzzled Piccaninny,
*   " Own Mittys Blubber Dub" yawned Pekinese,*
"What that mean?" asked startled Piccaninny,
*   "Mistress's Beloved Dove," said learned Pekinese.*
"You know lots!" said dazzled Piccaninny.
*   "Some are born with brilliant brains," said modest Pekinese.*

"Squat down talk," said lazy Piccaninny,
*   "Come walkee, walk," danced nimble Pekinese,*
"Not want walk: just had my dinner."
*   "I dine late," said lofty Pekinese.*
"What for din-din, when you get your wish?"
*   "Big bowl, temple rice, spicey stuff - & fish."*
"G'num! G'num!! G'num!!!" said greedy Piccaninny.
*   "Chow! Chow!! Chow!!!" said polished Pekinese.*

---

[20] Although this poem may seem unutterably cute and cloyingly sentimental today, it is typical of the period when E.H. Shepard's illustrations to the Christopher Robin books, and the etchings of children by James H. Dowd, to say nothing of Mabel Lucie Attwell, were so popular. The phrase "earthquake-shake-make booties" lingers in the memory!

Piccaninny wasn't dressed in a way to look his best,
     For he'd bits of grass & cobwebs in his hair:
Though he'd <u>such</u> a rich Papa, & a diamond-decked Mamma,
     And a Nanny doing crochet in a chair,
Still, he'd torn his coat in playing, & his hat had gone a-straying,
     And his collar - and his tie were - anywhere -
And he'd spoilt his shoes, boat sailing, & both his socks were trailing:
     So he didn't look like Master Millionaire.

Then Six-Foot-Three in Blue, who has eyes for all we do,
     Thought "I'd better see that everything is square:
It may be his dawg - or not, but since I'm on the spot,
     I'll go and put a question to the pair."
So Six-Foot-Three in Blue, took big strides up to the two,
     And his voice, though mild, gave Piccaninny a scare,
Saying, "Well my lad, <u>you're</u> muddy - just a reggilar brown study -
     And your Ma'll take a hayrake to your hair!"

"Now you tell me what is true, & a word or two will do,
For least said soonest mended, anywhere:
I've no wish to stop your playing, now's the time to go a-maying:
But the Park & <u>all</u> that's in it, is <u>my</u> care.
You're a very little lad, but your training may be bad,
And the value put on Pekes far tops <u>my</u> screw;
Don't you hang your head that way, but just answer what I say,
Does the little fancy dawg <u>belong to you</u>?"

Then that clever Pekinese, gave a winning little wheeze,
And his grin at Six-Foot-Three betrayed no awe,
"Park Lord, I am not reckless, palace name is on my necklace,

And my Mitty-slave is yonder, - wagging jaw -
Do not think that I'm offended, your remarks were well-intended"
(Here he proffered Six-Foot-Three his paddy paw).
"Pray proceed upon your duties, in those earthquake-shake-make booties,
I salute you as the Guardian of the Law."

Then Six-Foot-Three in Blue thought "That's really very true,
I may walk along my beat with mind at ease,
No need that I should foller, he's got Park Lane on his collar,
And Her Grace is chinning yonder, near the trees."
So Six-Foot-Three in Blue touched his helmet to the two,
And they played at "Catch-your-Tail" till teatime came.
And the very next fine day, if your Nanny walks that way,
Perhaps they'll let you join them at their game.

Tramp's Testament

"Peace on the uttermost border,
Strength on a road untold."

Bright in the sun the white roads run, & which one is the best?
North, East, West, South, there is food for the mouth - & joy for the eyes
- & rest.

Three to refuse, & but one to choose; one life for lion or lamb:
"Little I care the way I fare - so I bide not where I am."

North to the hills, where the snow dark rills hold flavours of methodice,
Or East to the coast where the fishers boast that seldom a fool comes twice -
West where the ray of the dying day, paints heaven in panoram
"Little I care the way I fare, so I bide not where I am."

Breeze in the South is soft as the mouth your bairn holds up at night,
And a woman there, with fading hair, would think me the welcome sight -
Or West I'd float, in a cockle-boat with a sail like an oraflamme
"Little I care how far I fare - so I bide not where I am."

(On a rusty bike, with a trusty tyke, and a pipe between my teeth
A stack for my bed, & the rain overhead - & the good hard road beneath -
And a king might find things less to his mind, as he rules over shows & sham -
"Little I care how hard I fare, so I bide not where I am."

When the sands have run & the trek is done, the best is kept for the end:
Whatever I lose, or like fool refuse, there's a bounty I cannot spend:
Be it North a rift in a deep snowdrift, or East the trough of a wave:
A ditch in the West - or in South moss best, I'll get me the gift of a grave.

No need my bones should be under stones, I was always for open air,
And if Corbie find my eyes to his mind - they are things I can easy spare!
For late I'll lie, when the sun is high, like a petted pup in a pram -
"Little I'll care 'twas far to fare, for peace will be where I am.."

July 30th. 1932.

———————————————

Valentine Echo -
We only talked of trifles,
But mind & heart spoke through
A voice of quiet music -
And smiled in eyes of blue -
Fate grants no second meeting,
But Memory hears anew
Soft speech - "far above singing " -
Sees eyes of hyacinth blue.

———————————————

A prose para from Emily Dickenson's letter -
> *The birds that Father rescued*
> *Are trifling in his trees:*
> *(How flippant are the saved!)*
> *Why they were even frolicking,*
> *Where we dare only kneel.*
> *About the place where he is graved*
> *They skylarked - over bold!*
> *Nature is far too young to feel,*
> *Or many years too old.*

Garden Contents [crossed out and replaced with] *Garden Inventory*

> *Laburnam's golden showers*
>   *'Mid hawthorn's scented snow,*
> *Borders of gilly-flowers,*
>   *Sweeter than spice-winds blow.*
> *Fat folded buds of roses,*
>   *Promise of joys to be,*
> *Pansies in kitten poses,*
>   *And foxgloves for the bee.*
> *The lilac's cones of sweetness,*
>   *And London Pride's pink mist*
> *The tulip's dutch completeness,*
>   *Aubretia - white - moth-kist.*

So many years -
How short they seem,
Lie all behind me -
So few more years,
Brief as a dream,
At most, can find me.

Sept/32

The Valley of Shadows (pic by Evelyn De M.)[21]

Dark is the Valley - the Valley of Shadows,
Weary of heart & of life is the king:
He sits among ruins & thorny the meadows,
The meadows unfruitful, forgotten of Spring.
A green snake is keeping the palace's portal,
The lizard is warden of desolate halls,
And wine has no savour, & Love the Immortal
Seems fading at even, as fast the night falls.
O dark is the Valley, the Valley at even
The King's brow is clouded, the King's heart is black,
His down gazing eyes give no glance to the Heaven
Where angels are winging their homeward bound track -
Sure in this dark hour at the brink of the grave -
The slave seems the Monarch, the Monarch the slave.

---

[21] Evelyn de M. - probably Evelyn de Morgan - a family friend through the Burne-Jones, William Morris connection.

Clay goes a-wooing,
 Courting comely Clay:
Clay vows in sueing -
 "For ever & a day" -
Clay weds at noonday -
 Clay dies ere night,
Clay graves above clay
 "Till the dawn is bright."

Or -

Clay weds at noonday -
 The lovers sever:
Love has his June day
 Death has Forever.

"Oh Hill Perfection - far above the sky line,
 When may I climb to you?
To revel in your woods of fir and high pine -
 To feel your silvery dew?
I tread a footpath dreary past abiding,
 When may I leave it best?"
That path is Patience, & its faithful guiding
 Will lead you to my crest."

        25.12.32.

The Quest of the Magi - (Persian Variant)

Led by the light of a visioned Star,
Gaspar, Melchior & Balthazar,
Kings of the East have come from far
To Bethlehem, where the shepherds are,
Bearing gifts to the Avatar,
Of gold, frankincense & myrrh.

II

"How may we know what gift to bring?"
"Comes He as Healer, Priest or King?"
"One by one, let us test this thing,
Prove if the Star be heralding,
Monarch, Physician, or Hallowing -
By gold, frankincense or myrrh."

III

Counsel taken, the camels kneeled,
Bales uncorded and sacks unsealed,
Coffers opened their wealth revealed,
Best that the kingdoms three could yield,
Gums & spices & gold annealed:
Tried gold, frankincense & myrrh.

IV

Gaspar took myrrh, in a tripod mould,
Heavy as aged hands could hold -
His face was an ivory image old,
With a century's lines 'neath the turban fold,
As he entered first to the Sight foretold,
With myrrh, not incense nor gold.

V

Balthazar's gift was a perfumed gum,
Stacte, onycha, galbanum,
Frankincense for burning till Angels come,
From the seventh sphere of Elysium,
Winging prayer to its arcanum,
Hail myrrh! Frankincense! & Gold!

VI

Melchior's offering, a golden hoard,
Tribute of prince to his Overlord,
Loyal hand on a golden sword,
Heart with homage & fealty stored
Soul a-flame for the Great Award
Lo! myrrh, frankincense & gold!

VII

Gaspar returned - no longer old
But radiant as one who is seraph-told,
His days in the desert are all uprolled,
Since his guided flock is safe in the fold,
And the Pearl of Price is within his hold -
(Laud, myrrh, frankincense and gold!)

_or_

Gaspar returned - no longer old
But radiant as one who is seraph-told,
His days in the desert are all uprolled -
Eyes of Balthazar did glory hold,
Melchior's bow shone like burnished gold -
(Fine gold, frankincense & myrrh!)

VIII

Hands of Balthazar were raised in prayer,
His face shone glory that fills the air
When the very desert seems Heaven laid bare
For the sun sheds splendour everywhere -
An instant only, ere night is there -
Hail gold, frankincense & myrrh!

IX

Forth strode Melchior, a king indeed,
Strong hands swung to his body's speed,
Young eyes shone with an answered need,
One beholding - fruit - flower & seed -
Birth - life - death - & the spirit's <u>creed</u> -   [?]
Hail - myrrh, frankincense & gold.

X

Gaspar, the elder, bowed his head -
"The Healer of Nations is here," he said
"Strength to the weak, to the strong Bread,
Light to the blind, & Life to the dead,
I laid my myrrh neath his Holy head -
Not gold, nor incense, but myrrh."

XI

"Nay, in Priesthood the Godhead dwells,
Light & Perfection His Breastplate tells,
Blue scarlet & purple of Tyrian shells
His robe with pomegranates clashed golden bells
As I burned frankincense in thuribles -
Frankincense - not gold - nor myrrh."

XII

"Sure" said Melchior - "the old are wise
But I saw the King of the Earth and Skies,
A youth my age & about my size -
He touched my sword & my gift did prize -
For my golden crown on his Thronestep lies,
Red gold - not incense nor myrrh.

XIII

Each must a different tale unfold,
"He is a Healer, wise & old."
"Your unbelief as a sin I hold,
He is High Priest - of Grace untold."
"He is a King, young, glad & bold."
Nor incense - nor myrrh - but gold."

XIV

"List" said Gaspar - "were it not good,
That we hush to silence this angry mood?
And go together in brotherhood,
To learn, as brethren, & children should,
This miracle in amplitude
Of gold, frankincense & myrrh.

XV

Three crowns lay in the cold star-shine -
Six hands knitted in secret sign,
The stable was sweet with the breath of kine,
And three Kings knelt - where the Babe Divine,
Twixt Faith & Chastity crystalline
Clasped gold - frankincense & myrrh.

XVI

To each his symbol for guiding sign -
The orbed Sphere & the Mystic Trine -
The thorn crowned Spear - & the Perfect Vine -
Creator and Paraclete - Lord Divine -
<u>Quest</u> [?] wounded Lamb - & the Heavenly Wine -
Hail gold - Frankincense & Myrrh.

XVII

To us these emblems for Token clear
The Trine Eterne and the Circling Sphere -
The brooding Dove - in the noonday near -
Our Father - & Comforter - Shepherd Dear -
The Bread of Love & the Wine of Fear -
Hail gold

XVIII

May we interpret their gifts of sense?
Gold is for Love & for Reverence
Prayer is the savour of frankincense
Myrrh for the Death that shall bear us hence -
May Love & Prayer be our Guide & Defence
Laud Gold - Frankincense & Myrrh.

A Biography

by

Alice Macdonald Fleming

Her memorial poem for Rudyard, was based on his

A St. Helena Lullaby, first published in *Rewards and Fairies*,

which is a résumé of the life of Napoleon.

Did she feel that her brother was also a great man,

stricken and despised at the end of his life?

Her talks and writings about him after his death were concerned

with their early life together when success and fame were

on the horizon, and illness, sorrow, and disillusion

had not touched either of them.

A BIOGRAPHY

1865 - 1936

BOMBAY   1865-1872

"How far is Poets Corner from a baby in Bombay?"
I can't explain, I cannot say - the paths they wind about.
But Mother, call your son again or else he'll run away.

(When you're full of mischief you must play it out.)

SOUTHSEA   1872-1877

"How far is Poets Corner from a lonely bullied child?"
A certain kind of wisdom is given when you weep:
And though the fog is round you, your Star is undefiled.

(How bitter is a stranger's bread, a stranger's stairs, how steep.)

WESTWARD HO   1878-1882

"How far is Poets Corner from a clever boy at school?"
So much to see, so much to learn, its very far to go,
But put your heart in all you do, and cease to play the fool,

(When you've done with Westward Ho, its Eastward Ho.)

LAHORE AND ALLAHABAD   1882-1888

"How far is Poets Corner from a Stunt Sahib in Lahore?"
Oh, very far those cool grey stones, the glass reads ninety-eight,
The browsweat clouds your glasses while the hand-pulled

punkahs snore.

(When you take the yoke in youth you must bear its weight.)

LONDON   1889   (aged 24.)

"How far is Poets Corner from the "Rudyard Kipling Boom?""
A bubble reputation may burst as soon as blown.
But you have got your web to weave, the warp is on the loom.
(Your work to you is Bread of Life, while flattery's a stone.)

AMERICA   1899

"How far is Poets Corner from New York and a sick man?"
Not the mere Atlantic, its the Seven Seas that mourn.
Three continents are frantic, - there's a Kaiser's telegram.
(You live, - but half your joy in life has gone, beyond return.)

WESTMINSTER   1936

"How far is Poets Corner from a coffin 'neath the Jack?"
So near that we may count the steps that bring you to the stone.
"Lest we forget. Lest we forget." Tears, and a crowd in black,
(And the choir's singing verses of your own.)

? ? ? ?

"How far is Poets Corner from a happy spirit freed?"
Further than mind of man conceives, astronomers are dumb.
Your works will live behind you, but you are off at speed.
(To learn how solar systems work, - until The Kingdom come.)

                    ALICE MACDONALD FLEMING.

[Retyped copy of an original two-page typescript by Trix.]

IF

"O God, why ain't it a man?" - R.K.

(To a young C.O. now enjoying complete exemption.)

If you can keep your job when all about you
   Are losing theirs because they're soldiers now;
If no Tribunal for C.O.s can flout you,
   Or tilt the self-set halo from your brow;
If you hold forth, demand your soul's pre-emption,
   And play up conscience more than it is worth,
You'll win your case, enjoy "complete exemption",

   And - at the usual price - possess the earth.

If you can take from college and from city
   Culture and comfort all your conscious days,
Take all and render nothing, more's the pity,
   But cunning preachments of self-love, self-praise;
Exempt you are, forsooth, and safely nested,
   Above your priceless pate a plume of white,
Protected by this symbol all-detested,

   Your worst foe - self - is all you need to fight.

If you can claim to follow Christ as Master
   (Tell us when he shirked service or grim death),
How dare you plead for freedom from disaster,
   And, wrapped in cotton-wool draw easy breath

If you evade - not touching with a finger -
  The heavy burdens other young men bear,
We dare not breathe the ugly word "malinger",
  For fear, perchance, your craven soul we scare.

If the girls in uniform do not distress you,
  If you can smile at verbal sneers made plain,
If you don't wince when soldier friends address you,
  Proffer bath chairs and greet you as "Aunt Jane",
Then rhino hide is nothing to the human,
  Holier than they are, grudge ye not their fun,
But laddie realise the average woman
  Gives heartfelt thanks that you are not her son.

(With due apologies to my brother, who wrote the
original "If", and who did not love shirkers.)

                    Alice Macdonald Fleming (Kipling)

A True Tale -

Won'ts[22] - (Women's Outfitted New Troops.)

What fills the housewife's heart with doubt? What makes her want to scream?
It isn't ekeing rations out, or missing fruit and cream,
Its when two burly men appear, and say - with bended brows,
"We're billeting some Won'ts round here - How many can you house?
They must have three meat meals a day, and one that's light and cold;
They tidy their own rooms, they say, and do as they are told,
You'll find them pleasant helpful girls, they'll stay three months - or more -
Their Commandant will put you wise. Good day - I'll send you four."

They came, they smoked, and swore & groused: they "smelt most awful vile"
Of perfume, powder, lipsticks that showed for a half a mile,
They talked of "ports", they <u>couldn't knit</u>, or put away a chair,
Their appetites were perfect - but their manners were - not there!
O! the Won't! O! the Won't! Never heard the word that's "Don't."
Doesn't know the Scotch for "Thank you", hasn't learnt the use of "Please";
She'll sit and smoke for hours, with her idle hands in front,
Doesn't mend if stockings ladder, from her ankles to her knees!

They claimed late passes twice a week, to share in midnight dangers:
I thought a nightly half past ten, enough for little strangers.
My husband said, "Please turn off lights, and don't shout on the stairs."
They said - "A good kick in the pants would cure the old man's airs."
O! the Won'ts! O! the Won'ts! O the sprawling, brawling Won'ts!
With their smoking, & their croaking, while they picket maids who knit:

---

[22] A parody of Rudyard's *OONTS - (Northern India Transport Train)* - the lifelong habit of expressing herself in verse didn't desert her in the difficult days of raids, shortages and billeting. It was her safety valve, no doubt, but still an echo of her brother.

Your clicking gives us willies, do something else or shunt!"
Yet - they're not such film-star lovelies that they needn't do their bit.

On Sunday they went back to bed, from 10 till 1 o'clock.
We woke them up at dinner time - Poor girls! It was a shock
But since they'd only breakfasted on puddings - black and bacon -
They sat up & took nourishment, to keep morale unshaken.
O! the Won'ts! O! the Won'ts! O! the lazy-daisy Won'ts!
Saying "Rules are made for breaking, so their sense we cannot tell."
They "haven't any use for Church" - but when they've got "the dunts" -
Call loudly on their Maker, with a word that rhymes with Bell!

Final Chorus

O! the Won'ts! O! the Won'ts! O the silly-billy Won'ts!
Wearing powder, paint & lipstick! Dirty faces on parade.
We're sorry for the youngsters, and would help them do their stunts,
But, those who wear the Uniform, should keep the Rule that's made -
Yes - when they wear King's uniform, obedience is their trade.

[Hand-written by Trix on four loose sheets, tucked into the back of the blue exercise book containing *Verse and Worse*.]

Butterflies[23]

I

Where are the butterflies?
Why have they fled our skies?
Why should they now despise
   Heather and ling-land?
Or has a tariff set
Some new-enforced war debt
Kept them, with deep regret
   Summering in England?

II

Or has the wireless
Taken in great excess,
Made them desire less
   Mountain and woodland?
Or have our petrol fumes,
Baleful as breath of tombs
Motors like clacking looms
   Made this no good land?

III

All winged life is not spent,
Moth still in bines content,
Brown bees on honey bent,
   Raid foxglove copses;

---

[23] Published in *The Scotsman*, 17.9.32, in response to a letter about the dearth of butterflies in Scotland, in spite of a fine summer. Anything which caught her fancy would set her writing verse.

Wasps clad in penal stripe
Cluster where fruit is ripe
Or drowse with opium pipe
   In meconopsis.

IV

Maybe the rage for flight,
Speeding more swift than light,
Flying with all your might
   Rules Land of Fairy -
Oberon's speedboats need
Countless Ithomides
Swallowtails splendid speed
   Admirals airy!

V

Where are the butterflies?
Chalk Blues, like Summer skies
Vanessa's peacock eyes
   Rhopalocere?
Lovely Nymphalidae
Papilionidae
Mocking Danaidae
   Lepidoptera?

Trix, aged 18, on Yorick, taken in Lahore in 1886.

Part Three

Prose
of
Trix Kipling

Introduction

THE sketches and short stories that follow are undated, typed carbon copies, which suggests they may have been submitted to magazines. They have "From Mrs. Fleming, Tisbury, Wilts" written in pencil in the top left-hand corner of the title pages of most of them. The most likely period of writing seems to have been late 1901/02 when Trix had recovered from her breakdown of 1898-1901, but was still with her parents in Wiltshire.

Reading between the lines suggests that the series of monologues is an attempt to exorcise the tensions and frustrations of life with her rather dour, undemonstrative husband, and the periods with her lively but demanding mother, against a background of disapproval from her father and brother. All through her life, except when she was incapacitated by illness, writing seems to have been her safety valve.

It is interesting to compare her use of experiencing life in an Indian hill station with Rudyard's early stories - although, of course, their purposes are very different. His comment on fashion in the poem, *The Vanishing Figure*, shows him at his coarsest, while her references to damp fringes will stir an echo with everyone who has suffered from a perm which frizzes in the wet!

The setting of the monologues is her life with Fleming, moving around India for his work with the Survey. "George" is an undemonstrative man saddled with a chattering, silly wife which suggests that, apart from the dramatic and humorous possibilities of such a pairing, Trix, consciously or unconsciously, thought herself stupid, either to have married Jack in the first place or to be unable to control her frustrations.

Some of Trix's typescripts, with her own hand-written alterations, are shown as facsimile reproductions, reduced to fit, on the following pages.

Notes

p.176 - Cabinet photograph, size 7" x 5".

p.217 - "Rose in June" was her own nickname in Dalhousie in 1884. Her birthday was June 11th.

p.219 - "unlucky enough to renew a broken engagement . . ." as Trix and Fleming had done.

p.229 - Stinginess over stamps has the authentic ring of a real-life irritation.

p.234 - "You never take an interest in anything I do . . ." A cri de coeur from Trix, I think.

p.235 - Mountmellick work. A type of embroidery developed in the 1840s at Mountmellick, near Waterford, Ireland. Thick white cotton thread is used for flat and raised stitches on white cotton fabric. Used for bedspreads and smaller pieces. Trix was an accomplished needlewoman.

p.236 - "I never knew anyone like you for saying a pleasant thing disagreeably, and it is a habit you should fight against, dear, for it makes the people around you very unhappy." Comment superfluous.

ON THE LADIES' LINKS.

-----‡‡‡‡‡‡‡‡‡-----

~~Any Wife to any Husband.~~

    Are you going to play golf with me this evening, dear? That <u>is</u> nice of you! I want you to show me a lot of things George dear, can you lend me a ball? I never seem to have any somehow. Oh that's all dented and quite dirty; I'll take these two nice new ones. Is that <u>my</u> cleek with the leather coming off the handle? I thought it was yours. Now George, we really don't need two caddies. I know its "only two annas each, "but what is the good of spending four annas when two will do? Clubs might get mixed up. Well, even supposing I did play with your clubs I shouldn't do them any harm. How faddy men are!

    "Come along. Yes, I dare say that is Mrs. Birkmire over there, but if you go off to speak to her, we shall keep the whole green waiting. I do hate this first shot, it makes me so nervous to know that all those people are looking at me. There! Look where it it's gone to! George what does 'square leg' mean? I don't understand. I'll keep the score. You were four ~~four~~ for that hole: three was it? I thought it was four, and I was seven, because of that tiresome round leg ball.

    "Wasn't that a good drive of mine? I'll pace it. It was quite twelve yards! Oh bother! My ball has stuck in

I

Note: A reduced facsimile reproduction of Trix's original typescript, including her own handwritten alterations.

a horrid little hole. George, George come here and tell
me. Ought I to play with a cleek or a niblick? There!
Now its gone into the road. Tell that bullock man to stop.
I don't like walking into all that dust. Will it count
against me if I send the caddy to bring it back? What a
shame! Fancy I'm eight for this hole , how dreadful!
Three for you again? Well you _are_ lucky!

. . . .

"we cross the road now. Look, there's Miss ~~Kinson~~. *Watson*
Who is that man she is playing with? She is wearing a
regular garden-party ~~dress~~; it's silly to get up like that,
when one really means to take exercise, isn't it? Oh, have
you played? Why, I've actually not hit the ball at all!
I don't know what's the matter with me to-day, the last
time I went round I got on awfully well. ~~Cleek do chokra~~

gin me the brass thing. no the iron thing
~~petal ke/ no lohar ke chiz~~ You know what I mean perfect-
stupid. ly well, don't be ~~bewakuf~~ *underneath.* Oh it does hurt one's shoulder
when one hits the ground, jars it fearfully. What did you
say, George? 'Golf is not agriculture.' Why, of course,
it isn't; what do you mean? Have I cut up the turf? Oh,
just that bit of grass, what does it matter? I'm sure
there is grass enough in the maidan. Number five is a
very exciting hole. Mind you don't roll down into that
ditch, I mean your ball. There, of course, I've gone on
the race course I always do, its too bad having the race
course there. They might move the railings, and spare us

2

Note: A reduced facsimile reproduction of Trix's original typescript, including her own handwritten alterations.

just that little corner, I'm sure the course is big enough
and wretched people come and ride over our greens, so it
would only be tit for tat. Oh, there is *a* Baboo right in
front. How am I to play? *Tiresome man - Bother him* No indeed I won't 'blaze away',
for I can hit much further than that, and I might kill him.
Do shout, George! I shall have to then. Hi! Five! Five!
He doesn't understand, Isn't 'Five' the right thing to call
out? Oh 'four' is it? I knew it was some number. I don't
see anything to laugh at, and if you mean 'before¦you
should say so; I hate slang.

Is that Captain Desmond on that big brown beast? Yes,,
it is; who is the lady I wonder. She looks rather smart,
I wish I could make out who she is. Oh, I forget I was on
the green, I thought I was making an approach shot, and
I've gone miles past the hole. Tiresome! have you really
done Number Six in two? I was almost sure I saw you playing three, but of course you know best, and its only a
game, and does not matter in the very least.

"Now, this is the longest hole on the links. Do I
stand in the right position when I drive, George? You are
not helping me a bit. Swing the head of the club more round
behind me? It won't go any further, Oh, I can't twist any
more, and my sleeve is cracking, as it is I heard the
stitches go. Indeed, George, I never wear my things tight
this blouse is perfectly loose, only I always have them
made on a fitting lining, they look so much neater. If I
would think a little less about trying to look pretty, and

3

Note: A reduced facsimile reproduction of Trix's original typescript, including her own handwritten alterations.

just that little corner, I'm sure the course is big enough
and wretched people come and ride over our greens, so it
would only be tit for tat. Oh, there is a Baboo right in
front. How am I to play? *Tiresome man - Bother him* No indeed I won't 'blaze away',
for I can hit much further than that, and I might kill him.
Do shout, George! I shall have to then. Hi! Five! Five!
He doesn't understand, Isn't 'Five' the right thing to call
out? Oh 'four' is it? I knew it was some number. I don't
see anything to laugh at, and if you mean 'before!you
should say so; I hate slang.

Is that Captain Desmond on that big brown beast? Yes,,
it is; who is the lady I wonder. She looks rather smart,
I wish I could make out who she is. Oh, I forget I was on
the green, I thought I was making an approach shot, and
I've gone miles past the hole. Tiresome! have you really
done Number Six in two? I was almost sure I saw you playing three, but of course you know best, and its only a
game, and does not matter in the very least.

"Now, this is the longest hole on the links. Do I
stand in the right position when I drive, George? You are
not helping me a bit. Swing the head of the club more round
behind me? It won't go any further, Oh, I can't twist any
more, and my sleeve is cracking, as it is I heard the
stitches go. Indeed, George, I never wear my things tight
this blouse is perfectly loose, only I always have them
made on a fitting lining, they look so much neater. If I
would think a little less about trying to look pretty, and

3

Note: A reduced facsimile reproduction of Trix's original typescript, including her own handwritten alterations.

"No, thank you, I haven't the slightest wish for a drive. You'd better go to the club, and I'll go home and sit in the verandah, all by myself!"

-----‡+‡+‡+‡+‡+‡+‡+‡‡-----

5

Note: A reduced facsimile reproduction of Trix's original typescript, including her own handwritten alterations.

ONE DOZEN - CABINET SIZE.

-----‡‡‡‡‡‡‡‡‡‡‡-----

SCENE:- A dining-room.   TIME:- Thirty-five minutes
late for breakfast. George's wife enters swiftly with a
great rustle of silk. She wears a long-trained pink
satin gown and has a diamond star in her hair.

-----‡‡‡‡‡‡‡‡‡‡‡‡-----

"Oh George dear, I'm most awfully sorry to be so
late, but you know what it is to dress in a hurry, nothing goes right. I'm sure I've done my hair six times
and I'm a perfect object all the same. Why do you look
so astonished, don't you remember that I am going to
be photographed this morning? It isn't that in the
least! I hate dressing up as you call it, but if one
doesn't put on an evening gown the photo looks old-
fashioned in six months, and if one takes the trouble
to be done at all one may just as well do it properly.
You don't see any necessity for more photographs? Oh,
George, that's just like you and I went into the matter
with you so thoroughly before I arranged to be taken! I
have not been done for two whole years and it would be
so awful if anything happened to one and there was not
a recent photograph. Yes, I daresay <u>you</u> are quite

willing   1

Note: A reduced facsimile reproduction of Trix's original typescript, including her own handwritten alterations.

willing to take the risk, but mother is simply longing
for a new photo of me, and I do my hair quite differ-
ently now and I'm ever so much thinner. *Take care.* Kaberdhar khit-
matghar if you spill rumble-tumble on my gown I'll kill
you. No, I'm not going alone: as I knew it was no good
asking you, Amy Forbes has promised to call for me.
She's a very nice girl. No, I suppose she's not very
young, poor thing, and she's not a bit pretty, but she's
awfully sweet!

"Handsome eyes did you say? Why her eyes are quite
tiny and her lashes don't curl in the least, you do admire the very strangest people! I believe she was engaged once and he broke it off or she did, or else it
was her people, I can't remember, but it doesn't matter
much. George, do you like those photos with the head
quite turned? I mean sitting with your back to the
camera thing and looking right over your shoulder - so.
I know one never sits like that really, but it looks
nice I think. Looks 'like a dying duck in a thunder-
storm' I wonder why, when you try to be funny, you
are always so rude.

"Come in, Amy dear, how nice of you to be so punc-
carriage/. tual. Call the gharri please, George. I suppose you

2

Note: A reduced facsimile reproduction of Trix's original typescript, including her own handwritten alterations.

will have gone to office before I come back, so good-
bye. Mind, dear, your foot is touching my train, this
brougham is very small. It's sweet of you to come with
me. 'You like seeing all the photos'. Oh but I want
you to look at me, not at the photos, and tell me if I
am standing nicely and so on. Have I done my hair well?
It took me ages! Oh please put up both the windows
it will be rather stuffy, but if it's at all damp my
fringe will get wild and it will spoil my fan, and it's
only just come out from being re-curled.

"Here we are. Oh what a nice long mirror, one
can't really dress properly without a long glass and
George won't let me get one because we are going to be
transferred next year. I knew a woman once who had a
full length triple mirror and it was perfectly lovely,
one saw oneself from head to foot all round! Is my hair
right? Are you quite sure my fringe hasn't come out
of curl? I brought tongs and a lamp on purpose. Oh,
your hat is quite straight and you are not going to be
photo'ed so come along. What a funny horrid smell, there
always is in a photographers' studios, I suppose it is
something to do with the camera. Good morning. I
want you to photo me half length and some big heads too,

3

Note: A reduced facsimile reproduction of Trix's original typescript, including her own handwritten alterations.

you know: I rather like profiles. Shall I sit in this
chair? Now do take care that my sleeve doesn't come
against my waist, it makes one look so huge. It strains
my eyes to look higher. Shall I open my mouth or keep
it shut, I don't like smiling photos. Have you done
two,that was quick! Oh please wait a minute, I must see
if my hair is all right before you take any more. Did
that look nice, Amy? What is the matter? What are
you staring at? His photo, whose? Captain what? I
can't hear if you whisper like that and the man has gone
off to the black-hole or whatever you call it, to look
at those photos so you needn't mind. Oh, Captain Arnold.
Well, he can't be very handsome if he is like that, do
you know him well? Oh was that the man you were engaged to, was he nice? But if he was fearfully poor
and his people objected as well as yours you were well
out of it dear, you would only have been wretched. Two
years ago was it? Why you must almost have forgotten it
and he is quite certain to, Those sort of things never
make any impression on a man. Is my fringe all right?
Will you do me standing this time with my fan held
like this? Why will my hand be out of focus if I hold
it there? Amy, Amy, is that nice? Have you taken four

4

Note: A reduced facsimile reproduction of Trix's original typescript, including her own handwritten alterations.

already. Oh, the head-dress has caught in my fringe net. I must put it on again.

"My dear girl, you are not crying, are you? What is the matter? It must be a new photo taken of him since, for you never saw it before? Very likely, and he looks quite fat and cheerful, so he evidently isn't pining, and you must summon all your pride and not mind. Oh, they all say they will wait for years , that doesn't mean anything. Look at his buttonhole, he wouldn't have been photoed like that if he hadn't wanted to give it to some one very special: I daresay he is engaged again to a girl with money. You mustn't say you wish you were dead, that's absurd, dear, as well as quite wicked, I'm sure you've got a very happy home. 'Nobody loves you', what nonsense, I don't know what I should do without you to help me with the flowers at dinner parties and do up my hats for me, I'm awfully fond of you. Ah, don't kiss me, I've just got this wretched net on, and here's the man.

"That last was a failure? What a bother. Don't you think if you brought up that palm and let me sit on that sofa so, rather in profile? I want my feet to show. You would have to put the camera further back to get them in and then my head would be smaller. That

5

Note: A reduced facsimile reproduction of Trix's original typescript, including her own handwritten alterations.

seems funny, doesn't it Amy? There ought to be room
enough, it isn't as if I wore "sixes" in shoes, I take
narrow "threes". Wait one minute, I'm not ready, my
watch bracelet has slipped right round!

"That ought to be a good one, don't you think,
Amy? Do attend! You've looked at that photo long
enough to know it by heart. Oh, you can't <u>buy</u> it,
fancy asking for it, and if I did, it would seem just
as queer and my husband would be furious!

"Poor dear, it does seem hard that you shouldn't have
have it when you want it so badly? Have you a rupee
with you? That's all right, put the photo in your
pocket, and put the rupee where it was. That's quite
honest and no one will know. Hide it quick, he's coming.

"Well, it's a comfort that those are nice, are you
sure you don't want to do me again? It might save trouble, for if these aren't very good I shall insist on
a second sitting. I suppose you know best. Now do
let me have them as soon as you possibly can, it's most
important. Good morning.

"Take care, Amy, you are simply squashing my train!.
You were afraid of sitting on that photograph? Well, I
should think that would not matter half so much! Do
you think they will be good, I do hope so!"

Note: A reduced facsimile reproduction of Trix's original typescript, including her own handwritten alterations.

REALLY ORIGINAL.

-----‡‡‡‡‡‡‡‡‡‡‡------

TIME:- Saturday afternoon. George returns early from
office   to find his wife surrounded by volumes of "Academy
Pictures.

She speaks:-

"The amusement Club means to give a Fancy Ball

after all, George, it's to be on the 20th. That's not

very long real notice, seeing that they particularly want

people to wear fancy dress, not just powder or Windsor uniform

and so on; I wish I could make up my mind what to go as.

"No, indeed, George I can't wear my old dress, I

haven't got one. Oh, you mean that Dresden China thing?

Why I wore it to rags it was utterly done for before

I picked it to pieces. I had been to at least half a

dozen balls in it, three at any rate, and I didn't want

to be known as the perpetual Dresden Chinawoman. Besides

it was made for a Calico Ball and I want a handsomer

dress now, silk or velvet, or something. I can't go

tripping about always in blue and pink cotton as though I

were seventeen, and I wonder that you want me to for it

is always you who talk about "mutton and mint sauce", and

make jokes of that sort if you think people dress the

1

Note: A reduced facsimile reproduction of Trix's original typescript, including her own handwritten alterations.

least bit too young. It was a very pretty little
frock, I got the chintz at Whiteley's, stripes of tiny
rosebuds on a pale blue ground. Amy Forbes made me
rather a sweet workbag out of the panniers of it. But
I want something really original and out of the way
for this time; I've been looking through all these
books of pictures trying to get ideas, but artists must
be stupid, for there's hardly a figure here that would
make a really telling fancy dress. Look George, most of
the people wear such floppy vague sort of draperies; they
wouldn't be at all nice for dancing in even if one could
make them keep on.

"The Spirit of the Summit" has a lovely face, and
the name would be awfully effective in the printed list,
but that arrangement over her head is like an ayah's
chudder and I suppose all those draperies are meant to be
very artistic but there isn't the least fit or style about
them, and I should think one would be very likely to
catch cold. No, it won't do.

"News from Trafalgar". Oh that's rather sweet, and
one could make that large patterned gown out of art-
muslin, the six annas a yard kind. It's got a little

2

Note: A reduced facsimile reproduction of Trix's original typescript, including her own handwritten alterations.

train and a deep flounce, but not very large sleeves so twelve yards would do it easily. But those Empire dresses look very bunchy, except in pictures, and this girl has a spinning wheel and I couldn't take that about the ball room with me even if I had one, which would be rather difficult. Besides that girl's hair is much darker than mine and all cut short.

"Wouldn't it be nice if we went as some famous couple? Antony and Cleopatra, or Romeo and Juliet, or Romulus and Remus? No, I forgot they were both boys and the wolf would be an impossibility. What is the joke now, George? Didn't they kill a wolf or have a tame one or something?

"Here's a pretty picture, "The Honeymoon" by Marcus Stone, how would this do? My dress would be very soft white muslin and I think you'd look rather well in one of those old-fashioned coats with a high cravat; your hair wouldn't have time to grow as long as that but I suppose you could get a wig.

"You don't feel inclined to make a fool of yourself? Nonsense how can you expect a fancy ball to be a success if everyone is so self-conscious. It's only for a few

3

Note: A reduced facsimile reproduction of Trix's original typescript, including her own handwritten alterations.

hours.   I don't much like the idea of an Empire gown

they never look really tidy, and that's a fearful hat

she's holding, all those roses and feathers suggest a

costermonger.   I think I'd rather have something modern.

We couldn't go as the "Heavenly Twins" could we, George?

I should like something up to date. A "Yellow Aster"

would sound well, but yellow never suits me.   I saw a

picture of a "New Woman" costume in the Lady the other

day, with one foot got up like a man's showing under

her robe and a halo on her head and books under her

arm: it wouldn't amuse me to walk with a lot of heavy

books, and a halo looks hideous in profile.

Some sort of a game isn't a bad dress: how would

golf do? Only I suppose one would have to be in grass

green and that's not pretty. I've seen a man got up

as "Billiards", green cloth, all trimmed with pockets

and balls, a cue and a rest in his hand and the pool

basket on his head. Wouldn't you like that, Goerge?

You are very hard to please.

I knew a girl once who went as a "Champagne

Bottle," dark green satin with gold lettering, and a

gold cap for a cork. It's a very taking dress, but

I'm not quite slender enough for it: she had a waist

like a wasp. I'm sure one constantly hears of new ideas

4

Note: A reduced facsimile reproduction of Trix's original typescript, including her own handwritten alterations.

if one could only remember them. Someone once told me how to make a lampshade-dress out of that crimped paper: it sounded pretty, but I shouldn't care to wear it, it would crackle and crunch so when one danced.

"George do make a suggestion. What, go as the Infant Prince? How can you be so absurd? Why he's a baby boy, and it wouldn't be in the least respectful, indeed I should call it taking a great liberty.

Flower-dresses are always pretty, a "Basket of Violets" or a "posy of Roses". Oh, George, you remember that very fat woman up in Simla ages ago, what was her name? She went as "Sweet Violets". Her skirts were very short and as she passed me I heard someone say quite loudly, "I thought violets had slender stalks", and as she was wearing green stockings I really felt sorry for her.

"Incroyable" is too hackneyed for anything, and so are most of the peasant dresses. I really wish I hadn't pulled my "Dresden China" to pieces, I daresay it would have done up once more perfectly well. I might get a dhirzie to copy it from the photos I have of it.

"I am taking no pains to suggest a costume for you? Oh George, I thought of heaps but you refused to have any one of them. I know what will do splendidly

5

Note: A reduced facsimile reproduction of Trix's original typescript, including her own handwritten alterations.

go as someone out of the Ark, a toy ark I mean.

"It's a very simple dress and so cheap, a long shapeless coat of glazed calico, yellow or brown, with big buttons down to your heels, and a mushroom hat aspinalled to match, one of your solah topees will do, and you can call yourself Shem, Ham or Japhet whichever you like.

"You'd rather be excused? Why. It would do beautifully, and you wouldn't need to be funny in a dress like that, the more wooden you seemed the better. Well since you won't enter into the spirit of the thing you'd beter go as "Evening Dress in 1895", or as I've got some pale blue silk, one of your dress coats could be done up as Windsor uniform.

I do wish I had my "Dresden China" dress still: it will be absurd if people expect that I'm going to get an elaborate costume just before I go home. I'd much rather wait and bring out a really pretty one, and I don't care to get another calico arrangement.

Do you know I believe my pink satin would look sweet with powder: it's rather quaintly made and I could arrange a fichu on the bodice and wear either roses in my hair or a big black velvet hat. Yes, I'll do that: no-

6

Note: A reduced facsimile reproduction of Trix's original typescript, including her own handwritten alterations.

thing is so becoming as powder, and I'll call myself
either "Lady Dorothea" or "An Old Picture" or something.
Don't you think that it will do perfectly well George,
dear?"

———————————✥✥✥✥✥✥✥✥✥———————

7

Note: A reduced facsimile reproduction of Trix's original typescript, including her own handwritten alterations.

IN THE MERRY MONTH OF MAY.

--------✝✝✝✝✝✝✝✝✝✝✝--------

TIME: - Six o'clock in the evening. SCENE: - A Ralli
cart driving along various well-known roads.

George's wife speaks:-

"This has been a terribly hot day, hasn't it,
George? You were very busy and did not notice it particularly. Now that is just where you men are so fortunate: you can simply bury yourselves in your work
and forget the heat, while we poor women only sit at
home and suffer. I was gasping to-day, literally gasping. You know we always think the drawing-room is a
cool room, and to-day, although it was shut up since
quite early, it was over 90. I suppose I shall grow
a little more used to it as the hot weather goes on.
This is the 12th of May: it's awful to think that we
have at least five months more of torment before us.

"There are very few people out this evening. No,
dear, it's not early, it's past six, and there is
nothing 'on': it only means that most of the people
have gone away - lucky wretches! Everyone who can

1

Note: A reduced facsimile reproduction of Trix's original typescript, including her own handwritten alterations.

manage it goes away in May: indeed, I think it's shame-
ful the way the women all leave their husbands and
rush off to the hills. Your friend, Mrs Birkmire,
started for Simla yesterday: she is to be away the
whole season. Perhaps that's how she manages to keep
 that wonderful complexion you admire so much, though
I suspect it's a case of "where nature fails art
steps in!" She's got rooms at the Grand Hotel, , and
her husband won't be able to take any leave this year:
she **will** have a good time! She asked me why on earth
I stayed down, and I said I did not like the idea of
leaving you all alone, and besides we really could not
afford it.

"Was it wrong to say that, George? Why it's the
truth, you are always telling me that we must be careful. We are certainly as well off as the Birkmires -
Oh, are we? That is nice! but no one would ever
think so: why her frocks alone -

"Please don't be cross dear. I feel perfectly worn
out and if I attempt to argue I know I shall get a
blinding head-ache.

"Do let us stop and have Billy picked up, he is
panting like a steam engine. It is really cruel to
make dogs run in this weather. I know that fox-terriers

2

Note: A reduced facsimile reproduction of Trix's original typescript, including her own handwritten alterations.

are supposed to stand the heat well; but if you had to
run in a fur coat that was drawn up to your nose and
pulled over your ears I think you'd find it trying.
Do stop! Come along poor old Billy then. Oh, good
gracious beast, don't try and sit on my knee! I'm
quite hot enough without nursing you, "Take him between your feet, George, and if he does mix himself
up in the end of the reins we can untangle him again.
Talk about women fussing over trifles!

"No thanks, dear, I'd rather not walk at all, it's
much too oppressive. I find it quite hard enough to
keep cool sitting still. If you want to walk let the
syce lead the pony; the trap certainly shakes awfully when only one person is in it, but I hate driving,
and I daresay I shall get used to the shaking presently and my head does not ache - yet.

I don't know what you mean by saying 'See the pale
martyr with his shirt on fire': is it one of your Club
jokes? It's vulgar enough for anything.

"There is another thing that is so pleasant for
you men: you always have your club to go to when you
want to read the papers and see people. Oh Ge orge,

3

Note: A reduced facsimile reproduction of Trix's original typescript, including her own handwritten alterations.

you know I wouldn't join the Amusement Club for anything, Mrs Lennox behaves as if the whole place was
her private property and I cannot stand her: she is
one of the few women I dislike. There's Mrs West,
she's going to Darjeeling soon, her people are up
there. I'm rather glad she's going away, I never
liked her. Look, look, There's that awful Minnie
Watson driving with Captain Desmond again! That's
the third time this week. I'm sure she asks him to
take her, isn't she a plain little thing?

"Want of charity. Oh, George, I despise scandal!
But when I am doing my best to talk brightly and amuse
you after your long day in office, you call me 'spiteful! I'm sure my life is not so interesting and bright
that you need object to my noticing what is going on
round me, One has to live without pictures or music,
or museums or -

"I am perfectly well aware that there is a museum
here. I went once and I saw a lot of steps and a sta-
tue of the Queen, and there was the skeleton of an
aligator with all the anklets and beads and bangles
they found inside it, of people it had eaten. I call
that disgusting.

4

Note: A reduced facsimile reproduction of Trix's original typescript, including her own handwritten alterations.

"The worst of the hot weather is that it is so absolutely monotonous. It's all right for you: men are
different and you have your work. I haven't given up
my accomplishments, but how can I possibly paint in
a darkened room, and if I let the light in it's like a
furnace. That's what makes the hot weather so trying,
the feeling that you are a prisoner from nine to five:
I sit and long to go out!

"You know the only time I tried going out in the
morning I got a fearful sun headache. That's another
thing I often think of: it's so dreary to feel that
if I were ill there is no one to do anything for me.
Amy Forbes is devoted to me, but she's up in Naini
Tal. I haven't a single real friend here now, and
the ayah is an idiot. I want you to remember, George,
if I get cholera or anything you must send me to the
hospital. I should feel very lonely and forlorn of
course, but I should have a much better chance of
life. Thanks dear, I feel all right, only very lan-
guid and weary, and of course in the hot weather one
may be quite well one day and dead the next, so it's
better to say this while I am able.

"Are we going to the band? Always the same routine,

5

Note: A reduced facsimile reproduction of Trix's original typescript, including her own handwritten alterations.

it's like a treadmill. Oh the band was different in the winter: there were lots of people and the dresses were pretty: now there is hardly anybody and they all wear white muslin and sailor hats. One is bound to look hideous at this time of year with one's hair all out of curl. The worst of it is I tan so and it's quite bad enough to endure discomfort and dreariness without being disfigured for all the rest of the year.

"Why George dear, what makes you imagine that I want to go to the hills? I wouldn't for the world, I never thought of doing it. It would be dreadful to leave you alone with no one to cheer you up. I wasn't grumbling, I was only stating facts. Surely you don't expect me to say that I enjoy the heat.

Well, just to show you how utterly untrue it is that I want to go away, I'll tell you something that I meant to keep a secret? I had a letter from Amy Forbes yesterday begging and imploring me to go and stay with her. Mrs Forbes doesn't like Naini and she would come down for three months, only she does not want to give up the house and she can't leave Amy alone. She says it would be absolute charity if I would come up and take care of Amy. Amy's much older than I am, you know, but I'm married and that makes the difference

6

Note: A reduced facsimile reproduction of Trix's original typescript, including her own handwritten alterations.

She says they know lots of nice people already and
have great fun boating and going for picnics: so you
see if I could have borne the thought of leaving you
I should have told you of this.

"No dearest I have not answered her letter yet.
Of course I shall say "No". What would you do without me?

"Well, if Mr Locke chummed with you that would
be very niceand of course you'd spend all your time
at your beloved Club, but still you would be so lonely with no one to tell all your worries to and help you
to look at the bright side of things.

"Yes darling, it certainly is a splendid chance
of getting a thorough change, and I should be as happy
with Amy as I could possibly be away from you, but I
don't think it would be right to leave you.

"Dear George, it's sweet of you to put it
lke that. If I really felt that you would be happier
and freer from anxiety, I should feel it was my duty
to go. You could send me up your socks to mend, wo't
wouldn't you? Don't let the bearer tie up the holes
with string.

"Dearest, don't you think I had better send a
telegram to Mrs Forbes this evening? It would be so

7

Note: A reduced facsimile reproduction of Trix's original typescript, including her own handwritten alterations.

tiresome if she asked anyone else.

"My black serge and the grey hopsack are quite
good still. If I get a pretty crepon gown, that ought
to do. Do you like green with black guipure?

"But I'm so dreadfully afraid that you won't
be able to get on at all without me to cheer you up,
you poor dear boy!"

-----:1:::::::::::----

8

Note: A reduced facsimile reproduction of Trix's original typescript, including her own handwritten alterations.

HIS ONLY COMFORT.

-----‡‡‡‡‡‡‡‡‡-----

SCENE. The drawing-room of a little house in
Nainá Tal: George's Wife speaks: -

Now Amy dear, don't talk to me, I must write
to my husband. You can't understand what we find to say
every day? Why I should be miserable if I did not get a
daily letter from George! He started the habit when we
were engaged, and I <u>make</u> him keep it up. It's only like
writing a diary you know, and it is so nice for me to know
exactly what he is doing. I can't think what he would
do without my letters; when he is alone like this they
are really his only comfort!

Yes, of course I tell him everything too, except
just the little things that might worry him, it wouldn't
be kind to write those, and men are so funny, when the best
of them, one never knows what they won't fuss about!

(Writes). "My own darling George" (Speaks)
Amy can you give me a nice J pen? Thanks dear. Do you
like these writing boards? They are very useful; this is
real Russia leather with scissors and everything that one
wants. George gave it to me last Xmas; it's awfully
nice, but I was a little disappointed for I wanted one of
those bangles with a green chrysophrase heart.

(Writes.) "Many thanks for yesterday's letter, but
it was fearfully short, I do wish you could manage to
spare me a little more of your time. You say you never
go out after dinner so I don't see that else you have
got to do in the evenings except write to me."

(Speaks.) You seem very deep in that book, Amy,
what is it? Oh, "A Yellow Aster", is it pretty? That
reminds me I mean to go in for botany, Mr Vincent wants

1

Note: A reduced facsimile reproduction of Trix's original typescript, including her own handwritten alterations.

to teach me, and he says there are all sorts of lovely rambles about here. Do you like him? I don't care for civilians as a rule, but though he is one, he has really nice manners. He is clever too, which makes it all the funnier. I think he's very good-looking, I always admire dark eyes. George's eyes are rather a light grey, but he's ever so much taller than Mr Vincent.

(Writes.) "Amy and I are very busy as usual, we seem never to have an idle minute. We read a great deal and lead a thoroughly simple healthy sort of life, - (speaks) Where did you put those new chocolates dear? Thanks, I do like having a box of sweets near me to nibble at, it gives one something to do: that's why men are so fond of smoking I suppose. These are very good pralines. George is so funny he hates to see me eating sweets, he says it is so bad for one!"

(Writes.) "With lots of riding and boating. Amy rows awfully well now, and we have great times on the lake." (Speaks) Have you any plans for this evening? Oh if Nellie Paget is coming to tea, you two girls won't care to have an old married woman listening to all your talk, so I'll go out with Captain Desmond in a canoe. I want to learn how to manage a canoe. I won't tell George, it would only make him nervous. He is so absurd about always expecting me to break my neck or something.

Oh no, Captain Desmond isn't in the least noisy really, it's only his manner. I have known him for ages, long before I was married. I'm afraid George almost dislikes him, but that is not my fault. Poor fellow! He tells me all his secrets, and I give him good advice. You know he never met me until <u>after</u> I was engaged. I suppose it was fate. Of course <u>I</u> never cared for him,

2

Note: A reduced facsimile reproduction of Trix's original typescript, including her own handwritten alterations.

but it seems so strange and so sad that one should be
able to influence a person's whole life, when one only
likes them. It's so unequal, but how is one to help
these things happening?

What Amy? "It's very unsafe and uncompromising to make
protestations after a girl is engaged or married." My dear,
you ought not to talk like that about things you don't
understand, and it is such a mistake for a girl to be
cynical, and although you <u>are</u> older than I am, you will
count as a girl until you marry, I only say this because
I am fond of you, and don't wish you to stand in your own
light, and it is such a pity for a girl to get the
reputation of being jealous and spiteful. Now Amy don't
be silly, I never said you were old and ugly. You often
don't look a day older than twenty-three, and you look
quite pretty in that new big hat. Have some chocolate
and do let me finish my letter.

(Writes) "I can't say I admire your taste in playing
golf with Minnie Watson, however I hope you keep your
temper better with her than you do with me. Why don't
you play real golf on the big links?

"I want you to get me some bright cornflower blue
serge, with a very large rib, if I write for it V.P.P.
they will probably send me last year's rubbish, and you
might ask them if they have any <u>good</u> dress linen the same
colour. I enclose a memo about the number of yards and the
names of the five shops I want you to try at." (Speaks)
Are you sure that dharzie can make boating shirts nicely
Amy? I can't stand things that fit badly.

(Writes.) "Do try and remember to send me the
khansamah's accounts every week, I'm sure you are being
<u>robbed</u> , and do take care that that horrible syce you
are so fond of doesn't charge you for gram enough for

3

Note: A reduced facsimile reproduction of Trix's original typescript, including her own handwritten alterations.

two elephants instead of two ponies. You ought to live
for next to nothing now, and I think Rs 32 the dozen for
whiskey is perfectly <u>sinful</u>, surely you can get a cheaper
kind. Have you sent the trap to be repainted? You don't
need one while I am away, and I think it would be a splendid
chance to have Punch and Judy's shoes taken off, and let
their hoofs grow for a couple of months. You don't care
for riding alone, and I should think you would enjoy
going on your bicycle everywhere or walking, Thanks dear,
I shall be glad to have some more money next week, it
seems to melt away. Don't be disappointed at not hearing
from me to-morrow, for we are going to a big picnic, so
I shan't have time to write. And now good-bye, with
<u>best</u> love.

                     Your ever loving wife, Connie."

    (Speaks) There, that's done! Yes, it <u>is</u> rather a
bother writing every day, but I make a point of doing it,
for I know how eagerly poor George looks out for my
letters. I must run away and change, for I asked Captain
Desmond to come in to lunch. You don't mind dear do you?"
                                     F.

-----‡‡‡‡‡‡‡‡‡‡‡-----

4

Note: A reduced facsimile reproduction of Trix's original typescript, including her own handwritten alterations.

JOURNEYS END IN LOVERS MEETING.

-----‡‡‡‡‡‡‡‡‡-----

TIME. - The middle of August. SCENE. - George's bungalow.

George's Wife speaks. -   "Dearest George, it is so nice to come back again. How huge the house looks after that cottage at Naini, and how well furnished! I think the Forbes are rather stingy, though you know he has 3,000 a month, for when I wanted Amy to buy some ordinary little wicker - I have not told you how I think you are looking. Oh awfully well, simply flourishing, and I was expecting from your letters to see a sort of bogey, quite wasted away. Of course you are rather pale, but that's the hot weather, and if only you wouldn't have your hair cut like a convict you wouldn't look at all bad.

"And how do you think I'm looking? You don't see much sign of the 'bright colour' I was boasting about? Naturally not, after a journey at this time of year ; but up in Naini they used to say I was as pink as a rose! Who said so? Oh, Amy and lots of people.

"Is there any news down here? Well, it's something to hear that the place is fuller than it was when I went away: so it won't be quite so deadly dull. I want to join the Amusement Club; it's much better than doing nothing, and it will be easy enough to find people to propose and second us. Perhaps I did refuse to belong to it once: but it's possible to change one's mind, I suppose, and I am really tired of being a hermit crab. I mean to go out a great deal this winter.

"Oh, <u>you</u> needn't trouble to come if you don't care to. I forgot that you are only strong enough to play golf with Minnie Watson, and find a dance much too ex-

1

Note: A reduced facsimile reproduction of Trix's original typescript, including her own handwritten alterations.

exhausting! I can easily find someone else to go with.
Mrs Conlan Bennett is coming down in the cold weather,
and we're great friends. I must have told you about her,
she's perfectly charming, not a bit handsome, but awfully
smart, with the most lovely clothes. I don't think I've
ever seen her without an accordeon pleated chiffon bodice
except in the morning or boating. Her husband is away on
a tea garden, I've never met him. She only came out
last winter, and she can't stand the place he's in for
more than a week or two, it's awfully out of the world.
She isn't in the least a mofussil sort of woman, her waist
is only twenty inches, and she's much taller than I am.
I asked her to come and stay with us in October, till she
finds a place that suits her here. It's impossible to
feel dull when you are with her, she has so much 'go'.
She has roused me up and done me a great deal of good;
it's no use behaving like a middle aged woman when you
are really quite young. Well, if you call twenty-five
old - women at home are quite kittenish when they are long
past thirty, and Amy Forbes -

"Your manners have not improved while I have been
away, George; it sounds so boorish to say things suddenly like that. You know I am very fond of Amy! I have
been devoting myself to her all this time, and she was
miserable when I left. She came to see me off all the
way to the tonga place, and her eyes were so red that
Captain Desmond said - Why of course he was up there, I
must have told you that he was. I don't believe that
you half read my letters, I know that way you have of
tearing up a letter as soon as you have skimmed through
it, I call it so unkind.

2

Note: A reduced facsimile reproduction of Trix's original typescript, including her own handwritten alterations.

"I have kept every single one of your letters to
me, and your telegrams about the remittances, and everything; they are all tied up with ribbon in my dress-
basket. But why shouldn't I? A letter is the property
of the person who gets it, and if I mayn't keep my own
husband's letters, I wonder whose letters I may keep.

"I can't remember the exact date that Captain
Desmond came up; I don't chronicle his doings. I can
inform you that he is coming down next week if you care
to know that.

"Now George darling, you are not going to be cross
with me before I have been an hour in the house, are you?
I was only chaffing, but you have been so much alone,
you poor, dear boy, that you have got quite solemn and
stodgy; you really must go about a little and get brightened up. Who had I better write to about the Amusement
Club?"

"It isn't only that they give cinderellas, and
have good tennis courts, but one can get books there.
'It will be a new thing if I take to reading'. Oh George,
I read dozens of books when I was in Naini: "A Heavenly
Woman'and 'The Superfluous Twins', - and - Well you know
what I mean, and I've got a book full of dried flowers,
petals and stamens; and things neatly stuck in, like
embroidery patterns gone mad. I love botany. No indeed,
it was not Captain Desmond, it was Mr Vincent who taught
me, and he was so patient and nice.

"I wonder who could take an interest in stamps,
that's quite different, you can't go for beautiful rambles and gather stamps on the hillsides. You spend fortunes on your collection and mine has cost nothing, not
even the magnifying glass, for Mr Vincent gave me a

3

Note: A reduced facsimile reproduction of Trix's original typescript, including her own handwritten alterations.

little beauty set in silver.

"Oh, look George! My beautiful Japanese jar has had the handle knocked off. Wait till I see the bearer, I will give it to him. Seeing that this is the rains I should never have imagined there could be so much dust in one room: I don't believe the bearer has done a hand's turn, except to break things, all the time I have been away. You might have looked after him a little, George. You used to see him dusting every morning? Oh that was make-believe to take you in; beyond putting every single one of the photographs to stand on their heads, he has done nothing. I shall have the whole place cleaned to-morrow morning, all the pictures taken down, the China washed, and everything Yes, I thought so. The curtains eaten through and through, and in nearly every letter I used to tell you to be sure and have them aired once a week. And they came from Liberty's only two years ago, my poor pretty curtains!

There the punkah rope has broken, beastly thing! It's awful to think that they have been swinging ever since April.

"I don't at all see that it's worse when you haven't been away; you have got accustomed to it, but when you first come back you see how horrible it all is, and feel it terribly.

"Grumbling and fault-finding and making things uncomfortable? Do you mean that I do that? Oh George, you are enough to break one's heart! They all said how sweet it was of me to come down, and I was having such a good time, and everyone was so kind and jolly, and now this is my welcome here!

4

Note: A reduced facsimile reproduction of Trix's original typescript, including her own handwritten alterations.

m "You wish I had never gone away. How selfish you
are! What I wish is that I had never come back."

-----‡‡‡‡‡‡‡‡‡‡‡‡‡‡‡‡‡------

Note: A reduced facsimile reproduction of Trix's original typescript, including her own handwritten alterations.

2

PASSED WITH HONOURS.

-----╪╪╪╪╪╪╪╪╪╪╪-----

George's Wife speaks:-

"I had a letter from Amy to day, George; the
Ambulance Class exam. hed just come off, and she was
feeling very nervous about it. No, I didn't go to any
of thelectures while I was up in Naini; I went through
the course in Simla ages ago, before I ever met you, so I
did not care to bother about it again.

"Did I ever show you my certificate? I used to
be so proud of it, I wonder where it has gone to. It's a
big card with the badge on it, like a hot-cross bun,
saying that I am competent to render "First Aid to the
Injured" and signed by three doctors, I ought to have
it somewhere unless I cut it in two for packing photographs to send home; perhaps I did that. But the lectures
were really great fun, though the Surgeon-Instructor that
was what ~~what~~ he called himself, was very strict. Yes,
indeed they were well attended; all the big-wigs went,
only ladies of course, and sat in the front row; and
when we got as far as bandaging they used to do it in
order of precedence. It was a little unfair, for there
was only one A.D.C. to bandage, and as you can't put on
more than eight bandages at once, we girls had to do
each other and it was rather dull.

"Good gracious, yes, of course the people who were
bandaged kept all their clothes on; only if a girl was
wearing a habit we made her do subject, it was so difficult to get those funny triangular rags fastened properly
over a fluffy frock. I never learnt anything about head
bandages because they spoilt one's fringe so, we all refused to have them on.

1

Note: A reduced facsimile reproduction of Trix's original typescript, including her own handwritten alterations.

The poultice lesson was rather messy, linseed and bread and pobby things like that; I never remember if you put the water into the linseed or the linseed into the water, but if you get them well mixed together it can't matter much. Besides we never got a chance of practising, the Members of Coundil's wives were all so busy, and one would have thought they ought to have learnt how to make poultices ages ago! The best of it was that when they had made them there was nobody to try them on, for even an A.D.C. wouldn't like a poultice put on outside his coat, and it wouldn't be much use as practice. So they just showed their poultices to the doctor, and he said they were very excellent, and some of them said they were going to take them home as patterns: only a wretched dog got in, before the end pf the lecture, and ate them all up!

"He did really, George, at least he did not finish all the linseed, and he left the mustard to the last, for that was what we heard him choking over: but he gobbled up the bread ones and the rags they were spread on too! I don't think I could endure a mustard plaster if I was really ill, it smells so exactly like roast beef.

"Yes, some of them used to say very absurd things. There was one lady, I can't remember her name, she had beautiful fair hair, when she was asked what she'd do in a case of snake bite, said she should tie a ligature tightly round above it! Wasn't that ridiculous?

"You don't see the joke? It seems very sensible to you? Why, George dear, ligature is stuff you pour out of a bottle, like lotion.

Oh liniment? Yes, that was what she said, and she meant ligature, wasn't she silly?

2

Note: A reduced facsimile reproduction of Trix's original typescript, including her own handwritten alterations.

I happen to have heard that everlasting saying about
"a little knowledge" before, but a little ignorance is
much worse; and it's so nice to know about not holding
up peoples' heads when they faint and giving them brand
when they're bleeding to death, and that sort of thing.
And it's most important about the normal temperature, an
all that.

"What? You don't believe I have a notion what the
normal temperature is? Yes I have, it's 89. No; that's
too much, we should always feel hot if it was that; it
must be 60 or sixty something. Well, you needn't laugh,
I've got it all put down in a dear little book he gave
us at the end of the course as a memento. I haven't
looked at ut for years, but it's awfully useful to have
it handy in case of an emergency. I really must find it
I'm sure it's packed away in one of my boxes.

"The exam; at the end was awful, though it was rather
fun too. We wrote long papers answering questions
about what to do for drowning and broken bones. I
only got one thing wrong; I said old beer bottles would
do for splints, and it ought to have been those straw
cases that come outside the bottles. Then there was the
vive voce, two doctors, and they asked us one question
each and made us do a bandage. What was my question?
Oh, it was something about bones; I knew it then. Tibby
and Fibby, or names like that. Yes, that was it, tibia
and fibula, they are in one's spine, aren't they?

"I nearly got spun over my bandaging, though
Captain Foy just saved me. You remember Captain Foy,
George, wasn't he handsome? Rather coarse looking? Oh
no, trust one man not to admire another! He was very
striking, and he had the most lovely dark eyes.

Note: A reduced facsimile reproduction of Trix's original typescript, including her own handwritten alterations.

"He wasn't supposed to care about girls, I know, but he always used to dance with me, and he danced like a dream: I have never met such a perfect dancer before or since, and our steps suited beautifully!

You don't see that this has to do with ambulance? Now George you mustn't be jealous, I hadn't even seen you then. Well, they told me to do an arm sling, and poor Captain Foy was waiting very meekly in his undress uniform. I was awfully nervous, and as I stood on tiptoe to get the thing round his neck he whispered, ''Tother way up'! So I turned the bandage, and did it all right, and they said it was very creditable. Of course he really knew more about it than any of us did, but I don't think he helped the others like that.

"Yes, we all passed, you can't wonder at it, for we had all worked so hard. It was a funny coincidence, when the list of marks came out the names were as nearly as possible in the order of precedence, but then, of course, they all sat in the front row.

"Where did my name come? I lost a few marks over those tiresome old beer bottles, but I passed, passed with honours. What are you laughing at now, George?

-----++++++++------

4

Note: A reduced facsimile reproduction of Trix's original typescript, including her own handwritten alterations.

A MINISTERING ANGEL.

-----ↁↀↁↀↁↀↁↀↁↀↁↀↁↀↁↀ-----

TIME - 3.30 P.M. SCENE - The guest chamber.
Mrs Conlan-Bennett is "resting" in an elaborate
dressing-gown, while George's Wife "takes care"
of her.

George's Wife speaks -

"Now you must lie still and keep quite quiet until
dinner time. I knew you had a dreadful headache the minute
I saw you this morning, your face was ghastly pale and
your eyes all red: even George noticed how funny you
looked, and he never sees anything generally. Shall I
close these jillmills? When my head is bad I like to be
in the dark and keep perfectly quiet, it's much the best
way. There, now I'll shut the other. Oh dear, how that
banged! Wouldn't you like another pillow? Are you sure
that thin dressing-gown is warm enough? If you catch a
chill you are bound to get fever at this time of year:
let me throw this shawl over you. No? Well I'll put it
close to your feet in case you want it presently. This
is a wretchedly small sofa. I really think you would
be more comfortable lying on the bed. You are quite content and don't want to move? That's right dear, and now
you must try and go to sleep. Is there nothing I can
get you? Smelling salts. Oh how wrong of me to forget
and I brought the bottle in on purpose and put it on the
table. Where has it gone to? I'm sure I put it on the
looking-glass. Oh bother! I've knocked it over and
it's rolled right under your sofa. Don't move dear, I
can get it without disturbing you. There! Did I shake
you? I'm so sorry.

"I think you must have got a touch of the sun:

1

Note: A reduced facsimile reproduction of Trix's original typescript, including her own handwritten alterations.

I'm afraid riding in the morning doesn't suit you. You
always come in looking utterly fagged, and that shows it
doesn't. Of course you are not used to the plains, and
they are so different from the hills; I think too unless
you first come to India when you are quite a girl you
find the climate very trying. You have promised Captain
Desmond to take "Black Knight" over the paperchase course
to-morrow? You had much better write and tell him you
can't, ot let me do it for you.. It's really very wrong
of him to ask you to ride "Black Knight", for it's a
perfect brute of a horse; he wouldn't let me get on it for
worlds, and you know what a fearless rider I am. You
like Captain Desmond, don't you? That's right, he's a
dear fellow and he is always so nice to my friends. Amy
Forbes is awfully plain and not a bit amusing, but just
because I was staying with her in Naini he made a point
of asking her for three waltzes at every single dance,
and I know he is quite willing to ride with you every
day. I hate going out in the morning myself, it's what
makes so many women look lined and wrinkled, missing
their proper sleep and they try to make up for it in the
afternoon, but sleep then is very unrefreshing and
tremendously fattening. What did you say dear? You
want some Lavender Salts, I'm afraid I haven't got any;
I never use them from year's end to year's end, and
George says only hysterical geese need them: you know his
funny teasing way.. Let me find yours. No your keys are
not on the dressing-table; yes they are, behind your
powder box. You have the most lovely silver things; the
sight of them always makes me wildly envious. Now which
is your dressing bag key, this one? It won't open. Ah that's
right. No sign of your salts, what sort of a bottle are

2

Note: A reduced facsimile reproduction of Trix's original typescript, including her own handwritten alterations.

they in? Was this bag one of your wedding presents?
It's a great beauty, mine has got sadly xhabby. Here
are the salts, right down at the bottom of course. Isn't
your head getting better? Let me take down your hair and
brush it very gently, it would be no trouble and I never
can bear the feel of hairpins when mine aches. You'd
rather not? I'll put some Eau-de-Cologne on your forehead
then. Oh how funny you look with your fringe pushed
back: no one would know you. I never imagined you had
such a high forehead. Your head is simply burning hot,
do let me get you some ice. There is a proper ice cap
somewhere, one of those red India-rubber things shaped
like a Tam O'Shanter. George found it a great comfort
the last time he had fever and the poor dear boy used to
look so jaunty and "Hieland" with this red "Tammy" on
his head and a plaid over him. It messes one's hair
dreadfully, but it's very soothing: would you really
rather not have it?

"Now I'm going to sit down and write a note to
Captain Desmond saying that you are certainly not going
out with him to-morrow, and I think the morning rides will
have to be stopped altogether. I should be awfully sorry
though, it's so good for George to see him riding with
someone else. You must have noticed that George is
desperately jealous, especially of poor Charlie Desmond,
and it is so ridiculous, for he is a perfect gentleman
and would never say a word that - but you know how funny
one's husbands are. I can't understand jealousy, I
don't see how love can exist without the most absolute
trust, and I always tell George that with his sort of
nature he ought to have married a hideous old woman and
then perhaps he would have been happy! The absurdest

3

Note: A reduced facsimile reproduction of Trix's original typescript, including her own handwritten alterations.

thing is that he is jealous backwards, I mean he simply
can't stand any of my old chums. I often feel sorry
now that when we were first engaged I told him the names
of all the men who had proposed to me, for when he sees
any of them he is so stiff and queer. Isn't it a
strange thing that of the whole lot there is only <u>one</u> who
has married, and his wife has heaps of money and is fearfully plain; all the others are single still. It's pleasant to meet them again and talk about the old days: it's
so hard for me to realise sometimes that I am grown up
and all my fun is over. Of course I married very young.

    "You are feeling sleepy? That's good, let me stroke
your forehead very gently and softly and that will send
you off. Do you believe in hypnotism? I often think
that I have a great deal of mesmeric power and I should
so like to get it cultivated when I go home. Often
and often I 'will' George to do things and he does them,
but he never guesses it of course.

    "Oh no dear, you are not keeping me from doing
anything. I like staying and taking care of you. I love
nursing, it's one of my talents: if I could ever spare
the time I should go in for six months' training at a
children's hospital, it must be so sweet.

    "Can't you get to sleep? Poor dear, perhaps you
are feverish and ought to have some quinine or phena-
cetin or antipyrin, only you mustn't take that if your
heart is not strong. Do you think yours is strong?
Your lips are a funny pale colour sometimes.

    "Would you like me to read to you? I often read
Gaorge to sleep on Sunday afternoons, I can read for
four hours without my voice getting tired. What's

4

Note: A reduced facsimile reproduction of Trix's original typescript, including her own handwritten alterations.

213

this book? It does not dound very exciting or thrilling,
so it will do nicely and I shall expect you to be asleep
in five minutes. <u>The Prisoner of Zenda</u> by Anthony Hope.
Chapter first. Oh goodness! it must be tea time for I
hear George's wheels coming in at the gate; you won't
think me unkind for running away dear? I'll bring you
a nice cup of tea directly. No indeed, the <u>ayah</u> shan't
bring it. I will wait on you myself! You are sure there
is nothing wlse I can get you? I'm coming back very soon."

-----‡‡‡‡‡‡‡‡‡-----

Note: A reduced facsimile reproduction of Trix's original typescript, including her own handwritten alterations.

HEARTFELT CONGRATULATIONS.

----‡‡‡‡‡‡‡‡‡----

TIME. - 11.30 A.M., SCENE. - A drawing-room
Satin shoes on one chair, long gloves on another;
evening dresses everywhere.

GEORGE'S WIFE SPEAKS. - "Oh is that you, Amy
dear? Come in. I'm so thankful it's only you, for
just look at the state of the room, and the bearer is
a perfect idiot about understanding dwarza bund. I'm
hard at work airing all my things, they've been shut
up since April, you know, and I thought it was a good
plan to have the boxes brought in here and overhaul them
thoroughly.

What, dear? You only came down from Naini the
day before yesterday? Why, of course, I quite forgot
I hadn't seen you for ages, I'm awfully glad to have you
back; I thought you weren't coming till much later.
It's dreadfully stuffy here still, you'll lose all your
colour before the cold weather. Don't you think I'm
looking wretchedly pale? Captain Desmond was saying so
only yesterday.

I do hope it isn't too early to get out one's
frocks. Mrs Conlan-Bennett is coming to stay with me
next month, and she is so particular about clothes that
I must make haste and have these rags done up respectably.
Don't you envy the people who can get new things every
winter? Mine were quite fresh and pretty when I put
them away, and now they are all crumpled and squashy,
and not fit to be seen: I packed them so carefully too,
with heaps of tissue paper. Oh there's a moth! Kill
it Amy, quick! I suppose now I shall find everything

1

Note: A reduced facsimile reproduction of Trix's original typescript, including her own handwritten alterations.

riddled with holes; but I like it better than smelling
of camphor, everyone knows then that one's frock isn't
new. Have I tried "Napthaline?" Is that the stuff that
looks like fluted candle ends and smells like museums?
George has it among his thick clothes, but I simply
couldn't stand going about smelling like stuffed birds!

Amy dear, look at this pink satin. Do you think
if I had it done up with - why what is the matter? What
are you holding your hand out for, you funny girl! You
want to show me your new ring? Oh, that little pearl
half hoop, it doesn't look new. Did your mother give
it to you? What does the third finger of the left hand
mean? Why, it's the wedding finger. Oh Amy not really?
Do you mean to say you are engaged? Well I am surprised!
Who is he? Captain Arnold, the man you were engaged to b
before? Only fancy! It's awfully nice that he should
have gone on caring for you all this time; and I suppose
if you are fond of him you really like it better than if
he had been someone quite new. "He has come into some
money", that's nice! "His aunt died; what a good thing!
Oh, so he wrote to you, and then came to Naini; had he
seen you before he proposed again? No; well very likely
you have hardly altered at all; I always say you are
one of those girls who looked no younger when they were
seventeen and won't look any older when they are forty.
Is that the very same ring you had before? Oh you ought
to make him give you another, pearls mean tears; and now
that he is better off you could have a handsome one.

Yes, you do look wonderfully happy; and when is it
to be? Not till the autumn: Oh what a pity! I hoped
you were going to say this Xmas for then your trousseau
mighth have given me some notions for my cold weather

2

Note: A reduced facsimile reproduction of Trix's original typescript, including her own handwritten alterations.

clothes: I am so bothered about them. You see I mean
to be ever so economical this winter because I am going
home in the spring, and I want to get a regular outfit
then. It is so unsatisfactory ordering frocks from
little shreds of patterns; and George says that whatever
I manage to save out of my dress allowance between now
and March he'll double, I've only saved fifteen-eight
thus far; and thirty-one rupees won't do more than get me
a hat. Do you think you could curl up these white
feathers for me, darling? You have such clever fingers,
and I should like to wear the hat at the races if they
aren't too limp. I got it last year, and it's awfully
becoming.

You mean to go out very little this winter because
he's up on the frontier. Who? "Arthur." Is that his
name? Arthur Arnold, it sounds very solemn! I went out
tremendously after I was engaged, and had the greatest
fun, George was away in camp all the time. But what I
really wanted to ask you, Amy dear, was about this pink
satin. I only wore it four times last year, and I really
must make it do for my Drawing Room gown. It's a lovely
shade at night, pink always suits me. All my first
season they used to call me "Rose in June". Wasn't it a
pretty nickname? Yes, my birthday is in June, but of
course they meant my complexion. Do you think if I had
sleeves of a soft pale green, like a moss rose it would
be pretty? I can wear all shades of green, most people
find it trying, I know, but it's quite my colour. Perhaps
it might look a little patchy though, I thought of
creamy lace.

Oh yes, I know that Honiton flounce of your mother's,
she wears it constantly, it's a lovely pattern, but it's

3

Note: A reduced facsimile reproduction of Trix's original typescript, including her own handwritten alterations.

gone very yellow. Frankly, dear, I don't think it would
look at all well on a white satin wedding dress. White
satin is hideously unbecoming by daylight, unless people
are very young and have exquisite complexions, but of
course one has a sentiment about wearing it. Everyone
told me I had never looked so well as on my wedding day;
there's my dear old dress turned into a dinner gown, it
fits beautifully. Shall I try on the pink satin? I will
in a minute, if you like, and then we can decide whether
cream lace or white chiffon and pearl passementerie will
look best. I'm not very fond of pink and white though,
it's rather common, and always reminds me of a Neapolitan
ice.

Oh, you are not going yet, Amy, do stay and help me
put these things away, you know how badly I fold frocks.
You haven't written to Arthur yet? Bother Arthur! I shall
be quite jealoud of him I see. Girls always get so selfish when they are engaged, you can tell him that from
me! He doesn't know who I am? What haven't you shown
him any of my photos? You are a queer girl, I should
have thought you would have told him all about me seeing
what friends we are. It's a perfect shame that I can't
be your bridesmaid simply because I'm married. Is he
tall, Amy? Just your height? Goodness, that's very
short for a man; I always feel glad that George is so
tall, it looks better.

Oh, wait one minute, does this pink satin look
dirty round the edge of the train? I should hate to
have it shortened; but still if it's grubby I must. You
think it will do, so do I, things always look cleaner
at night. I wonder if these sleeves are old fashioned -
they are very pretty. You really haven't time to see me

4

Note: A reduced facsimile reproduction of Trix's original typescript, including her own handwritten alterations.

in it? It would only take two minutes. You can't
possibly? Tiresome girl! Well the next time you come
please write "Arthur's" letter first. I feel sure I
shall call him Arthur, do you think he will mind?

Good-bye, darling, since you must go; mind you
come to me whenever you feel happy and want to talk and
confide. It's been so sweet to hear you pouring out all
that is in your heart, and you know how lovingly I sympa-
thize. Do come to lunch to-morrow, there's a dear, and
we'll really settle about the pink satin. Now be sure
and tell him to send you another ring, for pearls do
mean tears, and it's quite unlucky enough to renew a
broken engagement without having any more bad signs,
Come early to-morrow and I'll try on the pink satin
first thing, and we'll have a grand confab. Goodbye,
darling.

-----‡‡‡‡‡‡‡‡‡-----

5

Note: A reduced facsimile reproduction of Trix's original typescript, including her own handwritten alterations.

CHARACTER DELINEATED.

-----++++++++++++-----

SCENE:- A Fancy Fair in aid of a most deserving charity: the inevitable embroideries and "hand-painted"trifles are displayed among much "art muslin" drapery. Button-hole sellers and fillers of raffle papers are painfully numerous, and there are many "side-shows". George's wife, in silk attire, hesitates on the brink of the "Sibyl's Cave".

-----++++++++++++-----

"What's going on in there? Oh, Captain Desmond look at that exciting placard. 'The Sibyl of Chiromancy! Where is that? I've forgotten all my geography. "Your Fortune Told! Your Character Delineated! Your Fate Revealed! Only Two Rupees". Do let's go in. Who's the woman, who is doing it I wonder. Some stranger who's quite new to the place? Oh that's all right: I was afraid it might be Mrs Birkmire, she gives her-self the greatest airs about her palmistry, and it's all such nonsense. Isn't it funny how some people be-lieve in palmistry and are quite silly about it? I've seen a man look quite vexed because he was told he was going to do something awfully bad and then get a blow on the head and die raving mad. Of course I don't be-lieve in it in the least, but I've got a very lucky hand so I never mind having it looked at.

Note: A reduced facsimile reproduction of Trix's original typescript, including her own handwritten alterations.

"Can we go in now? Gracious, how dark this little passage is! Is this the Cave? Why it's only a little tiny room with a big shaded lamp: I wonder why they call it a Cave. I knew she'd be in a Greek dress. I am so tired of Sibyls in Greek dresses: why do they never get themselves up as gipsies or in powder?

"I want you to tell my fortune please: delineate my character you know. Am I to sit in this chair? Must I take my gloves off, both of them? Oh dear, and they have got such a lot of buttons! Please undo this wretched thing for me, Captain Desmond. You can only tell fortunes alone with one person? Oh do let Captain Desmond stay, I don't mind his hearing mine in the least: I've got no dreadful secrets. It makes you nervous and you always insist on having no listeners? Oh well, I suppose it is more mysterious: you won't mind waiting just outside, will you?

"Now, which hand do you look at? Both, how funny. Are they different? They're not always red like that you know. It's because I've pulled off my gloves in such a hurry. 'My heart governs my head?' Yes, I'm afraid it does, I'm dreadfully impulsive: but don't you think a woman ought to be, and of course I'm very sensible all the same. I'm going to be married twice

Note: A reduced facsimile reproduction of Trix's original typescript, including her own handwritten alterations.

aren't I? People always tell me that. You can only see a faint indication, but doesn't it show how old I shall be? Between forty five and fifty? Oh dear, not till then! 'Very fond of society'. Oh yes, I am, how could you tell? 'Very fond of dress and pretty things, and my talents have not been cultivated to their fullest extent. Oh you are a witch! How <u>did</u> you know that I was awfully lazy at school, the other girls used to do all my exercises and things for chocolate. 'Rather indolent?' Yes, you are right again, I hate getting up in the morning. 'Very talkative'. No, that's the first thing you've said wrong, I should say I was much too thoughtful to be talkative: I'm a woman who thinks a great deal. 'Warm-hearted, with a strong tendency to jealousy'. Oh, I'm not jealous a bit, George never looks at anyone except me: I don't know what jealousy is. Am I a flirt? 'Yes'. Oh what a shame! A bad one? 'Yes, a coquette?' Oh palmistry is wonderful, I must go in for it, does it take long to learn? Tell me something about my past. Was I ever engaged before? 'Once when I was between seventeen and twenty?' Oh yes, I was nineteen: do go on. 'Broken off because of a misunderstanding?' Yes, I changed my mind. I found he

3

Note: A reduced facsimile reproduction of Trix's original typescript, including her own handwritten alterations.

had a most ghastly temper, but it was awfully romantic
to begin with, he had only known me a week when he proposed. Can you tell me anything more? 'An illness
in childhood, not a very dangerous one?' Yes I had
measles when I was eleven. Oh you are marvellous!
'Not at all reserved, in fact unable to keep a secret.'
Oh no, that must be a mistake, I'm tremendously reticent,
look again. 'It's most clearly marked that I should
find it difficult to keep a secret.' What nonsense,
why there's a man here, a young Civilian, a Mr Archer,
 I suppose you have never met him: well, he's tremendously popular, and if the news of his engagement got about
the whole place would ring with it. He told me all
about it more than a month ago, and I have not breathed
it to a soul. So you see I can keep secrets after all!
No, indeed, he was not chaffing me; it's perfectly true
he met her up in Simla and her name is Leelee Mason.
I suppose that's short for Eliza! and he says she's not
a bit pretty, in fact when he first met her he thought
her exceedingly plain, but awfully bright and jolly.
That's all very well, but I do think a man ought to
 admire the girl he is going to marry just at first,
for if he doesn't he'll probably think her hideous later

4

Note: A reduced facsimile reproduction of Trix's original typescript, including her own handwritten alterations.

on!

"What, time is up and other people are waiting to
come? What a bother! you haven't told me half enough.
Do come to tea with me some afternoon and then you shall
tell me everything about my hand. Good-bye and thank
you very much: you haven't said anything about the
strong influence I have over people. I'm mesmeric
really, I think, but of course you haven't had time.

. . . .

"It was simply wonderful, Captain Desmond. I
shall always believe in palmistry after this; she
described my character as if she had known me for years
and told me heaps of true things about the past. How I
was engaged when I was nineteen, and why I broke it off,
and how old I was when I had measles and heaps of things.
She was only wrong twice; she said I was talkative and
jealous. Oh! come this way quick; Mrs Birkmire has
got hold of George, and if I don't interfere she will
make him buy all the rubbish on her stall. He always
says she's so charming, and she's got an awful Cockney
accent, and I think she has a very common sort of face,
don't you?

5

Note: A reduced facsimile reproduction of Trix's original typescript, including her own handwritten alterations.

"How are you getting on, Mrs Birkmire, aren't you
dreadfully tired? You must have been working hard,
you poor dear, for your face is simply flaming! Stand
still a second, I want to put your hat straight, it's
all over on one side, There, that's better. Do come
and have your fortune told, George, the Sibyl is splendid
I don't know her real name. She is a very plain girl
with dark hair. 'Miss Mason just come down from Simla?'
Oh are you sure? What's her other name? 'Leelee Mason?'
Is THAT Leelee Mason? Oh my goodness! No dear, I
didn't speak and nothing's the matter, only I feel
absolutely done, and I don't care to stay here any
longer. Do you mind taking me home George dear?"

-----++++++++++-----

6

Note: A reduced facsimile reproduction of Trix's original typescript, including her own handwritten alterations.

THE SEASON'S GREETING.

-----‡†‡†‡†‡†‡†‡†-----

TIME:- Directly after lunch. George is smoking a cigarette while his wife sits before a writing table overflow-
ing with Christmas cards.

She speaks:-

It's rather unlucky that Christmas Day falls on a
Tuesday this year, for I know you like me to do nothing
but talk to you on Saturday afternoons, and I really
must send off my cards to-day so as to be quite sure that
they will go in time. You see, dear, I really can 't
help it.

"You are perfectly happy sitting quiet?" that's
very nice of you!

"It doesn't often happen that you are left in
peace?" Now George I know your way of saying nasty
little things when you are put out, but even you can't
feel jealous or slighted because I am busy over a lot of
silly old cards. Look, I got all these for one eight!
Thirty two of them! I really meant to get two packets
at a rupee each but they'd only one left, so I took
an eight annas packet instead, and it's very nearly as
good.

"I think you might praise me for being on the cheap
as you call it, this year instead of laughing. I spent
fortunes on cards last Christmas, and when you come to
think of it it's really not worth while.

I made out a list this morning, of all the people
who sent me cards last year and I can't think where it's

1

Note: A reduced facsimile reproduction of Trix's original typescript, including her own handwritten alterations.

gone to. I'm sure the bearer throws things away. No,
George, it's not my untidiness. I lose things constantly
and it's all the fault of that horrid old bearer of yours.
Yes, I'm perfectly well aware that he has been with you
for ten years, all the more reason that you should send
him away and get someone with a spark of intelligence
for a change. I do wish you would just look through
the wastepaper basket and see if your treasure has thrown
it in there; it's the sort of thing he's always doing.
It's quite a long list written in blue pencil on a whole
half sheet of Bally foolscap. I'm not swearing; what a
low imagination you have; don't judge everyone by
yourself.. I meant Bally paper Mills foolscap.

Just see what a collection of rubbish! I never can
get my wastepaper basket emptied every day, the wretches
leave it for weeks.

All our servants know that they may do exactly
as they like, for you are too lazy ever to say anything
to them, and they don't pay the least attention to me.
Haven't you found that list yet? I must try and manage
without it, only please don't talk so much; I do want
to get this business done.

Cards are much prettier than they used to be.
Don't you remember the old style -snow scenes and robins
and plumpuddings, dancing polkas, and church bells and
frosted holly that came off on one's fingers; now they
are like valentines and birthday cards mixed up together.

The verses are awfully silly, though, who is one
to send a thing like this to? -

    "Prithee receive this unpretending card,
    Prithee believe it carries my regard."

And the picture's rather pretty, green chrysanthemums,

2

Note: A reduced facsimile reproduction of Trix's original typescript, including her own handwritten alterations.

ᵗ

look George.

I wish that I had remembered to get some of those
Autograph Cards; those ones that have "With all good
wishes for Xmas and ˉNew Year from", and then you write
your name, only they are much more expensive. Most of
the ones that I've got are so dreadfully festive! I want
something pretty but rather sad to send to that nice
little Mrs Darby I met in Naini; she lost her eldest
boy two months ago you know, and I can't send her a Cupid-
creature dancing on roses and -

> "Radiant may the gladness be
> That Christmas time shall bring to thee!"

for a motto though its one of the best cards here. I
know, I'll send it to Amy Forbes, Amy Arnold I mean. There,
how do you spell Punjab? With a "pun" or a "pan?" I
daresay she will be feeling very dreary as her beloved
"Arthur" has been sent off to Waziristan, but still she
ought to like a cheery card.

These white flowers wouldn't be bad for Mrs Darby
only they've got "God bless you," in big letters on the
outside and that looks like condolence and would remind
her of her trouble. Here's a nice folding one with swal-
lows. I don't think birds could hurt anyone's feelings,
do you George? What are the words -·

> "Merry and happy bright and gay
> Be each hour of Christmas Day."

Oh dear, that won't do; I wonder who ever expects to
have a Christmas of that sort after they are grown up!
Ah, this is better; a basket of daisies "With best wishes
for your happiness. I'll put in "best love" up at the

3

Note: A reduced facsimile reproduction of Trix's original typescript, including her own handwritten alterations.

top.

It's not humbug in the least George. People expect it, and it would seem unkind not to do it, and
"love" all by itself looks snubby. I put "very best
love" to my own people.

Look, if one cuts a little scallop out of each end
of the envelope and writes, "Cards only" it will go for
half an anna, isn't that a good dodge? "Looks rather
mean?" I don't see that at all, everyone does it and
my allowance doesn't run to these lordly ideas. Of course
if you like to give me all the stamps I should need
sending them the other way, you may. I know before I was
married postage stamps were a matter of course like the
air you breathe, or iink, or bread and butter, or any
of the other things one never dreams of buying. Father
never thought of locking his up; I always looked on stamps
as common property. It seems so funny of you to lock
them up in your office box. I suppose we are all stingy
about some one thing, though I don't know which is mine
is, and it is easier to get a ten rupee note out of you than
a half-anna stamp.

"You don't care to run the risk of finding out
when you particularly want stamps that I have not left
you one?" Oh yes, for goodness sake let us leave that
subject alone, I always buy my own stamps and I shall be
glad if you will allow me to send things in my own way.

There isn't much compliment about a Christmas
card after all, for one generally sends them to people
one doesn't care to write a regular letter to; if I try
to pick out something appropriate for each one it will
take me all day. What a nuisance one's friends are! I

4

Note: A reduced facsimile reproduction of Trix's original typescript, including her own handwritten alterations.

know what I'll do, I'll fasten them all up and then I'll
address them; it will save a lot of trouble as I shan't
know which one I have sent to any one and so can't worry
as to whether they'll like it or not. Don't you think
that is a good plan, George? But I wish I could find
that list; I'm sure I shall leave some out, but I daresay it will turn up in a day or two when I am not looking for it; and then I shall be able to polish off the
ones I have forgotten at the New Year. It's very convenient the way New Year always comes a week after Christmas.

    I think you might help me with all these envelopes,
George instead of sitting looking cross, but of course
you can go on sulking if you like. I suppose it amuses
you and it certainly does not hurt me."

------;‡‡‡‡‡‡‡‡‡----

5

Note: A reduced facsimile reproduction of Trix's original typescript, including her own handwritten alterations.

KEEPING A DIARY.

----~+++++++++----~

TIME - After dinner. SCENE - The Drawing Room.

George's Wife speaks:-

"I'm going to keep a diary this year George, don't
you think it's a good plan? I got one while I was out
shopping to-day, it was only a rupee, and it's rather
a nice one! Look, there's a week on a page, but you
have to write Sunday all across the top, else it only
gets three lines instead of six, and that's rather
absurd, for in India, at any rate, one does just as much m
Sunday as on any other day, if not more. I wish the
outside was a prettier colour, I shall get awfully tired
of seeing this dull green book lying about on my writing
table long before the year is over. If Amy were here
I'd make her cover it for me with a bit of silk, but I
never can be troubled to do little things like that, they
are so finnicking, and she really enjoyed them. I often
wish she hadn't married, I really miss her more and more
as time goes on and you simply wouldn't believe what she
saved me in the way of doing up hats. That's the worst
ef India, as soon as you have made friends with a person
and got quite fond of them they are sure to go away, or
else you do.

"Now don't talk, I must begin my diary. To-day
is January the 14th, isn't it? I wish I'd remembered to
get it sooner, for it will be rather hard to remember
what we've done since the New Year. I suppose I'd better
write my name and address on the first page of all,
there. I knew a girl once who always kept a diary and
used to write a motto at the beginning of each, something

1

Note: A reduced facsimile reproduction of Trix's original typescript, including her own handwritten alterations.

in Latin about every day a line. "Nulla dies sine
something" or something like that. Do you know what it
was George? No? No, well it doesn't matter much. She
was a funny sort of girl. I wonder what has become of
her, she married someone at home. Her motto ought to
have been "every day a page," for she used to write
yards all about nothing. She had a blank book you know,
not a tiny little space for each day like this and she
put down thoughts and feelings and what people said to
her and everything. It's very ridiculous to do that and
she put real names in too, only she used to turn the
book upside down and write them in that way. It was a
little puzzling at the first glance of course, but nothing was easier than to turn the book and read them. You
see what I mean George, the whole sentence was written
ordinary way, only the name upside down. I don't think
real names are fair. I know when I put them in if the
thing was the least bit secret I always wrote them backwards, that's a very good way. Yes, I tried keeping a
thought and feelings diary once, because she asked me
to; we thought it would be nice to exchange them at the
end of the year, but I soon got tired of it.

"You can't imagine anyone doing such a dishonoura-
ble thing as reading anyone else's diary?" No dear, of
course not, but she used to read hers aloud to me time and
again, and she constantly left it lying about, and when
a thing is tossed about it can't be very secret.

Now let me set to work at this. What did we do on
New Year's Day? You golfed of course and I went to the
Races with Mrs Birkmire's party. I never saw her look so
plain as she did that day. What did I wear I wonder,
it will make it more interesting to read after if I put

2

Note: A reduced facsimile reproduction of Trix's original typescript, including her own handwritten alterations.

down my frocks, I think it was that fawn crepon: no, it
can't have been for somebody told me I looked like a
lily, so it must have been my white and green.

"Who was the fool who said that?" Indeed I don't m
mean to tell you, and you needn't call him names for he's
very nice and very good looking: it's very silly of you
to be so jealoud, dear! We dined with the Forbes that
night, rather a jolly dinner, I don't remember who took
me in: some one called Anstruther or Crookshank or Shepherd, or some name like that. Never mind, I know I wore
pink. That day is filled up beautdfully, but one has to
write very small.

Now for Wednesday, 2nd. - The mail came in
that day, or was it Tuesday? I know I got a lot of
cards and two or three letters, who were they from George,
do you remember? I'm sure I heard from mother, I'll
write down that I did at any rate. Did we go to
tennis that afternoon? It's awfully hard to remember; or
was that the day I went out to tea and you fetched me and
came very late. Do try and recollect, you are not
helping me a bit. Perhaps it would be easier if I did
to-day and yesterday and tried to fill up backwards.
It's funny how hard it is to remember, and if I leave
blanks on the first two pages it will look very bad. I
didn't think it would be such a bother.

Oh George, isn't this strange, January 25th 9.26
p.m. Greenwich. Conversion of St. Paul. Now, how can
they tell that St. Paul was converted at twenty-six
minutes past nine at Greenwich? Why Greenwish can't
have been discovered in those days! They oughtn't to
make fun of things like that. Do look, it's really there.

What, that round dot means that there isn't a moon?

3

Note: A reduced facsimile reproduction of Trix's original typescript, including her own handwritten alterations.

Then why can't they say so instead of mixing up St. Paul with it? I didn't get a diary for that sort of thing.

Oh dear, I wish I knew what happened on the afternoon of the 2nd and the 3rd; why I'd quite forgotten. You keep a diary don't you George? Do lend it to me for a few minutes just to let me see where we went those, days, I won't actually copy it of course.

"You do keep it; you keep it locked up in your office box and you mean it to stay there?" That's very disobliging of you. If you keep a diary that you are afraid to let your own wife see I think you ought to be ashamed of yourself.

"It wouldn't help me at all for it's only letters and business memos and scores at golf." Oh pray don't apologise, I didn't suppose fpr a minute that there would be anything in it about me; I know the office box is much more important to you than I am. I wonder you don't go and lock yourself up in it. I should not mind if you did! I wish I hadn't bought this diary now every time I look at it I shall remember how disagreeable you were about it. You never take an interest in anything I do, George, and it is so disheartening!   F.

-----††††††††††-----

4

Note: A reduced facsimile reproduction of Trix's original typescript, including her own handwritten alterations.

A CHEERFUL GIVER.

-----‡♦‡♦‡♦‡♦‡♦‡-----

TIME - 9.30 p.m. George is reading the "Pioneer"
while his wife does Mountmellick work, one stitch
every other minute.

"George, did I tell you that Amy Forbes is going
to be married this winter after all? She says that
Arthur, that's the man she's engaged to you know, wants
it to be in December, and her parents have given in.
It's just as well, for of course she is not growing any
younger, and when a thing has been broken off once there's
always a risk in putting it off again.

Now, of course, the next thing will be to think
of a wedding present, they are really a most awful
nuisance; we have had to give two this year already.
What did you say George? It ought to be something
handsome because I stayed with them so long up in Naini.
Yes dear, if you'll give me thirty rupees to-morrow I'll
go out and look for something pretty.

You meant a silver tea-set or a good ring or
bangle? Why George that would come to hundreds, and
when you come to think of it I don't see that we are
under any great obligation to them. It was very convenient for them having me to look after Amy, and of
course I paid my own jampanies and my own pony, so there
was only the house, which they would have been obliged
to keep on in any case, and one's food, and that was
always perfectly plain. I am very fond of simple things;
but still, in India, when one has a joint and pudding
dinner every day one gets tired of it. I'm sure if we
had "broon custel" once we had it three times a week!
It's to be hoped "Arthur" likes it, for it's Amy's one
idea in the pudding line, and she is a very self-satis-

1

Note: A reduced facsimile reproduction of Trix's original typescript, including her own handwritten alterations.

fied sort of girl, she would never let me help her to
order meals.

Why not give her a set of entree dishes? Oh you
extravagant boy! I'm delighted to hear you have so much
money to spend, I thought you were anxious to save as
we are going home next year. You are particularly hard
up just now? Very well then, let's get something sensible and reasonable, tea spoons or salt cellars or - .

She is sure to have dozens? Well if she has she
can always change them, and I don't see how you can have
too many spoons or salt cellars.

"Why not give her a clock? Certainly dear or give
her a brougham or a saddle horse while you are about it!
If you give an absurdly good present people will only say
you are trying to show off, besides she is going to have
a very quiet wedding, so really anything will do.

I may get what I like so long as I don't
worry you? There, if you had only said that at first
it would have saved a lot of time. I never knew anyone
like you for saying a pleasant thing disagreeably, and
it is a habit you should fight against dear, for it makes
the people round you very unhappy. Now we really must
make up our minds about Amy's present; it's very silly
of them to be married near Xmas time when people always
feel poor. Wedding presents really are a tax when you
come to think of it. I'm afraid Amy isn't artistic enough
to care for Indian silver, and the English shops are
fearfully expensive She has seen all my things unluckily, for you know George I have several of my wedding
presents that we have never used, and which are quite
good enough to give away.

You wonder I talk of sending second hand things?

2

Note: A reduced facsimile reproduction of Trix's original typescript, including her own handwritten alterations.

Do you indeed? Perhaps you have forgotten that the
first time I opened the muffineers your dear friends
the Carringtons sent us, one of them was half full of
pepper! That did not look very much as though it had
been new. And there was Mrs Clarke, who is roll—ing in
money, she sent me a brass inkstand that she had evidently
cleaned out for the occasion, for there was a lot of
water in it. Well when rich people do that sort of thing
I fail to see that there is any harm in our doing it. I
do wish I had not shown Amy all my things, but it was a
long time ago and I daresay she has forgotten them.
Only this morning I got out a little cruet-stand that I
thought would do her beautifully. Look George, you see
it's awfully quaint, pepper and mustard in things like
duck's eggs, and one broken in half for the salt. We've
never used it for I can't stand anyt_hing on the table
that isn't either silver or cut glass, and I'm sure Amy
would admire it tremendously. "Fearfully vulgar looking
and not half good enough?" Well Mr Lester gave it to me
and if it was good enough for him to give to me, I
should think it would be good enough for me to give to
Amy.

"The stand is all tarnished?" Oh of course it
isn't bran new but still I think it would do perfectly.

I shall be very glad to keep it since you sneer at
it like that, and I cannot see how you can call me "mean"
when I unselfishly offer to give away one of my own
things to save you from buying something.

Thank you, I am quite ready to "keep quiet". It's
no pleasure to me to talk to a man in a raging temper,
very much the reverse, I don't wish ever to speak to you
again.

3

Note: A reduced facsimile reproduction of Trix's original typescript, including her own handwritten alterations.

George, George, what shall we get for Amy? George dear, don't be sulky, it's awfully easy to tease you. Now do put down that paper and think of something for Amy. I should like it to be jewellery, she's got very little, but though I have got a gold brooch I have hardly worn at all, it's one of those wretched date things. I suppose I could not have 1888 altered to 1894, could I?

Do give me that Pi. Oh I don't want to read it, I want to see the advertisements. Look, there is a sweet little sugar bowl for twelve rupees, let's give her that, or a butter dish, or this silver shoe horn and button hook. Perhaps she would not care for that though, as she has very ugly feet.

It's just like a man George, to taunt me about what I can't possibly help: but though my feet may be long, they are slender and well-shaped, Amy's are square and flat.

I think we had better decide on the sugar bowl, we are not likely to get anything cheaper and I'm sure it's very. pretty, only I'm afraid she will have seen the advertisement, they take the Pi too. I do wish jewellers would not illustrate their things or not put in the prices. Really what a nuisance wedding presents are, I am all at sea again. I wish I was one of those lucky people who had written a book, it must be a tremendous saving for they can go on giving it away for years; presentation copies they call it. And the people who paint too can just send a sketch. I would have given Amy one of my latest photos in a pretty frame, but the wretched girl has got one already. Happy thought! George dear, wouldn't it be nice for me to be done again, quite a large photo you know, and give it to her, I'm sure she'd love it?

4

Note: A reduced facsimile reproduction of Trix's original typescript, including her own handwritten alterations.

"You'd rather I did not do anything so ridiculous?"
then please think of a present for Amy yourself. I'm
simply worn out making suggestions for you to carp at.
You may give her a diamond tiara or a service of plate
if you like; I shan't bother myself any more about it!

                                                    F.

-----‡‡‡‡‡‡‡‡‡‡-----

5

Note: A reduced facsimile reproduction of Trix's original typescript, including her own handwritten alterations.

AT A TENNIS TOURNAMENT.

-----+:+:+++++++:+-----

SCENE:- The Tennis Club's best tennis court, surrounded
by rows of spedtators watching the Champion and the
would-be Champion bounding with the bounding balls as
they play the "finals"! George's Wife speaks:-

"What a lot of people there are here, I'd no idea

there'd be so many; I'm very glad we came. Can you,

see an empty chair anywhere, George? I do think one

of these men might move, instead of pretending to be perfect-

ly absorbed in the game. "We are rather late". Well, I

can't help it if they <u>are</u> playing the second sett; I real-

ly cannot go out before I have had tea this weather for all the

tennis in the world. 'I could have got tea here'. Oh yes,

and typhoid to follow! How is one to know where they get

the milk from, and the water probably comes from the

nearest gutter.

"Look at Mrs Birkmire over there in a striped gown with

a bush of pink roses on her head. I suppose she calls it

a toque, but the effect with her complexion is simply weird.

I want to go and talk to her; come along, George.

1

Note: A reduced facsimile reproduction of Trix's original typescript, including her own handwritten alterations.

"Well dear, how do you do? What a nice place
you are in for seeing. We came too late to get a seat,
and it's very disappointing, for standing always killed
me. Oh thank you, Mr Dimsdale, it's very good of you
to give me your chair. There, that's all right: I
thought he was never going to take the hint.

"Don't you feel the glare in your eyes dreadfully?
I wish now that I had put on a veil. Which of these men
is which? Is that the champion serving? He's got a
very nice face. Poor fellows! they must feel fearfully
nervous with all these people looking on and clapping
whenever they miss a ball. I shouldnt be able to play
a stroke. It does look awfully easy though, the way
they play it. The umpire must have a very bad time of
it perched up on that table and obliged to watch every
single stroke and call the score every minute, especially when it's always going back to deuce in that confusing
way. They ought to give him a prize or something for
doing it.

"Do look at those people's heads opposite turning from side to side: it's exactly like a clock-work
toy, I should think they will all have stiff necks to-
morrow. It's making a toil of a pleasure to watch each
stroke like that.

2

Note: A reduced facsimile reproduction of Trix's original typescript, including her own handwritten alterations.

"Why are the men crossing over? It's rather nice for now we shall see the other man better. Oh, I do hope he'll win, he's got such _sweet_ hair! They're playing for a cup, aren't they? Is it here? Yes, I see it, what a beauty! A thing like that is worth winning. It would look so splendid on a dinner table, although it would be no joke to get flowers to fill it. These white balls on the green are dreadfully dazzling: I am beginning a headache already.

"People are still arriving: it's really too bad of them to come so late, disturbing everyone else. Five, seven, eight, there's the _ninth_ white drill coat and skirt that has passed in the last five minutes, and all exactly alike, only some of them are well cut and some are too fearful for words. I cannot understand the fondness for white drill: it's very thick and stuffy to begin with, and after you have worn it half an hour you look as if you had walked out of a dirty clothes basket, all wrinkles and creases. It seems to need a dhobi perpetually running after it with an iron.

"What is the matter George? Why are you saying 'Hush?' I can't see why I shouldn't talk if I want to: we're not in church. Crossing over again? They look very hot and they must be very tired. Why can't they

3

Note: A reduced facsimile reproduction of Trix's original typescript, including her own handwritten alterations.

give them a little time to rest and have a peg? It would be a rest to all our eyes too. One of them is rubbing his hands in something. I wonder what it is. Goodness! What a big bath towel: it would have looked better if he had had two little ones instead.

"What did you say, Mrs Birkmire? No, indeed, I haven't got a lot of pretty things for the hot weather: you know I am going home, so I am trying to manage with what I have, wearing out last year's rags. Yes, this __is__ a new cotton, but it was so cheap and I think green and white always look cool. Do you really like it? Of course it's as simple as it can be. Now your frock is lovely, so stylish. I often wish I could wear stripes like that, but they make me look so dumpy. Yes, George I saw that rally: I thought it was a very good one. 'How do I get my sleeves to stick out? It's very easy, just have them lined with stiff muslin, but you know they won't stand out nearly so well after they have been washed. Cottons are very disheartening in that way.

"What, George? I __am__ attending, only it hurts my eyes to watch the whole time. What's the score? Haven't they nearly finished? Look, one of them is eating an orange and the other is sucking a lemon. I wonder if they arranged to have different fruit like

4

Note: A reduced facsimile reproduction of Trix's original typescript, including her own handwritten alterations.

that, or if it's only a coincidence.

"Mrs Chesterfield is wearing a very pretty hat isn't she? I like those big tulle rosettes. I'm sure it came out from home, one can tell a home hat in a minute. Your toque is perfectly sweet. I've been admiring it all the afternoon. You got it from Madame Cora? I always heard her taste was perfect: <u>do</u> give me her address, that is, if you are quite sure you do not mind. You'll write it down for me? That's awfully nice of you.

"What a comfort it is that it's getting cooler, but the dusk is coming: they won't be able to see much longer. George, what will happen if it gets too dark for them to play: will they finish it to-morrow? Play it all over again?' Oh not really, that would be a shame, and they ought both to be too stiff to move to-morrow. Why doesn't someone hurry up that man: if he wants his towel so often he ought to tie it round his neck, instead of lounging up to the table for it. I wonder if they are fearfully excited now that it is just near the end.

"Are you dining with the Argyles to-morrow, Mrs Birkmire? I wish you were, they give such jolly dinners. Isn't it absurd how Lent seems to be the regular

5

Note: A reduced facsimile reproduction of Trix's original typescript, including her own handwritten alterations.

dinner-party time though we are all supposed to be
fasting.

"What's the matter? What are they clapping so
for? Is it all over? Oh dear, it does hurt one's
hands to clap hard. It's nice to be allowed to move
about again, I got so tired of sitting in that chair.

"How do you do, Captain Desmond? This is the third
time that I've bowed to you this afternoon, I don't like
being cut by my friends.

"You were quite taken up watching the tennis? So
was I: I do enjoy seeing thoroughly good players, I
wouldn't have missed it for the world. I found the glare
very trying though, and I couldn't hear the score just
towards the end. Which of them is it that has won?"

----+++++++++++-----

6

Note: A reduced facsimile reproduction of Trix's original typescript, including her own handwritten alterations.

THE JOYS OF CAMP

In Anticipation.

George's Wife speaks:- "You wish we were not going
into camp next week? Oh George, I am so looking forward
to it. The freedom from worry will be splendid, and it is s
so good for one to be out in the open air all day long.
Of course I'm very fond of my own house, but I do get tired
of perpetually ordering dinners and keeping the servants up o
to the mark, and in camp I shall just rest. It will be a
sort of lovely lotus-eating.

No, indeed I shan't be lonely. Why it will be a
perfect treat not to have to go to the Club every evening.
I always know exactly who I shall see and what they'll wear,
and pretty nearly what they'll say. Besides you needn't
talk as if we were going to camp in the Desert of Sahara: one
is sure to come across people sometimes, and if you ask
Captain Desmond out for a few days shooting now and again
he'll be only too glad to come.

Oh yes, I have quite made up my mind to do without English
papers. They are just the same week after week, full of
fights and funerals and portraits of plain people who have g
got killed or done something or other. When I'm at home I
never have time to look at a picture paper, except the Queen
and I never miss them a bit there are too many other things
to do.

Note: A reduced facsimile reproduction of Trix's original typescript, including her own handwritten alterations.

I shan't find an embarrassment of occupations in camp?
Now George, for goodness sake don't try to set me against it;
to begin with; if a woman has resources she's never dull.
I mean to knit you splendid long golfing stockings with thin
legs and thick feet; I've got a book that tells you how to
do it, and I used to knit kettleholders when I was a little
girl, and that sort of thing always comes back to one when
one begins again. I shall take heaps of needlework too and
my banjo. Yes, of course I know that I've had it two years
and not got further than five chords, but I shall learn lots
of tunes this winter. Oh, you'll see, the days will be too
short for all I mean to do. Then there will be the marching,
the beautiful rides in the fresh cool of the morning, and
sitting under a tree watching them put up the tents.
I've often longed for a chance of roughing it a little and
I'm looking forwatd to it now tremendously, it will be the
greatest fun.

In Realization.
-"Oh George!! "

"Oh George, do you mean to say its time to get up
already? Why it can't be half past six yet, its quite dark
and icy cold. Do turn up that lamp, how am I to see ?

I've had a wretched night. As soon as the jackals left
off howling the pi-dogs began to yell, whenever they stopped

2

Note: A reduced facsimile reproduction of Trix's original typescript, including her own handwritten alterations.

the watchmen made a simply fiendish noise, and towards
morning the camels were something dreadful.

What did you say? You sent all the camels on last night
with the tents that were struck. Indeed I wasnQt dreaming
& did hear camels. Of course I can't tell if they were our
camels, but I heard some; I suppose even you won't lay
claim to possessing all the camels in Asia.

Oh dear, how I do hate dressing before daylight; for one
thing one never knows what to put on. Its bitterly cold now
but as soon as the sun is up I am sure to feel melted in this
thick serge.

No, I shan't ride this march: Skittles nearly pulled my
arms off yesterday. Yes, yes, I'm perfectly well aware
that one has to drive at a footpace along these unmade
roads, but I prefer that to being run away with and killed.
I daresay Skittles has a snaffle mouth, he may have a
snaffle nose if he likes or a curb eye, but that does'nt
prevent him from pulling horribly if he's the least bit
fresh You never do exercise the ponies properly, I've told
you so a dozen times.

Where is the shoe horn? I'm sure I saw it a minute ago
and now its gone. Bother. I can't possibly put on these
shoes without it, and all my other ones are packed up.

What nonsense, they are not in the least bit tight; a
well-cut shoe ought never to be put on without a corkscrew.

You needn't laugh in that silly way, you know perfectly
well that if I did say "corkscrew" I meant horseshoe.
Why there it is under your brushes, I believe you saw it
there the whole time.

3

Note: A reduced facsimile reproduction of Trix's original typescript, including her own handwritten alterations.

I do hate getting up at this unearthly hour of the morning I never feel really awake till after nine o' clock.

How absurd it is to try and do one's hair in a mirror the size of a cabinet photo. When one liveo like a savage one ought to dress like a savage.

Yes, yes George, I'm nearly ready. Do go and begin chota hazeri and give me time to put on my fringe net.

No, I certainly will not brush back my fringe. There is no reason that I should look hideous, though i am obliged to live in jungles. What does Noor Ali want now? The candlestick ? Well there it is, do give it to him, he is always fussing about something.

George. George. Oh George, do look on the ground and everywhere, I've just remembered that I put my brooch in the candlestick last night to keep it safe. Can you see it ? Can't you see it ? Oh don't say its lost. How tiresome, I wouldn't lose it for anything. It was those dear little pearl hearts on a safety pin that Mr Darcy gave me as a wedding present. It must have fallen somewhere quite near that tiresome Noor Ali ought to have seen it when he took the candlestick. What a nuisance he is.

How could you expect me to see it George ? You were worryi ng so that I hadn't a thought for anything, except keeping you quiet. I'll come and look for it.

Oh what a ghastly place to lose anything in. All dead leaves and anthills. George, tell them I'll give two rupees to the man who finds it, and call everyone to come and

4

Note: A reduced facsimile reproduction of Trix's original typescript, including her own handwritten alterations.

hunt. Make them take their shoes off, they are never likely to see it, but if they walk about I daresay it wil will run into one of them, the pin is very sharp, and if they have bare feet they won't break it. Oh I am sorry, it was one of my pet brooches, and Mr Darcy said w when he sent it that he had tried to get a broken heart but the jewellers didn't make them.' I prized that brooc

Yes I'm coming to chota hazeri, but surely you don't m mean to leave here till they have found my brooch.

Camp is no place for trinkets ? No, of course it isn' and that's why I sent nearly everything to the bank: my best rings, and all my evening bangles, both my necklaces and heaps of other things, but simply for decen decency's sake I had to keep a few rings and a brooch or two, and it just one of these few that Noor Ali throws away. Haven't they found it yet ? Tell them I'll give them five rupees, two isn't enough of a reward.

Do sit down again George, we're not going just yet. Oh George, do you remember that when I lost that ruby out of my bangle I had the whole house swept and the dust sifted over water, and then they found it. Let's tell them to do that. How do I propose to sift a few tons of dead leaves and anthills ? Oh so you think it wouldn't do ? What a barbarous country India is.

Must we really go? I do think you might wait another hour: I shall always remember this as the place where I lost my pet brooch. George darling , do say you'll

---

Note: A reduced facsimile reproduction of Trix's original typescript, including her own handwritten alterations.

give ten rupees to whoever finds it in the next five
minutes, and tell that idiot who is staring up at the trees
with his mouth open that its no good looking there: it
won't fall from heaven.

ccccc-----------

On The March

"George get your rifle, quick.   There's a splendid deer
in that cornfield over to the right.   A man ? Nonsense,
it couldn't be.   Oh yes, now that he is standing up I see
it is one.   How tiresome.   I should have liked a little
shikar to-day to make me forget my poor brooch.   A thing
of that sort makes one feel so stupid, though it certainly
was not my fault.   Whose was it then ?   Why your's of
course, for worrying me about that ridiculous candlestick.
   George, what makes you say that women have no sense of
justice ? Your'e getting into a habit of saying absurd
things, a propos of nothing at all

At the Next Camp.

   I don't like this camping ground at all, its much too
near the village, and these trees don't give the least shade
   Only till to-morrow ?   Well, I don't see the use of
needless discomfort even for a day, but of course my
opinion is of no importance.   The ground is nice and tidy

Note: A reduced facsimile reproduction of Trix's original typescript, including her own handwritten alterations.

at any rate.   I wish I'd lost my brooch here, there would
be some chance of finding it.

What was that you said George ? Well of course I am
feminine , I don't deny it for a minute, but I never thought
I should hear you swearing at me because of that.   Yes, you
did, you said something about "the infernal feminine"
I heard you, and I think it was a disgraceful thing to say,
and not at all nice.   What ? You said "eternal feminine"
I think that is just as bad, or worse if anything.

Oh George, George, there's a scorpion or something
dreadful in my handkerchief: it has just stung my nose.
Take it do.   Oh don't touch it.   Stamp on it hard and
kill the horrid thing.   Is my nose swelling , ?It isn't
unbearably painful yet, but it soon will be, and I do hope
it won't have to be cauterised.   I'd rather die than be
disfigured for life.   Oh George, why don't you stamp on
that handkerchief instead of stirring it up with a stick ?
Do you want to be stung by a venomous beast too ?   Do you
think I shall be disfigured for life ?   Oh don't touch
the handkerchief, kill it first.

What ? No signs of a scorpion, and a knot tied in the
corner ?   The creature couldn't be inside that, could it ?
Open it, only be very careful.   Don't stand so near me.
Why, there's my brooch.   Oh of course I remember nowB : I
took it out of the candlestick last night and tied it up
there to keep it quite safe, and then, when you fussed so,
I forgot it.

Note: A reduced facsimile reproduction of Trix's original typescript, including her own handwritten alterations.

"Much ado about nothing ? I think I behaved wonderfully
well, for I never knew I had it in my pocket all the time.
Let me see, you said ten rupees to whoever found it, didn't
you ? so you'll have to give me that. I'll spend it all on
chocolates and then I shall have something nice to eat in
these hateful jungles. How glad I shall be when we get
back to the station again. Even the old Club will be quite
exciting; I never thought there was so much deadly monotony i
in camp. Three months of it would kill me. Oh you needn't
complain, that's quite diffeoent, you @@'ve got your work
but I fand time hangs most dreadfully heavily.

Is my brooch put in properly George ? How lucky it was
that you did'nt stamp on it when you thought it was a
scorpion. You would have had to give me another."

f

IN DILKHUSHA COTTAGE.

-----‡‡‡‡‡‡‡‡‡‡-----

Scene: Dilkhusha Cottage, a little house set on a
hill: The rooms are few, the walls are bare, the floors
are covered with grey durries, the furniture is scanty:
most of the tables are lame on one leg, and many of the
chairs are ricketty. The front verandah is heaped with
boxes, all bearing severe traces of their journey up from
the plains, various servants stand about, looking ostentatiously helpless. George wanders to and fro with puck-
ered brows; his wife, in a very old frock, brandishes a
large bunch of keys and speaks with decision. . .

"Are you sure all the boxes have come, George? T
There ought to be twenty-six. Do count them. I've done

it twice, but I'm not sure if it's right. I believe I

counted you in the first time. What a shocking state

they are in! I declare if they'd been trundled up the

hill they couldn't look worse· Oh! do look here; my nice

new dress-basket has got an absolute hole in its lid, and

I only bought it last November, I wonder if its any good

writing to complain, for the dresses inside will be all

spoilt with dust, and they are my best ones too. I'll o

open it and see how much harm has been done, if you'll

only tell one of these creatures, who are standing doing

nothing, to unfasten the straps.

"You think we'd better unpack the things that really

1.

Note: A reduced facsimile reproduction of Trix's original typescript, including her own handwritten alterations.

matter first? Oh, of course, you don't care if my dresses are spoilt or not; but all the same you will be the
first person to find fault if you see me looking shabby.
Open anything you like; here are the keys. 1 can't remember which holds what, its more than a year since we
broke up house, and surely you can't expect me to remember every single box after a long time like that.

"No, George, 1 did make a list, a very careful one,
but 1've mislaid it somewhere. 1 saw it at home when 1
was getting ready to come out, and 1 put it away, but 1
don't know where its gone to now. 1t doesn't really
matter though, for everything has to be unpacked sooner
or later. Those two wooden boxes are full of kitchen
things, tell the servants to take them away and open
them. Why, of course, 1 <u>know</u> they are kitchen things,
what else could they be, and 1 don't want to look in and
make sure. If you like to keep a pack of hounds and
bark yourself, you may, but 1'm not going to.

"Now we really must get to work; we'd better do the
drawing-room first. 1 hate to have things hugger-mugger
when people come to call. You think the dining-room is
more important? That's just like a man, always thinking
of things to eat. You'd better go back to the hotel if

2.

Note: A reduced facsimile reproduction of Trix's original typescript, including her own handwritten alterations.

you feel like that, for you won't be at all well fed here for the next few days. No, it wouldn't have done to have stayed on at the hotel and settled down by degrees, its best to make up one's mind to be thoroughly uncomfortable for a week or two and get it all over. Men ought to be able to rough it; they can do it perfectly well if they are out in jungles, killing things, but when its a question of being helpful and obliging they grumble if they don't get five courses at dinner. Now, George, don't waste more time in talking, but tell the <u>kalai-wallah</u> to open that big box, the carpet and rugs are in it. There isn't a <u>kalai-wallah</u> here? Oh what a nuisance! All the boxes 1 want to open are tinned up. 1'm perfectly certain 1 asked you yesterday to be sure and have a man sent for, at least if 1 didn't 1 meant to,1 ought to have learnt by this time that its best for me to do every single thing myself. Do send for one now at any rate. A man has gone already? Well, 1 suppose we may hope to get one some time this afternoon. 1f we live about two miles out of the station we must take the consequences. You chose this house on purpose because it was so fresh and airy. Oh its airy, enough, a house perched on top of a hill generally catches every wind that blows. You thought it would be so much healthier

3.

Note: A reduced facsimile reproduction of Trix's original typescript, including her own handwritten alterations.

for baby than living near bazaars? Well, 1 never heard
before that it was good for babies to live in a thorough
draught; indeed,1 was thinking she'd better sleep in that
little inside room. The poor pet has never had croup yet,
but there is always the risk of it. Oh yes, dear; 1 know
you did your best, and what is the good of getting so
cross; you simply make me afraid to say a word to you. 1
daresay we shall manage somehow, one gets used to draw-
backs after a time: but 1 can't pretend 1 like the situation, and the road up to it is awful. Didn't you notice
it, its all huge rolling stones. We shall be lucky if
we get off without sprained ankles, and 1'm certain 1
shall never dare to go down it in a dandy.

 *'Why don't we do some unpacking instead of talking?'
Very well, take the keys. Oh, dear, where are they? 1
had them in my hand a minute ago. George, do look for my
keys. Why, you've got them all the time. You don't need
to open the box 1'm sitting on, there are heaps of
others and as 1 can't do anything till I get the carpets
1'd better not tire myself out.

 *What's in that box? 'Greeny blue rags, with a
wriggly pattern on them!' Oh, George, those are my new
curtains, and its such an exquisite design, they call it

4.

Note: A reduced facsimile reproduction of Trix's original typescript, including her own handwritten alterations.

'Lotus and River!' Let's take them into the drawing-room What a dingy little place it is! Do you think those rocks outside will come down in the rains? They look very like it. That's an absurdly high window for such a small room; its nearly up to the ceiling. 1 suppose this crooked rod in the corner is meant for a curtain pole. 1 just want to try the effect with the curtain thrown across it. Please put it up over the window, George; you can do it if you stand on a chair. Not high enough? Oh, but 1 must see how it looks: 1'll put these two square sofa cushions under your feet and then you'll be able to reach. There! Hullo, baby! Has zoo come helpems Muzzer then? Take her over there, <u>ayah</u>. <u>(A crash)</u> Oh, goodness, how you frightened me! Did you jump, George, or did you fall? You're not hurt, are you? What a mercy that you didn't tear the curtain! You've hurt your arm? What a bother! Oh do look at baby! Look how she's laughing! Clap hands, baby! Did a goosems Daddy go tumble-tumble and make a baby laugh? Isn't it sweet the way she notices everything? Little pet; she wants you to do it again.

"There's the <u>kalai-wallah</u> at last, and he's got the big box open. How it smells of napthaline! 1 wonder

5,

Note: A reduced facsimile reproduction of Trix's original typescript, including her own handwritten alterations.

if 1 shall ever be able to sit in the same room with that
carpet. Tell them to take it outside, George, and shake
it and beat it; but they mustn't put it in the sun, and
all the table-cloths and things must be hung over the
verandah rails, and a man must watch and see they don't
blow away. Oh 1 can't give my own orders, I've forgotten
most of my Hindustani, you say it.

"'Your arm is horribly painful?' Where? If its
only at the elbow its all right, you must have knocked
your funny-bone. Do you know why its called the funny-
bone? I didn't till quite the other day, its because it
borders on the <u>humerus</u>. That's one of the bones in one's
arm you know. It was Mr Trafford told me that on board-
ship; he was such a jolly boy always saying funny things
and playing practical jokes, and keeping everybody lively.
We missed him dreadfully when he left at Aden, and they
chaffed me about him like anything. We certainly were
great friends; he was so good to baby, and though there
were lots of other children on board she was the only
one he ever noticed. She used to scream with joy whenever she saw him, for he could hop all over the deck like
a frog; it was the funniest thing you ever saw, and
she loved it.

6.

Note: A reduced facsimile reproduction of Trix's original typescript, including her own handwritten alterations.

"You think that if I'd leave off 'relating my con-
quest' and do some unpacking, it might save time? Oh
George, dear, how funnily jealous you are! I am sure
even <u>you</u> needn't mind about poor Mr Trafford: he was
never the least bit sentimental or silly, only just the
day before he left he asked me to call him 'Bertie' and
I said I made a point of never calling people by their
names.

"'Did I call him Algernon then?' No; of course not,
how absurd you are! I called him Mr Trafford. Do you
know this sofa is not half as un comfortable as it looks if
one lies down on it? I'm rather tired George, I wish
you'd go out in the verandah and see if there's a man
there. I don't want my table-cloths to blow away, and
you might ask Noor Ali when lunch will be ready and if
they have got all the kitchen things out. What, he says
he couldn't find any <u>dekshies</u> in those boxes; they were
full of carved wood and nothing else? Oh George, I know
what has happened. Don't you remember the screen and the
gong stands that Colonel Willis sent me from Burma, and
we said we wouldn't bring them up because they were so
heavy. They have been sent instead of the <u>dekshies,</u> and
everything that we want is down in your office now, and

7.

Note: A reduced facsimile reproduction of Trix's original typescript, including her own handwritten alterations.

there is no knowing when we shall ever get them! You
needn't laugh. 1 feel much more like crying. 1 <u>did</u>
think you could be trusted to send off boxes. Now 1
suppose we shall have to go back to the hotel and wait
there for a fortnight at least.

"What, you are doing your best to tell me that Noor
Ali has opened two other boxes, and the <u>dekshies</u> are in
them all right? Then 1 hope you'll give him a really
good scolding for frightening me for nothing, its most
impertinent of him. Tell him we want lunch as soon as
possible, and say 1'm not to be disturbed until its
ready. I've had a very busy morning, and 1 know if 1
don't take a little rest now 1 shall have a dreadful
headache."

8.

Note: A reduced facsimile reproduction of Trix's original typescript, including her own handwritten alterations.

261

THE PLEASURE OF HIS COMPANY.

-----╬╪╪╪╪╪╪╪╪╪╪╪----

Mabel's Husband speaks:- 1t's not time to go yet, it's only half-past seven. Oh, its tonight we've got to dine with the Fosters. Why on earth can't people leave one alone, in the hot weather? 1 fail to see the pleasure of sitting in their stuffy rooms, talking a string of nonsense to some silly woman. When you've gone home you wan't catch me attending these feasts; they are part of the price one pays for the joy of one's wife's society. 1 don't remember saying that we must accept this time, because they had asked us twice before and we had refused. You have a most convenient memory!

1 suppose 1 must drive home, you will need at least half an hour for dancing in front of the looking glass, though what you do all the time is more than 1 can say. 1 never see any wonderful results to account for it.

Now for goodness' sake don't dress up to the nines, put on something simple, and 1 hate to see you plastered over with brooches and bangles. 1 wonder what you'd say to me if 1 arranged all my spare studs and pins about my coat.

1.

Note: A reduced facsimile reproduction of Trix's original typescript, including her own handwritten alterations.

We can go there in the cart, it's not going to rain and 1 hate jolting along in a ticca*. 1f you will kindly refrain from putting on a court train your dress will be all right. "So damp for your fringe?" Why can't you w wear your hair simply and naturally, instead of curling and frizzing it? 1f you do brush it straight back from your forehead 1 won't go out with you, that's all. 1t makes you look like a lunatic just escaped from Girton.

Now do try to be in time for once, what 1 hate in going to dinners isn't so much the things themselves as standing about waiting till you have finished decorating Then we always arrive late and you sail into the room, rubbing your chin against your left shoulder; 1 do wish you could remember to hold your head straight, it looks supremely idiotic and not in the least fetching.

Mabel! Mabel! 1t's ten minutes to eight. Are you nearly ready? What, we don't dine till a quarter-past eight? Why on earth didn't you tell me that before, then 1 shouldn't have dressed so soon. 1ts suffocatingly hot, and these clothes are fearfully thick. No, indeed 1 can't put on my thin dinnercoat, not to dine with that pompouss old Foster: he is a self-made man, who adores his creator and he would be mortally offended if 1 didn't appear in

2.

Note: A reduced facsimile reproduction of Trix's original typescript, including her own handwritten alterations.

tails.

You wonder 1 don't get a suit of paramatta. 1 daresay you do, anything is good enough for me, but 1 don't
choose to wear flimsy rags. 1f 1 am dragged out in the
evening, against my will, 1 prefer to be decently dressed
at any rate.

Just look at this shirt! 1ts all crumpled already,
and it will be like an accordeon before the end of the
evening. 1 wonder how often 1 have told you not to take
shirts from the dhobi unless they are stiff as boards.
Cut him eight annas for this one, and if he says he can't
starch them properly, sack him. 1 ought to have learnt
by this time that nothing 1 say is considered worth attending to, but still if you would bestow on your servants
a little of that sweet temper you reserve for your husband
they would obey you better.

Mabel, are you ready? Mabel, aren't you ready yet? 1
think you might have told me that you were waiting in
the hall. Hullo, so you are got up à la bébé, white frock
and blue ribbons: looks rather skimpy. Did you make it
out of old pocket handkerchiefs? There you go, your dress
lapping after you! 1 can't see the beauty of dragging
yards of good muslin on the ground, what would you say to
3.

Note: A reduced facsimile reproduction of Trix's original typescript, including her own handwritten alterations.

me if my coat tails trailed on the floor? Think of the amount of dirt and germs of disease you pick up and carry about with you.'

Come along, do, we shall be late. Haven't you brought a cloak; only that gossamer shawl? Well, don't expect me to pity you if you have neuralgia to-morrow, after doing your best to get it. Women seem to delight in doing the most absurd and irrational things!

Where is this house? "You don't know" and why don't you know? 1 thought a woman always took charge of all her husband's social duties; you are a regular broken reed to trust to. This it? Oh Lord, we're the first, 1 can't stand that, let's go for a turn.

1ts not really raining, just a drop or two. 1 suppose you're such a fragile flower you're afraid of melting.

Now for goodness sake don't start singing after dinner, there's no getting you to stop once you begin, and 1 don't want to stay till the small hours. Remember, 1've got my work to do to-morrow, 1 can't spend the day lolling about as you do. 1 know 1 shall feel wretchedly bad in any case, one eats prawns and drinks bad simkin and peach-brandy and all sorts of mixtures.

4.

Note: A reduced facsimile reproduction of Trix's original typescript, including her own handwritten alterations.

"Don't mix them?" That's really very clever of you, but one does it without thinking, I just take what I am offered.

That fool of a bearer has forgotten to give me my cigarette case, and old Foster is sure only to have poisonously bad cheroots, so I shan't even get my smoke after diiner. This is what they call pleasure.

I say, it's past the quarter! What a lot of gharries there are in the compound; it's going to be a big spread. Hurry up, don't be all night! There, why did you get out so quickly; you've sent your frock right against the wheel and got a great streak of mud all down it. I could not manage to save it; you should have had a cloak on.

Never mind, come along, we are the last. Your fringe is all out of curl and meshes of that "invisible net" of yours are showing across your forehead; it looks awful.

                                                          F.

-----++++++++++-----

5.

THE ART AND CRAFT OF PALMISTRY.

— — — —‡‡‡‡‡‡‡‡‡‡‡‡‡— — — —

Scene: The drawing-room of a little house in the hills, full of bamboo furniture, "draperies" and photo-graphs. A dinner of eight is nearing its close, the men having just left the dining-room.

Mrs Baird, the hostess speaks. She is small pale and plain, has an enthusiastic manner, and is addicted to the use and abuse of italics.

"I am *so sorry* I haven't got a piano, but you know they're an *awful* nuisance in the hills· They *never* keep in tune and one has to take *such* care of them, wrapping them up, and pans of charcoal and wadded covers just as if they were *babies!* But I *do* regret not having one now, I hear you play so *exquisitely*, Mrs Goold."

Mrs Goold, the wife of a genial and popular civil-ian, is a tall lady with a strong chin and a great deal of forehead; she wears a black dress and a species of cuirass in jangling jet.

"I think you have been misinformed, I never play."

Mrs B. "How *stupid* of me! But I feel *sure* you *sing*, it must have been singing I was thinking of, and you have *such* a singing face.

Mrs G. (grimly): "Really, but I never sing."

Mrs B. (suddenly): "Nita darling, did you bring your banjo?"

Miss Palmer, a young lady whose age may be described as "present day," having once been told that she resem-bles a well-known actress cultivates, photographic ex-pressions and poses, and arranges her hair with elaborate untidiness. She wears a flame-coloured gown and a trail of artificial poppies is wreathed round her.

"Oh no darling, the poor Jo Ban is so ill. Its vel-

1

Note: A reduced facsimile reproduction of Trix's original typescript, including her own handwritten alterations.

ʃ

lum is like a bag this damp weather. (Raises her eyebrows despairingly) It would be torture to play on it!"

Mrs B. (tenderly): "How fiendish! But what am I thinking of, I promised Captain Winthrop that you would tell his fortune. Have you ever had your fortune told, Mrs Goold? Nita is wonderful, quite weird at times! She makes me shiver. She does it by the hand you know. I knew a girl once who used to do it by coffee grounds, but I never could quite believe in that, though I have known her say some marvellous things!"

Mrs G.: "I cannot say that I am at superstitious."

Captain Winthrop, short and spare, a renowned steeplechaser with a reputation on the turf.

"Would you mind tellin' me my fortune, Miss Palmer?"

Miss P. (with her most appealing gaze): "I'll try, but I'm hideously out of practise. I can't remember when I last looked at a hand. If I have to read hands professionally, at a bazaar, you know I simply steep myself in palmistry. I read nothing else for weeks."

Captain W. (impressed): "By Jove!"

Mr Colville Parkins, a rising young civilian, very delicate looking with gold rimmed eyeglasses and the manner of one who instructs and corrects an ignorant world.

"In which of the many authorities on palmistry do you place most faith?"

Miss P.: "Oh Desbarolles is a great stand by, but he's wickedly long; as long as a novel of Zola's, only very dull. Of course I began with him, but some of the English books are quite good." (Arranges herself in a Sibylline attitude, Captain W. holds out a short square hand, the other men draw nearer.

Miss P. (in her light comedy manner):"Oh we mustn't have any listeners. I insist on being along with my victims always!"

Captain W.: "Clear out all you fellows, this is bizz.

2.

Note: A reduced facsimile reproduction of Trix's original typescript, including her own handwritten alterations.

f

Miss P. (intently, her eyes fixed on his hand):"Darling!"

"Captain W. (starting): "What did you say?"

Miss P. (more loudly):"Gertie darling, 1'm a demon to be so troublesome, but may 1 have a magnifying glass?"

The glass is brought and Miss P. gazes silently through it for two long minutes. Captain W. has time to decide that having your fortune told is much worse than being photographed, and almost as bad as going to the dentist, before she speaks, very slowly and musingly.)

"Yes, you have a fairly well balanced mind. That is to say you weigh your actions well before you perform them. Only where physical danger is concerned you are wickedly reckless."

Captain W. (impressed):"D'you know that's awfully true. 1 think over things like writin' a letter or goin' to church no end, and often don't do 'em, but if its a case of ridin' or pigstickin' 1'm on!"

Miss P. "Yes, that is so clearly shown. As to your heart line well, you might be a great deal more constant with advantage. 1'm afraid you're dreadfully fickle.

Captain W. (delighted: "Oh come now!"

Miss P.: Women influence you tremendously. (Looks steadfastly at his pink face and light eyes.) A dark pale woman, not exactly handsome but very bewitching will. . . "(pauses impressively.)

Captain W. (nervously): "Yes what?"

Miss P. : "No 1 don't think 1'll go on." (Notes a scar on his brow) "Shall 1 tell you something about your past?"

Captain W.: "Yes do: You've told me some awfully true things up to now you know."

Miss P. (with decision): "Not long ago you had an accident, something to do with a four-footed beast, that injured your head."

3.

Note: A reduced facsimile reproduction of Trix's original typescript, including her own handwritten alterations.

Captain W: "By Jove you are rum, Miss Palmer! 1 was
trainin' a little beast of a mare and she came down over
a hurdle and 1 came a most awful crumpler. Got the mark
of it still."

Miss P.: "That is deeply interesting, but still these
things are recorded. You have had several other accidents, in fact y ou have had many more accidents than illnesses."

Captain W.: "Never was ill in my life except a few
goes of fever."

Miss P. (as though not hearing): "A slight tendency
to fever is the only thing 1 can see on your health line.
(Gazes at him as she passes her fingers over his palm)
"You have a noble nature, reserved, passionate yet forgiving. You have many friends, friends who adore you, you
are keenly sensitive to music, and you have funds of reserve in your nature, deep wells of strong feeling, that
even those who love you best can only dimly guess at."

Captain W. (open mouthed):"By Jove that's all most
awfully true. Do go on?"

Miss P. "1'm afraid 1 mustn't now. 1 could go on
for hours, you have an intensely interesting hand, but
the others are waiting."

Mr C.P. (advancing with alacrity and holding out a
long thin hand): "My turn now, Miss Palmer."

(Business as before with magnifying glass.)

Miss P.: "Yes, you have a singularly well balanced
mind. You are acutely logical and you weigh your actions
well before you perform them. Mental actions that is,
for where physical danger is concerned you are wickedly
reckless."

Mr C.P. (approvingly): "Quite right, go on."

Miss P.: "As for your heart line you might be a
great deal more constant with advantage, indeed 1 might
call you "Tender but not true!"

4.

Note: A reduced facsimile reproduction of Trix's original typescript, including her own handwritten alterations.

Mr C. P. (delightedly) "1 shall begin to be seriously afraid of you."

Miss P. "Women have a tremendous influence upon you. (glances at his pale face and dark eyes.) There, was, no there is, a fair blue eyed woman, not strictly beautiful but with a bright, winsome face who. . "(pause.)

Mr C. P. (a little uneasily) "Well what about her?"

Miss P. (softly): "You know!"

(In the pause that follows this successful thrust she has time to notice an ink stain under a nail, and a yellow tinge between two fingers, and speak with authority.)

"Your danger is that you work too hard, you write too much, it is bad for your nerves; and you smoke far too many cigarettes."

Mr C. P.: "you are a witch Miss Palmer!"

Miss P.: "Oh no, you have such a sensitive hand, no one could help seeing it. Several illnesses are marked, are marked, chiefly from brainwork and mental strain."

MR C.P.: "You are quite right, 1 suffer very much from headache in the hot weather."

Miss P. (as though not hearing): "You have a strong tendency to headache which you should guard against. (Gazes at him as she passes her fingers over his palm) "Yoy have a noble nature, reserved, passionate yet forgiving. You have a gift for friendship, You are keenly sensitive to music and literature, and there are funds of reserve in your character, deep wells of powerful feeling that even those who love you most can only dimly guess at."

Mr C. P. (almost too surprised to be sententious) "I may truthfully say that you have converted me to palmistry, 1 never knew before that character could be delineated by it with such absolute fidelity."

Mrs B. "Has she finished? Isn't she wonderful, 1

Note: A reduced facsimile reproduction of Trix's original typescript, including her own handwritten alterations.

told you she was wonderful. Now **Nita** darling you must look at Mr Goold's hand and let us all listen. I know you like doing it quite alone best, but you can tell him something at any rate, and we do so want to hear."

Miss P: (in the tones of a gentle martyr(I'll try darling." (Takes Mr G's plump reluctant hand and strokes it slowly, while his wife looks on with a severe face, and lends a serious ear.)

Miss P.: "You have a splendid head line, you might do anything with a head like this, but the heart! (a burst of rippling laughter) Oh dear what a shocking heart! Chained and lined and crossed. Flirtations that begin at seventeen, and go on till after seventy!"

MRG. (feebly) "Not with the same lady I hope!"

Miss P. "Ah, don't try to laugh it off in that way! No, always with different ladies, for out of sight is out of mind with you even more than with most men!"

Mr G. (conscious of his wife's eye, and longing to change the subject) "Have I a good life line?"

Miss P. "Very fair, quite normal and ordinary, but your heart line is what interests me. Its so. . . and those lines which confirm it! Oh Mrs Goold, I hope you never go home and leave your husband out here?"

Mrs G. (severely) "I have done so on several occasions when my children have required my care."

Miss P. (through laughter) "Really! did you trust him alone? I wouldn't trust anyone with a heart line like that?"

Mr G. "Well Miss Palmer I think you are a little unkind with your vague accusations."

Miss P. "Oh, I'll be more definite then! Let me see, about five years ago I notice a very strong influence, a woman's influence. I think I can describe her, but not in English words, she was **petite, riante, tres spirituelle!** C'est vrai monsieur?"

Mr G. (pulling his hand away) "Its all rubbish! I

6

Note: A reduced facsimile reproduction of Trix's original typescript, including her own handwritten alterations.

beg your pardon but really you have been talking as much
nonsense to me as though you were a gipsy fortune teller!'

Miss P. "Gipsies tell the truth you know. And your
wife believes me, don't you Mrs Goold?"

Mrs G. (in an icy voice) "I have been very much en-
tertained.

(Rises and makes her adieux and the party breaks up)
Mr G. (nervously on the way home) "Did you ever hear
such nonsense, my dear, that silly girl ought not to be
encouraged."

Mrs G. (still in glacial tones) "There is many a
true word spoken in jest!"

Mr G. subsides, feeling that the shades of the
prison house are closing round him.

Captain W. to Mr C. P. as they stroll up to the Club,
united for once by a common interest. "D'you know that
girl told me some rum things, that had happened, and described people to me, it was quite jumpy!"

Mr C. P. "exactly my experience, but perhaps, the
absolute accuracy with which she described my character
was even more remarkable.

Both register a secret vow to call on Miss Palmer
next day.)

Mrs B. Bidding farewell to Miss P. who is the last
to go.)

Oh Nita you naughty girl, how could you make poor
dear Mr Goold so uncomfortable?"

Miss P. opening large innocent eyes, "Did I, darling
(to herself, as the rickshaw rattles home.) "What luck
that I should have been at Maidanpore just when Mr Goold
was flirting with that little Frenchwoman. He had for-

7.

Note: A reduced facsimile reproduction of Trix's original typescript, including her own handwritten alterations.

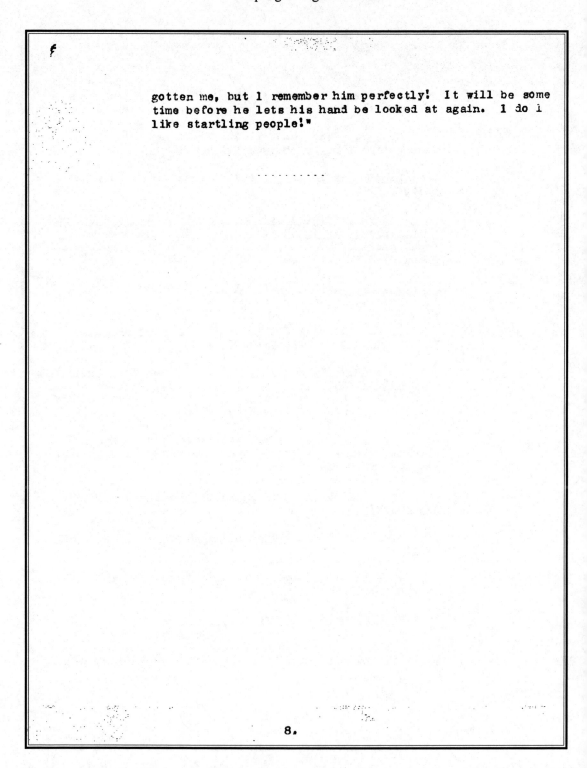

f

gotten me, but 1 remember him perfectly! It will be some
time before he lets his hand be looked at again. 1 do 1
like startling people!"

. . . .

8.

Note: A reduced facsimile reproduction of Trix's original typescript, including her own handwritten alterations.

Ⱶ

AT AN AUCTION IN THE HILLS.

-.--.--✝✝✝✝✝✝✝✝✝--.--.-

A large room three parts filled with rows of chairs, the fourth part behind the auctioneer's desk is devoted to an exceedingly miscellaneous collection of goods. The curious eye may discover a perambulator, a saddle, towels a pile of old clothes, tinned provisions, china teapots, solah topees, bronze statuettes, boots, umbrellas, books and other articles too varied to enumerate.

New Comer in calling costume greeting experienced lady in dark blue cotton and a solah hat: "So you see I've come after all, just to look on, for I suppose one can't be seen buying anything here."

Experienced Lady (coldly): "Just as you like, of course, but I got all those embroideries that you admire, here last year, and some very good old China too."

A Bride in white frock and sailor hat to a plain friend in tusser silk: "I'm so glad you could come, I should never have dared to come all alone and I've set my heart on surprising Fred. We looked at the things yesterday, and there is the most delicious set of dessert knives an and forks, with fruit spoons and everything in a case lined with green plush. I daresay they'll go very cheap, and they're just what I want. Come and sit close up to the desk. How does one bid, shall I have to call out my name every time?"

Friend: "Oh, no, put up your hand, and give a little nod."

Bride: "Is that all? How nice!"

Her Husband, a nervous and short-sighted young man enters at the further door, and recognises a chance acquaintance: "Hullo, you here? It's quite a gathering, I've never been to one of these shows before and I shouldn't have come now, only the fact is my wife saw a box of knife things she rather fancied and I thought I'd see if we could pick em up. No, I don't care to go any

1.

Note: A reduced facsimile reproduction of Trix's original typescript, including her own handwritten alterations.

f

nearer thanks, 1'm all right here." (remains standing at
the door)

Bride (suddenly): "1 do think wedding presents are
disappointing things; 1 got dozens of silly little
spoons, and shoals of salt cellars, but no fish knives or
dessert knives. People ought to be more thoughtful."

Friend who has no personal experience of wedding
gifts: "Yes, of course."

Bride: "Did I tell you that there are grape scissors
im that case too? But one never seems to need them in
1ndia, the only grapes 1 have seen out here were packed
in round boxes, like pills!"

The auctioneer enters with a smile, and taps his
hammer twice or thrice, in tuning fork fashion on the
desk.

Auctioneer: "Now ladies and gentlemen, please, we
have a great deal to get through this morning. We'll begin with five pounds of Kangra Valley tea, make a bid for
the tea, so much per pound, anything you like."

      native
Jocular shopkeeper at the far end of the room :
"Four annas!"

Auctioneer (slowly and impressively): "Was that you
Yussuf?" Yussuf subsides into uneasy silence, and bidding and general conversation proceed briskly until thirty
pounds of tea have been sold and the babel of tongues has
risen to something remarkable.

Auctioneer (driving imaginary nails all over his desk
as an appeal for silence): "Well, this is a regular mother's
meeting! Ladies and gentlemen, I should so like to be
able to hear myself speak! We should get on ever so much
quicker you know. Thank you."

Giddy girl to Sergeant's wife: "1sn't he fun?"
Sergeant's wife (practically): "'E knows 'ow to run
up the prices 'e does. 1 wish they'd get on to the 'ams
in canvas. Ten annas a pound isn't dear when you come to
think of it."

2.

Note: A reduced facsimile reproduction of Trix's original typescript, including her own handwritten alterations.

Her son: "Mother, ain't there going to be any refreshments?"

Sergeant's wife (emphatically): "Not for hours yet,
young man, and if you don't sit quiet and leave off kick-
ing your chair, 'ome you go."

*The auctioneer having disposed of a rifle, a fancy
dress, three dozen boxes of silk ties and five saucepans,
turns his attention to purely decorative objects. A huge
Mooltan jar, four feet high and broken at neck and foot
is hoisted precariously upon the desk.*

"Now here is an ornament for a house. Make a bid
for the vase. Anything you like, must be sold, there is
no reserve on any of these things. Its a bit bent, you
see," *(lifts off the broken neck)* "but a little stickphast
will put them to rights. Eight annas? Come now! Why the
ornament on the lid alone is worth eight annas. Twelve
annas? Can't take four annas bids for a thing like this
sir, one rupee is your bid. sTwo rupeesYussuf? Going to
the bazaar for two rupees! No advance? Two eight! Three!
Three eight. Four rupees. Four rupees no advance? Take
a last long look at it. Four eight. Five. Five rupees
in two places. Can't give it to you both. Six rupees!
Six eight, against you sir. Seven? Going for seven rupees no advance? Well this is a bargain! Seven eight!
Eight rupees. You don't get a bargain like this every
day. Eight eight! Nine. No advance! Nine, going for. -
Ten rupees? Going for ten rupees" *(hammer falls)* "Mrs
Stackpole Collins, The Towerobabel."

*The vase, in three pieces, is brought to the lady by
a staggering chaprassi, she tries not to look appalled by
its size.*

Candid Neighbour: "Well, l can't say l admire it,
and where do you mean to put it in your tiny little hotel
room?"

"Mrs S.C. "Oh it will look so nice standing in a
corner."

Her Neighbour: "It might in a corridor, but the
Towerobabel sitting rooms are so small. l hardly know
how you'll get it in, and it wants mending too."
3,

Note: A reduced facsimile reproduction of Trix's original typescript, including her own handwritten alterations.

MRS S.C.(hopefully): "1've got some gum, and it was so cheap."

Her Neighbour: "Do you think so? And 1 wonder how you'll pack it when you go down next month."

Mrs S.C.: "1 didn't think of that."

Her Neighbour: "Rather a white elephant, isn't it?"

Mrs S.C. is silent.

The Small Boy: "Mother, mother. When the refreshments do come what'll they be?"

His Mother: "Sherry wine, which you don't touch, mind that, and good 'ard biscuits, not sweet ones, don't you think it, an' ginger beer which you'll only get if you're good an' leave off bothering."

Bride: "I haven't bidden a bit yet, 1 must practise in case I shouldn't do it right when the knives come" (Raises her hand and nods with such energy that she becomes the purchaser of a twenty pound ham at twelve annas a pound.)

Auctioneer: "Name and address please."

The Bride gives it in so low and depressed a voice that it does not reach the ears of her distant husband.

Bride(sadly): "Bidding's awfully easy, but 1 didn't want this thing a bit. Fred hates ham and 1 don't care for it and the servants don't finish things up for you out here, as they do at home. Twelve annas a pound isn't much though is it?"

Friend: "You'll have to pay fifteen rupees for that ham."

Bride: "Oh, what a shame!"

New Comer (contemplating a large armful of purchases with the light of auction fever glowing in her eyes):It's the greatest fun 1 shall come every week. 1 haven't a notion of what 1've spent though."

4,

Note: A reduced facsimile reproduction of Trix's original typescript, including her own handwritten alterations.

Experienced Lady: "You'll get the bill on Monday morning."

(Refreshments are brought in, and as they are much appreciated by a large number of the assembly, the smell of sherry and the sound of the steady crunching of very hard biscuits fills the air.)

Small Boy: "Mother this ginger beer's lemonade!"

His Mother: "You be thankful for what you get."

Small Boy: "Mother, mayn't I have another glass of lemonade?"

His Mother (taking second glass of sherry): "No you mayn't, you've had as much as is good for you."

Auctioneer: "Now here is a beautiful set of dessert knives and forks with four fruit spoons all complete in plush lined case. This would make a splendid wedding present."

(The general public bids briskly up to seventy rupees, then it losses interest and the contest is between the bride and her husband, who outbid each other with zeal and enthusiasm.)

Auctioneer: "One hundred rupees. Against you, ma'am ma'am."

Bride (in a defiant tone): "A hundred and ten."

Her Husband (waving his stick and resolved to succeed at all costs):"A hundred and twenty!"

Bride (forgetting in her excitement that a bid need not be ten rupees: "A hundred and thirty!"

Husband (loudly):"Hundred and forty."

Bride (gasping): "A hundred and fifty!"

Husband (despairingly): "One fifty-five."

The friend suddenly stands up and gazes towards the

5.

Note: A reduced facsimile reproduction of Trix's original typescript, including her own handwritten alterations.

<u>doo r.</u>

<u>Bride (shrilly)</u>: "One hundred and sixty!"

<u>Friend</u>: "Kitty stop! That's your husband!"

<u>Auctioneer</u>: "One hundred and sixty. No advance!"
(Hammer falls).

<u>Bride</u>: "Oh why didn't Fred tell me he was coming. Oh
I wish I'd told him I was going! I never had a secret
from him before."

<u>Friend</u>: "I don't believe he's seen you yet."

<u>Bride (hysterically)</u>: "Of course he hasn't he's as
blind as a dear old bat. <u>(Clutches her dearly bought
dessert knives)</u> "Good bye Gertie, I can't stay, I'm
going to tell him. He's never been cross with me yet."
<u>(Goes out hastily, forgetting the ham)</u>

<u>New Comer (who has just bought twelve small vases on
a tin tray)</u>: "Oh dear, these are fearfully common when
you see them nearer to they looked lovely up there, and
I do believe this brocaded notepaper is rather monsooned,
I wish I hadn't bought six boxes of it."

<u>Experienced Lady</u>: "He said it was 'slightly damaged'.
Personally I make it a rule never to buy anything that I
have not carefully looked at the day before. You can
always do that." <u>(Bids with calmness and discrimination
for the old Cloisonné plate which is the reason of her at
tendance at the auction and carries it off in triumph.)</u>

<u>Small Boy</u>: "Mother, will there be more refreshments
by and bye?" <u>His Mother</u>: "No there will not, an' you
come along 'ome."

-----++++++++++-----

Note: A reduced facsimile reproduction of Trix's original typescript, including her own handwritten alterations.

A CHRISTMAS MINSTREL.

He was trying to write verses, a great many sheets
of foolscap before him were scribbled over with quatrains
couplets and half lines, but genius was not burning
and it seemed as though the Christmas verses might not
be written. There was no reason why they should
be, but he liked to send 'seasonable contributions' to
the newspapers and sometimes the newspapers published
them.

His wife sat near: she had been summoned to
play the part of audience and critic and until her
opinion was ~~called for~~ *required* she was busy making a new bonnet
for the baby.

"Look here," he said, "I think that in India
Christmas verses ought not to be too cheerful: one
always thinks of the people at home and so on and
the verses ought to express regret and that sort of
thing."

"Yes, dear," said his wife.

"Listen to this, I like the metre, it's got a
suggestion of Herrick about it."

1

Note: A reduced facsimile reproduction of Trix's original typescript, including her own handwritten alterations.

'Peace and Good Will to Men'
The Church bells say:
Be joyful then
To welcome Christmas Day!
But what if that *day* bring
Memorial
How shall we sing - -

"No, I scratched that out, the second verse goes on

like this -

'What memories does it bring
Of bygone years?
How shall we sing
Who cannot hide our tears."

"Do you think that'll do?"

"Yes, dear," said his wife.

"It's a difficult metre to manage though, I couldn't

make it long. I began another of the same sort.

"Now Christmas comes again
With festal cheer,
To end the pain,
Of one most dreary year."

"But I like the other beginning best, don't you?"

"Yes, dear," said his wife.

There was a few minutes silence, the pencil travel-

led slowly over the foolscap, and he consulted a little

2

Note: A reduced facsimile reproduction of Trix's original typescript, including her own handwritten alterations.

brown book. Its name was "Ballades and Rondeaus".

"A ballad with a pretty refrain goes well", he
said, "how's this for a start?

> 'The bells in the church-tower chiming,
> The redbreast birds that brave the snow,
> The Christmas songs of merry rhyming,
> The Christmas days of Long Ago.

"You see, 'The Christmas Days of Long Ago' comes
in as a refrain all through."

"Yes, dear," said his wife.

The pencil began to scribble on the margin of
the paper "climbing, sliming, timing". "That's an impossible rhyme" he said half aloud, "I must start again".

His wife did not say "Yes dear", for the baby's
bonnet was reaching a critical stage, but she nodded.

A little troop of jackals was singing part-songs
not far away:their lyrics appeared to require no
rhymes, whic h perhaps accounted for the ease and
spontaneity of them.

The writer began to read aloud again,

> ""On Christmas day, our thoughts must wend
> To many a long forgotten friend
> The air is thronged with memories With tender
> thoughts from overseas.
> The merriment that we intend -

3

Note: A reduced facsimile reproduction of Trix's original typescript, including her own handwritten alterations.

"No, that won't do. Jessy have you seen the other little book like this, 'Sonnets of this Century?'"

"Yes dear," said his wife and she gave it to him.

"The rhyme rules for sonnets are very strict", he said a little later with corrugated brow, "I can't get on any further with this –

'So Christmas comes, and mirth is now a debt
That we must pay, our duty to our neighbour:
Away with sorrow! Strike up lute and tabor!
Have you a grief? Your business is forget. –
Your heart is weary and your eyes are wet? –
Dry them and smile, nor count it wasted labour.'

The little white bonnet with its soft fur edging was beginning to look very pretty.

"Any rubbish does for Christmas: look at the things they publish", he said suddenly, "I shan't worry my-self about it. Listen to this Jessy –

"The year has sped its circling way
    Through autumn rain and summer heat,
And safely brought us Christmas Day
    The usual revels to repeat:
I wonder if we find them sweet –
    Oh hold as weary work well done –

"That'll do if I finish it?"

"Yes, dear," said his wife.

But it was hard to finish, so hard indeed that he

4

Note: A reduced facsimile reproduction of Trix's original typescript, including her own handwritten alterations.

ran his pencil through it and vaguely scribbled such
strains as these -

"On Christmas Day you must be glad
It were a treason to be sad'.

"No, that's too ordinary. I believe they like
comic things, American jingles like the last page of
Harper's.

"I'm not amused on Xmas Day,
Plum pudding does not make me gay,
Nor turkey make me smile'-

"I never found it so difficultto write a string of
verses before,"

He lit another cheroot and returned to the little
brown book: his wife was sewing the fur round the little
white bonnet, and thinking how well it would suit the
baby's blue eyes and fair curls.

"I've got it at last", he said, "A Villanelle, a
thing with two refrains. Listen -

CHRISTMAS AGAIN.

Christmas comes to us again,
   Borne upon the circling year,
Ah, the mingled joy and pain!

5

Note: A reduced facsimile reproduction of Trix's original typescript, including her own handwritten alterations.

"We, who bound in exile's chain
  Spend a weary life-time here,
Christmas comes to us again.

Can we raise a merry strain
  Far from those we love most dear?
Ah, the mingled joy and pain.

True, some pleasures may remain,
  Children shout with hearty cheer,
Christmas comes to us again.

It is foolish to complain,
  Learn the laugh that hides the tear.
Ah, the mingled joy and pain!

There's no moral to explain,
  For the summing up is clear:
Christmas comes to us again, -
  Ah, the mingled joy and pain!

"There, won't that do?"

"Yes, dear", said his wife. It was growing late,

but she was so anxious to finish the bonnet that she did

not feel tired.

He copied his Villanelle in a fair, round hand and

tossed it over to her with a wearied air.

"Do it up for me there's a good girl", he said,

"and I'll send it off to-morrow."

The string and the stickphast were at his elbow,

while she had to rise and put down all her work to get

them, but she only said "Yes dear", as she fastened up

the verses.

He addressed them with a flourish, putting his name

Note: A reduced facsimile reproduction of Trix's original typescript, including her own handwritten alterations.

in the left hand corner outside, for he was sure that
the Editor would remember him and open the packet
quickly.

"Oh, I'm tired," he said yawning, "but I'm glad I've
done those verses. I should think they'd take them,
think they'd be glad to get 'em, eh?"

"Yes, dear", said his wife.

He stood near her watching her busy hands.

"What are you fussing over?" he said genially.

"I've just finished it," said his wife proudly,
"it's a new bonnet for Baby, won't she look sweet in
it? I made it every bit myself from a paper pattern,
and it would have cost ever so much to buy."

He looked at the pretty thing with indulgent scorn,
and stirred the fur border with a cautious finger.

"Who would believe the amount of time and trouble
you women spend over trifles!" he said laughing.

7

Note: A reduced facsimile reproduction of Trix's original typescript, including her own handwritten alterations.

A SYMPATHETIC. WOMAN.

------++++++++++-----

Scene: The deck of an outward bound steamer, one day past Suez. It is nine o'clock and a broad track of moonlight silvers the rippled sea. Mrs Seymour, thirty years old, with eyes that have learnt the trick of pathos, reclines in a deck chair. Major Strood-Mayhew, R.E., stand near. He is thirty-five, the proud owner of a profile, a tenor voice and several grievances.

Major S.M. : "1 suppose you are going to this so-called concert they mean to have at the other end of the ship this evening? I heard nothing about it till about five minutes ago, it's all been managed by the great Colville as usual. (Laughs bitterly.) 1 should like to buy the fellow at my valuation and sell him at his own!"

MRS. S. (acquiescingly): "1 know."

Major S. M. "He's the sort of man who constitutes himself head of everything at once, and its sheer push that does it, for he hasn't the least idea of singing. 1 suppose he'll figure about six times in the programme in his usual way!"

Mrs S. (Sympathetically) "1 know."

Major S. M. (earnestly): "1t isn't as though he took the least trouble to find out if anybody else on board is musical: he's so perfectly satisfied with his own performances."

Mrs S. (scornfully): "1 know!"

Major S. M.: "Personally, of course, 1 haven't the least wish to sing, its a great thing not to be bothered; but I must say 1 was never on a ship before where 1 was not asked to sing, asked repeatedly too."

Mrs S. (tenderly): "1 know."

(Enter briskly Mr Ledlie of the Ineligibles. He is

1.

Note: A reduced facsimile reproduction of Trix's original typescript, including her own handwritten alterations.

twenty-five and possess⸍es⸍ a cheerful disposition, a small
stud of polo ponies and a large crop of debts.)

Mr L.: "That you, Mayhew? Just the man 1 was looking
for; they're waiting for you in the smoke-room, fourth at
whist. . . . There, thank goodness, he's gone. 1 do think
he's the most awful specimen!"

Mrs S. (laughing): "1 know!"

Mr L.: "Well, 1'm afraid 1 don't make much secret
of it, but you are no end quick at finding out how 1
really feel about things. You don't want to go to this
concert, do you? 1t will be an awfully poor show."

Mrs S. (resignedly): "I know."

Mr L.: "Let's stay here then. Do. Its ever so
much nicer. Isn't the moon jolly on the water? A night
like this makes one sort o' sad and thoughtful, doesn't
it?"

Mrs S. (Gently): "1 know."

Mr L. (musingly): "I just hated coming back to India
this journey. You see 1'd been having an A-1 time at
home; lots of shooting and staying about, and 1 met some
jolly people and made heaps of friends. One does feel
saying good-bye sometimes."

Mrs S. (con molto expresione): "1 know."

Mr L.: "You see 1ndia is no end of a way from England, and one can't help feeling after one's gone that
its a case out⸍of⸍of sight out of mind."

Mrs S. (les larmes d ans la voix): "I know."

Mr L.(drawing his chair nearer): "1 don't know how
it is, Mrs Seymour, but 1 believe 1 generally talk to you
about myself. You're awfully nice to talk to; you always
seem to understand how one looks at things."

Mrs S. (with modest emphasis): "1 know."

Mr L.: "Yes, that's it; and it just makes all the

2.

Note: A reduced facsimile reproduction of Trix's original typescript, including her own handwritten alterations.

difference; most women yarn away about themselves and don't
don't care a bit what you say. Now l wanted to tell you,
there's a girl at home that — What on earth is that kid
doing, tearing about at this time of night?"

(Enter very hastily Daisy Penfield, aged five, wearing a little red dressing gown and hotly pursued by a
Madrassi ayah.)

Daisy (breathlessly, flinging herself into Mrs Seymour's arms): "I ran away from ayah 'cause l wanted to
say good-night to you, and oh, do you know l saw such a
funny thing to-day? lt was a flying fish what the Quar-
termaster caught, and it had such funny wings like a bird,
only no feathers, and it felt all cold and flabby!"

Mrs S. (laughing): "l know."

Ayah (querulously): "My Missis saying, 'burra nartee
baba."

Daisy: "Don't ayahs talk rubbish? But if l go to
bed now will you make me paper-boats to-morrow, Mrs Seymour? Yes, and boxes, and frogs, and you said you thought
you had some beads for my dollie's necklace?"

Mrs S. (nodding): "l know."

Daisy: "Then I'll give you a real hard kiss."

(Enter Mrs Penfield, thirty-four, pale, thin, sharp
featured and sharp voiced.)

Mrs P. (crossly); "Go to bed at once, Daisy. What a
naughty child you are! How often have l told you never
to come up on deck like this? You spoil her, Mrs Seymour.
(Takes Mr Ledlie's chair; he grimaces and slips away.)
You seem very fond of children, but then you have none of
your own and that makes such a difference. Daisy simply
wears me out!"

Mrs S. (sympathetically.): "l know."

Mrs P.: l wanted to leave her at home this time, but
but my husband insisted on her coming out for another
year. We go to Simla all the hot weather of course, but

2.

Note: A reduced facsimile reproduction of Trix's original typescript, including her own handwritten alterations.

f

still the child's a fearful responsibility for me."

Mrs S. (kindly): "1 know."

Mrs P. (peevishly): "1'll never travel alone with
her again; she keeps me in a perfect fever of nervousness.
1'm always expecting her to go up the rigging, or over
the side, or something dreadful. If my husband were here
he could take care of her. 1 haven't strength for it."

Mrs S. (soothingly) : "1 know."

Mrs P. : "He wanted me to bring out an English nurse
for her, and it certainly would have been convenient to
have a maid to wait on me when 1 knock up. I have wretched health, but then they are such worries. They always
die of typhoid or get married at once, or something tiresome of that sort."

Mrs S.: "1 know."

Mrs P.(wearily): "But 1 do wish 1 had one now, for
Daisy pays no attention to the ayah. 1 suppose I must go
down and see if she is in bed yet. Yesterday 1 found that
she had made a tent with two umbrellas and a blanket and
was sitting in it, throwing my silver-backed brushes at
the ayah! It's very hard to manage a child like that."

Mrs S. (laughingly): "1 know."

[Enter Mr Adrian Ellington, C. S. Thirty-one, tall
and clean shaven, with an expression of weary superiority]

Mr E. (drawling slightly): "I have escaped at last.
How wise you were to avoid that terrible entertainment!
I endured a song of sentiment by Milton Wellings, sharped
throughout, and a patriotic ballad by Pinsuti, consistent-
ly flatted but when the idol of the second saloon rose,
with his thumbs in his waistcoat pockets, to sing 'Up
comes Jones,' I felt 1 could bear no more. It was too
terrible!"

Mrs S. (smiling): "1 know!"

Mr E. (sententiously): The isolation of India, the
utter lack of congenial companionship begins as soon as

4.

Note: A reduced facsimile reproduction of Trix's original typescript, including her own handwritten alterations.

one sets foot on an outward-going steamer. After the three months of civilisation that I snatch every three years, I feel that I am being driven back into the wilderness."

<u>Mrs S. (pityingly)</u>: "I know."

<u>Mr E. (complacently)</u>: "I may expect one oasis in my desert, however, this cold weather. I forget if you ever met the Allanadales. Old Lord Allanadale died two years ago and his nephew came in for the title.

<u>Mrs S.</u>: "I know."

<u>Mr E.</u>: "He is the dearest good fellow, as stupid as it is possible to be, and immersed in the desire of killing things; but she is an exquisite woman with lips like a scarlet thread and long, slender feet exactly alike; she never wears rights and lefts in shoes. A scintillating intellect too, one of the unique creatures of the earth!"

<u>Mrs S. (with admiring intonation)</u>: "I know!"

<u>Mr E.</u>: they mean to come out this cold weather. Allanadale dreams of tigers, and she intends to rise above the level of the ordinary tourists by avoiding the sights they come so far to see. I can imagine the vast infinite commonplace of India making even Julia Allanadale ordinary!"

<u>Mrs S. (hiding a smile)</u>: "I know.

<u>Mr E. (thoughtfully)</u>: "Lucknow, Cawnpore, Benares and the Agra sights must of course be taboo; they are visited in herds and droves. I am not altogether certain about the Taj, though. In a dark night, during a thunderstorm, dimly guessed at through flashes of lightning, I have known it to be quite beautiful. I was even able to forget the photographs of it, and the polychromatic pictures and the dreadful little white models. Yes, perhaps Julia, such a deliciously incongruous name for such a woman, might wait for a thunderstorm; but lacking that, I think it would be best for her not to see it."

5.

Note: A reduced facsimile reproduction of Trix's original typescript, including her own handwritten alterations.

MRS S. (absent-mindedly)!'I know.'

Mr E. (rising languidly): "Alas, ill fortune pursues me to-night, that depressing old optimist is coming to speak to you, and I would rather not stay to face him. You will forgive me, he afflicts me so."

(Enter Mr Hadlane, fifty-four, red-faced and grey-haired with brisk twinkling eyes.)

Mr H.: "It's warming up pleasantly, Mrs Seymour. I'm beginning to feel myself again - beginning to thaw after an English summer. It's my firm belief that a year in England would kill me. I can't stand the place."

Mrs S. (from behind her fan): "I know."

Mr H.: "What, are you laughing at me? I know its the fashion to run down India, but my opinion is that people don't know when they're well off. Think of a splendid climate, the perpetual sunshine, eh?"

Mrs S. (pleasantly): "I know."

MR. H.: "And then the servants, of course they swindle you, but they make you comfortable, and that's the great thing."

Mrs S.: I know."

M r. H; "I've had the same bearer for three-and-twenty years. Now I know that man will be one of the first people to come on board when we get to Bombay, and I shall be glad to see his villainous face again, heartily glad! NI spent six months at home and never had anyone to lace my boots for me all that time I'm not used to stooping. I haven't the figure for it, but what was I to do? There were housemaids in pink gowns and flyaway caps. I couldn't ask them to fasten my boots."

Mrs S. (soothingly): "I know."

Mr H.: "And the food. I went to stay with one of my sisters; hadn't seen her for sixteen years; had to go down, and her cook (at least the woman who spoilt the food in her kitchen, you couldn't call her a cook) gave

6,

Note: A reduced facsimile reproduction of Trix's original typescript, including her own handwritten alterations.

me what she considered a curry. A yellow stew, with a
wall of rice round it. Rice on the dish! There's
English cooking!"

Mrs S. (in sympathetic horror): "1 know."

Mr H.: "Then the getting about. 1'm not a rich man.
1 can't afford endless hansoms, at a shilling every five
minutes. When 1 am in town 1 have to go in omnibuses,
and very uncomfortable things they are, though they are
so wonderfully popular. Give you my word the last omnibus
1 was in, one of the red ones going along Piccadilly, 1
trod on the toes of a Member of Council getting in, and
nearly sat down on a former Lieutenant-Governor! How had
the mighty fallen, eh?"

Mrs S. (laughing): "1 know."

Mr H. "Mustn't mention names of course, but 1 can
tell you a much funnier thing than that. Last -(Mrs S.
rises and holds out her hand.) "What, you surely are not
going so soon, its hardly ten yet? Well, 1'm sorry you
are tired. 1 always enjoy a talk with you. Its something nowadays to meet a lady who holds sensible views
and expresses them well. Good-night!"

[As Mrs Seymour goes through the companion her arm
is seized by Miss Cheston, a tall young woman of twenty-
eight, with not enough nose and too much mouth.)

Miss C.: "You are going down very early to-night,
but 1 saw 'India for ever' victimising you, so 1 don't
wonder you fled. Its been very full this evening; that
concert was over in about half-an-hour, and then all the
men went off to the smoking-room straight. Let me come
into your cabin and talk for a bit? 1 haven't seen you
all day. How neat you keep it. That horrible Mrs Nut-
talls strews clothes all over ours. 1 can't stand that
woman!"

Mrs S. (soothingly):"1 know."

Miss C. (vehemently):Well, 1 can't help it; she's a
perfect cat! She makes me get up at seven every morning
and scolds if 1'm more than half-an-hour. Of course,
her dressing is a fearful and wonderful business, and she

7.

Note: A reduced facsimile reproduction of Trix's original typescript, including her own handwritten alterations.

wants time and solitude for it!"

Mrs S. (laughing): "I know."

Miss C. : "Did I tell you that she still sleeps
with a shawl over her head, even in this hot weather?
She says she feels the draughts? I only wish there ever
was a draught in our cabin. I'm perfectly certain her
fringe goes into a little box under her pillow every night
and I have my suspicions about her teeth!"

Mrs S. (still laughing): "I know."

Miss C. "But I wouldn't mind how artificial she was,
if she wasn't so spiteful. Yesterday she turned to me
before a whole lot of people, and asked in her soft cooing
voice if I was going out to be married. I said, Oh no!
I was going to keep house for my brother, and she laughed
and said: The one is always supposed to lead to the
other, but I'm afraid you may find that it no longer does!
It was horrid of her, wasn't it?"

Mrs S. (kindly): "I know."

Miss C.: "And if she sees anyone nice talking to me,
she makes a point of interrupting. But it was really
rather fun this afternoon, Mr Mansfield was so cross."

Mrs S. (archly): "I know."

Miss C. (giggling): "Then you saw it? I was afraid
everybody would, but what was I to do? I can't spend all
my time with one man - people talk so."

Mrs S. (pensively): "I know."

Miss C. (complacently): "He's quite furious! He
never came near me all this evening, but he's sure to make
it up to-morrow, and then Mrs Nuttall will begin gossip-
ing again. But I suppose one really need not mind: after
all it's only the penalty one pays for not being bad looking!"

Mrs S. (enthusiastically): "I know."

8.

Note: A reduced facsimile reproduction of Trix's original typescript, including her own handwritten alterations.

Miss C. (rising and glancing at the mirror): "Well, I really must go to bed. Good-night, you dear thing. I do like a talk with you. You've given me lots of good advice to-night, but then you do it so nicely and gently, that one doesn't seem to mind it somehow - Good-night!"

(Mrs Seymour alone claps her hands and laughs): "There, I've done it! I knew I could! I haven't said a word all the evening, except'I know,' and yet not one of the people who talked to me noticed it. In fact, I believe they thought I was nicer than usual, more sympathetic! I suppose if I cared to keep it up I should become rather a popular woman. And yet there are people who say that conversation is a lost art!"

F.

Note: A reduced facsimile reproduction of Trix's original typescript, including her own handwritten alterations.

The Little Pink House

[This story was published originally in The Pall Mall Magazine *circa 1894.]*

JOHN Port held a subordinate post on the Eastern Bengal State Railway; and the post carried with it, besides a certain number of rupees per month, a little pink house, that sat very flat upon the ground near the railway line. It was also near a tank, and had, in consequence, a green dank garden, where marigolds and poppies sprawled together, and big bushes, starred with the scarlet shoe-flower, grew in inharmonious fellowship with the magenta masses of the bougainvillea. A decaying tree trunk was glorified by the tangled wreaths and orange trumpets of the *Bignonia vernesta;* and there were many foliage plants, clumps of brightly coloured leaves, boasting long Latin names; but John Port called them, one and all, "burning bushes."

" 'Tisn't what you'd call 'omelike," said John Port to his pipe, as he paced among these flowering splendours; "but Ellen 'll make a difference, trust 'er."

And Ellen was on her way out, and every throb of the steamer's screw brought her nearer to the pink house, and the green garden, and the expectant man, to whom her coming was to make such a difference. It was four years since Ellen Gee had promised to marry John Port, four years since he had gone to seek his fortune in India. He was a steady hard-working man, and the fortune had not been long coming: the monthly salary, with good prospects, and the pink house and the green garden. In the pride of his heart, John Port sent home money, a cruel sacrifice at a time when sixteen rupees barely equalled twenty shillings, for Ellen's passage out.

"The idea!" said Ellen, when she received the money, and she promptly put it into the savings bank against a rainy day. Ellen had made her arrangements for the voyage; she came out in attendance on a delicate lady and two small children, and a second-class fare was gladly paid in exchange for her services.

"I only wish you could stay with me," said the lady; and she gave her five pounds at parting.

The marriage took place in Calcutta. John Port was nervous and excited, and the best coat of four years ago was already a little tight for him. Ellen was very quiet and composed, and wore a grey woollen gown.

They went straight from the church to the train, and as Ellen travelled without a ticket, she felt that she was indeed entering into her kingdom. Six hours of slow progress brought them to the little pink house, which Port had furnished as a man in his ignorance furnishes. Ellen was impressed by the four rooms and the verandah, but her quick eyes took instant note of the scaliness of the colour-washed walls, the inferior woodwork, and the clumsy doors that would not shut. But the servants astonished her beyond all things.

"Whatever 'ave you got all these people for?" she asked, as a row of four stood salaaming to her.

"Most men's wives 'as more," said Port.

"The more shame to them; if I couldn't manage to do the work of my own 'ouse, after all the time I've been a 'general,' it would be a pity."

"Some of 'em you must 'ave, and you won't feel much like working when the 'ot weather comes, you'll see," said Port, secretly filled with tender admiration.

"We 'ad it 'ot enough in the Red Sea, I'm sure," said Ellen; "and as long as I was looking after Mrs. Nugent, or doing anything for the children, I didn't mind it; but when I sat down with my 'ands in front of me it was awful. Keep busy and you'll be all right; that's what I say."

She had already changed her wedding-dress for a serviceable blue cotton gown, and she was on her knees as she spoke, dusting the long-neglected legs of the big square table; her sleeves were turned up, and she wore a large apron. John watched her in approving silence; she was certainly making a difference already. She went into the verandah to shake her duster, and Mrs. Gasparez, the wife of a ticket-collector, watched her from the house across the road.

"Ooh, thee bride is veree grand," she said to her husband that evening; "she has brought out an English maid with her; onlee fancy, and makes her work so hard alreadee!"

It never entered into the mind of Mrs. Gasparez that any woman could possibly use a duster on her wedding-day.

John and Ellen walked in their garden when the sun was low, and Ellen spied its flowery tangles with a practical eye. "It's a waste of land," she said; "couldn't we manage some greens instead of all that 'ighbiscus?" And John marvelled at her erudition. She had once attended a series of botanical lectures at Kew, organised by her Sunday-school teacher.

"Things will look more 'omelike presently," said Ellen, as she fastened strings outside the verandah for scarlet-runners to be trained upon.

She was bending over the strings as she spoke, and John stooped and kissed her smooth hair a little awkwardly. "I knew you'd make it seem different when you came, old girl," he said huskily.

"Oh, it *is* nice to be 'ere," said Ellen.

Three days later Mrs. Gasparez came to call, picking her way through the red dust of the road with little mincing steps. She was quite young and very stout, and her fat, brown face was naively and thickly coated with white powder; she had abundant shiny black hair and small goodnatured eyes. She wore a bright blue merino dress, trimmed with thin satin that crackled like paper, a cape on her shoulders jangled with beads, and there were red and yellow flowers in her bonnet. A little observation had corrected her mistake as to "thee bride's English maid"; and though she considered Ellen a person of low ideas, there was no one else to talk to, and she was prepared to be kind to her. There was no servant to be seen in the verandah, and Mrs. Gasparez raised her shrill voice in vain.

"Ooh, I hope this is not a veree great libertee," said Mrs, Gasparez, as, tired of waiting, she stepped into the little sitting-room; but the room was empty. She examined it critically. "Veree neat," she said, "but not at all smart; my, onlee two antimacassars!"

She sat down, very genteely, on the edge of a chair; her flounces crackled stiffly. Five minutes later the bride appeared; she wore a big apron, and she was turning down her sleeves.

"Ooh, I am sorree to have disturbed you; I see you have been unpacking," said Mrs. Gasparez, politely.

"I'm very glad to see you, and I 'ope I 'aven't kept you waiting long," said Ellen; "but I didn't see you come, and I couldn't make out what that boy Abdool was trying to tell me at first. I was out in the kitchen. Don't you find it very tiresome 'aving your kitchen so far from the 'ouse?"

"Ooh yess, but you will grow used to it presentlee. I am veree particular; I go into thee *bawachi khana* everee morning to see what my *bawachi*, thee cook you know, is doing, and sometimes in the afternoon also."

Mrs. Gasparez's voice shrilled into unexpected cadences, and she emphasised small words, and laid great stress on terminations, with that Eurasian accent which is as indescribable as it is unmistakable. Ellen's voice seemed very full and deep as she replied.

"I 'aven't got a cook; I don't mean to have one."

"My, how will you eat?" screamed Mrs Gasparez.

"Can't *you* cook?"

"My, no. I can make lovelee *metai*, sweets you know; but to cook thee meats, and thee soups, and thee curries, Ooh, no!"

"I don't like curries," said Ellen; "they're too spicy, and all odds and ends; you never know what you may be eating. John says he likes my cooking the best of any 'e ever ate."

"Ooh, but your hands!"

Ellen glanced from her own capable fingers to the tightly stuffed yellow gloves that lay on Mrs. Gasparez's blue lap: one of the seams had burst, and a ring with a vast red stone gleamed through.

"Use comes before looks," said Ellen.

"Ooh yess," said Mrs Gasparez, doubtfully.

" 'Ave you been 'ere long; do you like it?" asked Ellen.

"Onlee six months; it is veree dull, there is no societee. I often say to my husband, 'I think I shall run away.' You see we came from up countree, and there it was veree jollee, so manee people; here there are onlee four houses. I do not know what to do with myself ahl day long."

"I should think your children would keep you pretty busy," said Ellen.

"Ooh yess, there are four, but they are veree small; the babee is onlee three months old, and they have their *ayah*. You see they are so noisee, and I am *not* strong."

"I don't fancy these natives," said Ellen. "I shouldn't like to see their black 'ands touching any child I was fond of." And then she remembered the dark skin, which so clearly proclaimed Mrs Gasparez's connection with the country, and felt very uncomfortable; but fortunately, Mrs Gasparez considered herself purely European, and always spoke of the England that she had never seen as "home."

"My yess, they are fearful, you will see; your servants will always *dikh* you, worree you, you know."

"I shall 'ave just as few as ever I can do with. Wouldn't you like to see my kitchen? You see," she continued, leading the way into the next room, "I keep all the plates in 'ere, and shall do the pastry-making and so on 'ere; and I wanted John to let me 'ave a stove, but 'e says it won't do for the 'ot weather."

They went out to the mud hut in the garden, which served as a kitchen. It had been newly whitewashed within and without: and at the freshly planed table stood a depressed-looking scullion peeling potatoes; he had scrambled up from his seat on the floor at the sound of his mistress's voice.

"That's the only servant I've got in the 'ouse," said Ellen proudly.

"Ooh, thee hot weather will soon make you lazee," laughed Mrs Gasparez.

"Well, I made bread enough for three days yesterday, and baked it in that queer iron drum thing. John doesn't like the baker's bread 'ere; there was a beetle in the last we 'ad."

"Ooh, you will soon grow lazee, we shall see."

In the course of the next few months, something very like a friendship grew up between these two dissimilar women. John Port was often away, up and down the line, and Ellen became a frequent visitor at the house opposite. It was a larger house than her own, but it always appeared hopelessly crowded. The smell of savoury meats lingered in that house, and odours of garlic, kerosene oil, and bad tobacco strangely blended, never left it. The dogs and the children left bones about, to be tumbled over and kicked into corners; the clothes of the household seemed to have a habit of straying, and were to be met in unexpected places; the boots and shirts of Mr. Gasparez, the brilliant raiment of his wife, and the tattered little garments of the children had alike no abiding city. Nothing indeed was in its right place; the baby was lulled to fitful slumber in an arm-chair, while a tailor, hired for the day, squatted sewing on a child's cot. Mrs. Gasparez's abundant hair was generally brushed and oiled in the front verandah; and the three elder children ate strange meals, at odd hours, sitting on the floor of any room they happened to be in, surrounded by servants, puppies, and tame birds. Presently Ellen tried, both by precept and practice, to instil a little order into the chaos; but Mrs. Gasparez, stout in a white dressing-gown, only laughed at her efforts.

"Ooh, you are veree sillee! What does it matter? Wait till thee babies come to your house, and then you will not be so particularlee neat."

Although Ellen was too courageous to make any confessions, the cruel heat of a Bengal summer was a revelation of terror to her. She fought the heat with her favourite prescription of hard work; indeed, her husband, who was a great deal away, hardly realised how much she did. She cooked and cleaned, she mended and made clothes, she even washed clothes sometimes, earning thereby bitter headaches and the scorn of her neighbour; but a firm sense of right sustained her.

"Just think of what I'd be doing at 'ome, John," she pleaded, when her husband noticed that her fresh face had grown white, and her light step heavy. "I didn't come out 'ere to spend all your money on living like a fine lady; and yet 'ere I don't need to wash my own dishes, and that Abdool is learning to cook quite nice; 'e can do lots of things already. And as for the washing, wouldn't your sister think 'erself in clover at 'ome, with a sun like this to dry and bleach the clothes. You let me 'ave my own way, John; I can't sit idle, and I shall 'ave to be a do-nothing for a bit when the New Year comes"; and at the thought her needle sped more swiftly through the little white garment she was making.

John thought her looking ill, but he supposed it was natural and inevitable, and she never complained.

Then the rains came; at first a respite from torment, presently torment in themselves. A clinging penetrating damp infected everything. The tank overflowed, and the green garden became a dismal swamp, tenanted by many frogs, whose barkings kept Ellen from sleeping. A broad dado of damp showed itself on the walls of the little pink house, and a thin film of blue mould spread over their most cherished treasures. Ellen tried stoves in vain, nothing could get rid of what she called the "mushroom smell". John Port had several attacks of fever; sharp, short attacks such as he had grown accustomed to, and thought very little of, but it was terrible to Ellen to hear him raving in delirium. She attached no importance to her own sufferings from neuralgia, though a spike of pain seemed to be piercing through her left temple and was her constant attendant all the day long.

"I don't believe in giving in," said Ellen, when the autumn fever smote her in turn, and the ground seemed to glide from her tired feet, and objects were three times their right size to weary eyes, whose very lids felt hot. "Just think of the colds I should 'ave been getting at 'ome," she repeated, with persistent cheerfulness; "the influenza again most likely; and don't you talk nonsense about this climate being so bad for me," said Ellen to her husband.

After the first few months, after health and high spirits had flagged, came a terrible nostalgia, and that too was hidden from John Port. He never guessed the passion of longing for her own people that filled his wife's heart, and it was very rarely expressed in her letters home; but none the less it was an ever present pain.

"My, you are looking seedee!" said Mrs. Gasparez.

"I 'ave a little fever at night sometimes," said Ellen, "but it's nothing; and I suppose it will get cooler every day now."

"Ooh yess, it will soon be ahlright. And I have some news to tell you; my sister is coming to stay with me - my youngest sister, Miss de Cruz."

"That will be pleasant for you," said Ellen, heartily; "is she a nice girl?"

My yess! she is a beautee! eyes that big, hair so long, and her figure, Ooh, lovelee! She will have some monee too some day, for my old grandmother is very fond of her, and says she will leave her ahl she has, ever so manee rupees!"

Miss de Cruz was brought to call a few days later; a big girl, plump and shapely, with magnificent eyes. She yawned openly through Ellen's attempts at talk, and brightened to coquettish liveliness when John Port came into the room.

"That's a fine handsome girl, a fine strapping girl," said John Port later; then, with a clumsy laugh, "*you* aren't much to look at now, old woman."

"True enough," said Ellen, laughing back; and then she went away and looked at herself in the glass with new eyes.

"I do wish it didn't make one so plain for so long," she said to the worn face and ungainly figure she saw reflected there.

And all this while Ellen took no heed of the new world round her. She heard the wedding music from the surging ways of the native town, and she said, "Well, they *are* making a noise." She saw the dead, slowly borne past the little pink house to the funeral pyre, and she said, " They're going to burn 'im; isn't it 'orrid?" She lived in India, save for the wide difference of heat, discomfort, and loneliness, exactly as she would have lived in England. The only native with whom she held anything approaching to speech was Abdool, a craven representative indeed, and the conclusion she drew from her study of his character was that they were "a dirty lot", She took no interest in her surroundings; the little pink house in its wealth of strange flowers was only pleasing to her because it had been allotted to her husband, and she trusted the garden would look more homelike when a child played there. She watched the long line of rails down which John's train would come, without a thought of what the land had been before the wonderful iron road had traversed it. There was no romance for her in the widely varying tracts the train came through, and she had no desire to see more of the country in which her lot was cast. "The gorgeous East" held for her neither glamour nor glory. Her days were passed in an endless succession of small duties, and in secretly hoping that she should feel better to-morrow.

Towards the end of November, Abdool ran over to Mrs. Gasparez's house one morning with an urgent message.

"My," said Mrs. Gasparez, as she caught up a solah topee, " onlee seven months."

That was at breakfast time, and John Port was away up the line, and would not return till the morning of the next day.

"I *am* sorry to bother you," said Ellen, through her agony; "but I was that bad all night, and I did want some one to speak to."

"Ooh, I will stay gladlee," said Mrs. Gasparez, "and I will send for thee doctor, and you will soon be ahlright."

The doctor came presently, and went and came again; Mrs. Gasparez wept fluent tears over the sufferings that could not be allayed, even as she said, "Oo, you will be ahlright veree soon." Ellen lay with clenched teeth, trying not to writhe or cry out. "I do 'ate to give you all this trouble," she said often.

"But she was so strong," said Mrs. Gasparez to the doctor in the next room; "she worked so hard, she did Ooh, everything! I am not so strong, but I was never like this, never."

"She has worn herself out," said the doctor; "the climate counts for something, and she has never considered it."

Some time after midnight the child was born - a dead child; and the doctor went to Mrs. Gasparez's house for a little rest. Mrs. Gasparez sat nodding and blinking, and drinking strong tea, and Ellen seemed to be sleeping.

Just before dawn Ellen roused herself and talked for a few minutes to Mrs. Gasparez; she had a message to leave with her.

"Ooh no, you are not going to die," sobbed Mrs. Gasparez; "go to sleep again, and do not be so sillee; the next babee will live, and it will ahl be jollee."

Ellen smiled faintly. "Don't you forget," she whispered, and turned her head on the pillow; but instead of going to sleep her face changed and worked strangely, and Mrs. Gasparez ran out calling wildly for the doctor. Ellen's last doleful scene was acted alone, but it must have been a short one, for when Mrs. Gasparez and the doctor came back they found her dead.

John Port's train came in at seven o'clock. The doctor met him, and told him of his wife's death, but he did not realise or understand what had happened till he came to the little pink house. Abdool was in the verandah lamenting ostentatiously, but Port put him aside and went into the bedroom. It smelt stuffy and sickly after the fresh morning air, and it was exceedingly untidy; a white sheet was thrown over the bed, and Mrs.

Gasparez, her eyelids puffy with crying and want of sleep, came to meet him.

"I have a message for you," she said; "I was to give you her love, and she was veree sorree not to see you again, and she hoped you would not mind that the babee was dead, for it was reallee much better, and would leave you free to marree again. Ooh! she did love you."

John stood by the bed, and laid his hand on the brown hair, pushing aside the scarlet flowers, with which Mrs. Gasparez had surrounded the still face. "Never another wife for me," he said; "never another woman in your place, old girl, all my life long."

And through the window came the sound of the high-pitched voice of Miss de Cruz; she was taking a morning stroll with a devoted admirer.

"Ooh yess, Mr. Woods, that is ahl veree fine, veree pretty, I daresay, onlee you do not mean it."

*   *   *   *   *

It was in the spring, five months later, that John Port married Miss de Cruz; and Mrs. Gasparez explained to her friends, that "it was not such a veree bad match for Eulalee, for that nice wife of Mr. Port's who died, poor thing, was very thriftee, and she had saved, Ooh, quite a great manee rupees."

Beatrice Kipling.

ROMANCE OF A DOLI

[Is Trix making amends in this story to the Irishmen she turned down four times? The central situation of a hostile brother and an easily swayed father parallel Trix's own experience during her engagement to Fleming. It is interesting that there is no mother figure in the story. Although Trix's typescript is held together with a brass clip through all the pages, page 17 is missing. The poor quality of the carbon copies meant it was unsuitable for facsimile reproduction, but we have laid out the pages roughly as the document, together with the punctuation, underlining, and spelling etc. of her original typescript.]

Dullhouses, as its very name implies, is not a lively hill station. Its position, some hundred miles or more distant from the nearest line of railway, makes the journey from the plains so tedious, that the society gathered together on its heights is invariably small, if not always select; and time passes there with a decorous dullness, which though considered excellent for the bodily health, is undoubtedly trying to the mind and spirits of most of its visitors. It has been said, with some show of truth, that nothing ever happens at Dullhouses, and it has the enviable reputation of being the one hill station in Upper India which is absolutely free from scandal. Colonel Fogey can send his third wife, a girl some years younger than any of his daughters, to Dullhouses, at the beginning of the hot weather, in perfect security that when he comes up to join her a month or six weeks later, his arrival will cause no confusion of any kind in her arrangements, and that she will have been so lonely and bored by her existence there that he will actually be made welcome. The station, however, is not without its admirers who are never weary of praising its salubrious qualities - just as a woman is described - as being amiable, when it is impossible for even her best friends to say that she is either handsome or graceful.

In the days before lawn-tennis had broken out in Anglo-Indian society with the severity of a plague, which spares neither age, sex, nor condition, this charming place was even duller than it is now: and one morning, early in May, 1874, Dullhouses was surprised to find that something had actually happened in its very midst. The arrival of an empty doolie is not itself a startling or exciting event, but when, up to the moment of its emptiness being discovered, it was supposed to contain a lady, and when the *kahars* who had brought it in from Babool, a march of a dozen miles, swore by their gods in answer to the furious questioning of the gentleman who had ridden up at the same time, that the lady - and a very heavy lady too - had been in the doolie when they took up their burden; the affair became a mystery. There were pillows, rugs, an umbrella, a fan, and a lady's hat and cloak - but the lady herself was gone. If ever a man was in a foaming rage it was the brother of this missing lady as he realised what had happened. His knowledge of past events gave him a clue to his sister's disappearance; which however unwilling he might be to accept it, gave none the less a purpose and meaning to his fury. "D him" he said again and again through his set teeth, as he lashed the air with his riding whip. The doolie bearers, who had been at first so positive in their assertions, began to waver in their testimony under the influence of the Sahib's anger, till at last one more timid than the rest, had the truth shaken out of him; and with clasped hands, raised deprecatingly, confessed that the doolie was so light a weight when he and his fellows took it up, that they had thought they were carrying a little child. The ayah, fiercely interrogated, replied only by a whimper, and pitifully begged some one to fetch a doctor. She was, like most of her kind, helpless in an emergency.

Suddenly the Englishman turned and, without a word of explanation, mounted his horse, and spurred the tired beast down the road which he had just left; and on the silent morning air the sound of its feet were for some time audible above the hush which had fallen upon the chattering groups of natives. This scene, which took place at the entrance of the hotel, was not without more or less intelligent witnesses, and before the retreating horseman was five miles upon his way, a rumour of the occurrence had run over the greater part of the station. By sunset every one who cared to listen had heard the story with all the details of a good deal that had not taken place, in connection with it; but it was not for some time that the actual facts of this mysterious affair came to be really known.

Colonel Thornton, stationed at Ghurmabad had been a good deal startled, some little time before our story begins by receiving a photograph of his only daughter, Sybil, who had been sent home on the death of her mother, which had taken place some fifteen years before. Not having been compelled to take furlough by ill-health, he had from year to year postponed his intended visit to England, and had never realised the lapse of time, until this portrait obliged him to recognise the fact that the pretty child he remembered had developed into a charming girl, whom it would be

ridiculous to call a school-girl any longer. The
photograph was accompanied by a letter from his son, a man
of some twelve years' standing in the Civil Service, who
had gone home on six months' leave - who wrote that he
thought it time Sybil should come out to her father, and
that he intended to bring her with him on his return. This
barely left the poor Colonel time to turn round before she
would be upon his hands, and the prospect of a grown-up
daughter to look after appalled him; not that he was a bad
father: on the contrary, he was as good a one as a man well
could be to a child whom he had not seen for fifteen years,
and of whom he knew nothing. He had sent her what he
called birthday presents at least twice every year, and
whatever a man could do, in the way of indulgence by
written permission, he had never failed in; but none the
less he looked forward to the child's arrival in India with
more misgiving than satisfaction. Sybil and her brother
were on the best possible terms when they left England for
India; but long before they reached Bombay, the girl was in
the deepest disgrace. Robert Thornton had the misfortune
to be a bad sailor, and for three days he was absolutely
obliged to "seek the seclusion which a cabin grants." So
tottering on deck at the end of that ghastly time, he found
that his sister had not been ill for a moment, and had in
fact been getting on remarkably well without him. He was
not quite unprepared for this state of things, as a steward
whom he had questioned during his retirement had told him
that "the young lady was quite well and seemed enjoying of
herself uncommon;" but he had not expected to find her so
completely out of hand. She had run up an intimacy with a
lady from whom she seemed inseparable, and had even changed
her seat at table that she might have her companionship

there. There was no actual fault to be found with this.
The lady who shared Sybil's cabin was no longer young
though still charming, and was the wife of an officer whom
she was on the way to rejoin, rather it is true because he
had made a point of it that from any inclination on her own
part; a light-hearted, bright-tempered woman about whom
there was absolutely nothing to dislike. She was the
centre round which all the young people gathered, and made
of Sybil an especial pet and favourite; while the girl, who
was attractive enough on her own account, seemed to gain
additional fascination by this companionship. To her
brother's reproofs or reproaches she paid no attention,
making fun of what she pertly called, his "Deputy
Commissioner manner"; and his annoyance soon grew to actual
displeasure under the irritation of her gay indifference.

Among the passengers was an Irishman, a lively, good-
looking young fellow, of about twenty five, travelling for
amusement; as he said himself "going nowhere for nothing at
all;" and whose luggage was certainly of the slightest - a
gun-case, a billiard cue, and a portmanteau, being all that
he brought on board. He was a general favourite before
twenty four hours were over, and his very name, Blade Bone,
had an attraction for his young fellow-travellers, one of
whom gave him the nick-name of "Knuckle" on the spot. He
was as ready as anyone to join in the laugh at his own
expense. "Had a fool for my god-father," he said in
explanation of his absurd name, "just such another as
yerself, my dear fellow," he added with a wink at the wag
who had re-named him.

To his astonishment and indignation of Robert Thornton,
it was not long before he was obliged to recognise the fact
that between Sybil and Mr Blade Bone there seemed to be a

particularly good understanding. Wherever she might be he
was never far off; and they sang together, danced together
walked, and talked, and above all, laughed together in a
manner that Thornton decided was absolutely unpardonable.
He had never felt less like laughing in his life than the
day he made up his mind that he must speak seriously to his
sister upon the subject. But neither on that day nor on
the next was he able to carry out his intention. Much has
been said of the opportunities afforded by the intimacy and
life on ship-board, but no one who has not tried it can
realise the difficulty of finding a suitable time and place
for such an interview as Robert Thornton sought. He could
not invite his sister to his cabin, of which he had only
the privilege of a third share; nor could he offer to visit
her in her own. The ladies' saloon was closed to him by
reason of his sex, the dining saloon was never empty, and
he dared not risk speaking to her on deck, as he had some
misgiving as to the spirit in which she would receive what
he had to say. Towards the close of the second day, in
sheer desperation, he asked the Captain to allow him for
ten minutes, the use of his cabin; explaining in a few
words the circumstances which alone could excuse such a
request. The Captain - who had daughters of his own, and
whose experiences as a marine chaperon had considerably
developed his natural intelligence - at once consented, and
Sybil running lightly up the companion stairs heard her
name called. To her amazement she saw her brother standing
in the door of the Captain's cabin, and holding out his
hand he drew her within the curtain, that did duty as a
door. The place was retired enough, but not quiet.
Through the venetians came the sound of laughter and of
voices; for a group of young men had gathered just outside

the bulkhead to jest away the tedious half-hour before the
first dinner bell should warn them of the chief event of
the day: and to his annoyance Thornton could distinguish
among them the gay voice of Blade Bone. His face grew
sterner at the unwelcome sound, and he was about to utter
the words which he had, after much consideration, chosen as
a suitable beginning for his serious speech, when there was
a moment's hush, and a tuneful tenor, with an unmistakable
brogue, struck up a song, the words of which were
distinctly audible.

"On Agypt's banks, contagious to the Noile,
Great Pharoh's daughter wint to bathe in sthoile,
And runnin' on the banks to dhry her skin,
She hot her toe again' the basket that the babe lay in."

Sybil's face grew radiant as she heard the first words;
she laughed aloud and clapped her hands in approval of the
singer and his song. "Bob!" she cried "do listen to that
lovely song! The second verse is even better; he sang it
to me the other night."

Thornton was thunderstruck. All his carefully arranged
speech vanished from his mind; nothing remained but blind,
senseless rage. "Sybil!" he burst out - "do you mean to
tell me that this indecent Irish mountebank" - Mr Thornton
did not stop to choose his words; but he was interrupted by
his sister, more angry than she had ever been in her life.

"Yes," she answered a little incoherently. "I do mean
to tell you, and a good deal more; and he has something to
tell you too. We are only waiting till we get to Bombay."

The fatal pronoun had however told him more than enough
and as Sybil ran downstairs to hide her flaming cheeks in

her cabin, he took his way to his, cursing the ill-luck
that had induced him to undertake the charge of this
intolerably troublesome girl. He could hear the thunder of
applause that greeted the conclusion of the Irishman's
song, as he went forward on the main deck, and his
irritation was not soothed by the sound. The interview
which Thornton felt it necessary to have with Mr Bone was
eminently unsatisfactory. The latter frankly acknowledged
that he had asked Sybil to be his wife, but absolutely
declined to take an answer to this question from her
brother. He was offensively flippant in his manner.

"You've got a father haven't you?" he asked. "Well I'm
coming up your way, and I'll settle the thing with the old
gentleman himself, if that's all the same to you."

Sybil's friend, Mrs Masterman would give him no help when
he appealed to her to use her influence with that young
lady. "I never interfere with the course of true love"
she said assuming her most sentimental air.

"True fiddlesticks" muttered the unhappy brother.

Even the Captain had his little jest on the subject.
"I'll put the Irishman in irons with the greatest pleasure
Mr Thornton," he said, "if I can find any excuse."

By the time the steamer reached Bombay, Robert and
Sybil were scarcely on speaking terms, and nothing could
have proved the strength and sincerity of the lover's
feeling more than the patience and good temper with which
he put up with Thornton's treatment of him, which was
exceedingly contemptuous and irritating.

Thornton on his part, was nearly maddened by the way in
which Sybil declined to acknowledge his authority and Blade
Bone refused to recognise it.

When the brother and sister left Bombay for their long

journey up country, the lover was in the next carriage, with his gun case and billiard cue, the sight of which articles seemed to have a particularly exasperating effect upon the wretched Thornton. "You may depend upon it," he said gloomily "the man's a black-leg; that he gambles and races." - "I know he does," Sybil interrupted cheerfully; "he won a cup at Punchtown, and he's going to give it to me." She would have liked nothing so well as to tell her brother all that Blade Bone had told her about himself, it was the subject uppermost in her mind; but he gave her no encouragement. At each station, as soon as the train stopped, the Irishman's cheerful face appeared at the window of the carriage that contained his sweetheart; his hand brought her the early cup of tea, and he took his place by her side at every meal in the dreary refreshment rooms, making fun of the goat chops and vegetable curries which were the invariable dishes at breakfast or dinner.

Thornton was powerless to prevent all this.

"Confound the fellow!" he broke out on the second morning; "he behaves like an accepted lover." "And so he is," retorted Sybil; "I have accepted him."

The fourth day saw them at the end of their journey, and the same evening, when Sybil fatigued and excited by the meeting with her father whom she could not remember to have seen before, had retired at an early hour, Colonel Thornton and his son had an important conversation. The younger man told the story of what he considered his sister's misconduct, with some bitterness, and certainly did not spare the Irishman who was the cause of all his annoyance.

"Is he a gentleman?" asked the Colonel.

"Well," answered Robert grudgingly "he isn't a butcher, which with that name he ought to have been."

First thing next morning, before Colonel Thornton had had any opportunity of speaking to Sybil on the subject Mr Blade Bone's card was brought to him. The old gentleman was alone in the verandah in dressing gown and slippers, enjoying his early cheroot; and scarcely was the card in his hand when its owner stood before him. In spite of all that Robert had said to his disadvantage, and the conviction that he had forced upon his father that the Irishman's acquaintance was in every way undesirable, the impression made by the young man's appearance was distinctly favourable. For a moment the men stood opposite to each other in silence, and the elder could not but see that Sybil's lover had everything externally to recommend him. His figure was of middle height and muscular though slight of build, and his features though not handsome were of the best Irish type; the face fairly illuminated by the look of humour and good nature that shone in his blue eyes. But Colonel Thornton remembered all that his son had said the night before, and his eye falling upon the objectionable name so plainly printed on the card in his hand, he hardened his heart, and assumed as much dignity of manner as was compatible with his extreme undress. It was however wasted upon Mr Blade Bone who held out his hand with a winning air of friendliness.

"You have heard all about me I am sure," he began; "I can tell by the very look of you that your son has given you the worst possible opinion of me. Don't believe him now" he went on as he saw signs of relenting in the Colonel's manner; "ask your daughter - ask Sybil, the darling, what she thinks, and be guided by her entirely."

The fascinating impudence of this address was too much for Colonel Thornton, who, unable to resist the hand still held out to him, gave his own in a friendly clasp, and taking a seat pointed out a chair to his visitor.

When Sybil and Robert came to breakfast a couple of hours later, to the delight of one and the indignation of the other, they found that Mr Blade Bone filled the fourth place at table.

If Robert Thornton had not endeavoured so persistently to influence his father, he and Sybil would soon have settled the matter satisfactorily; but nothing would induce the younger man to look favourably upon the Irishman's suit. Though he had references which were perfectly sound, and which guaranteed the truth of all he stated of his income and position - one of which was excellent and the other undeniable - nothing in any way weakened the prejudice which Robert had conceived against him from the first. When he left Ghurmabad, at the end of a few days, though he had extorted from his father something like a promise that he would not sanction the engagement, and though the lover himself had gone gaily upon the shooting tour which he had come to India expressly to make, he had uneasy misgivings, which subsequent events fully justified, that this troublesome business was by no means at an end.

Colonel Thornton possessed one of those kindly impressionable natures, that shrink from giving pain as others from receiving it, and whose opinions are always influenced by the latest argument. No sooner had his son left him than his daughter's view of the situation commended itself to him; and in a fortnight's time it was with difficulty that he could recall the reasons against the marriage, which, when Robert had uttered them, had seemed so convincing. Two or three letters passed between them in as many months, but no reference was made by either to the obnoxious subject; the son trying to persuade himself that the affair was at an end, and the father too well satisfied with things as they were to run any risk of disturbing them. But the mail bag which carried this superficial correspondence contained also letters from Sybil and from Blade Bone, the perusal of which would have considerably disturbed the peace of the fool's paradise in which Robert Thornton lived.

If the ostrich be really stupid enough to hide his head in the sand to escape his pursuer, it is imaginable that he may be foolish enough to draw it out again to discover the exact position of his enemy; and this in effect was what Mr Thornton did.

Having curtly replied to an affectionate little note from his sister asking him to spend Christmas at Ghurmabad, that he was too busy for holiday-making, it occurred to him that he had thus thrown away a good opportunity of finding out if matters were actually as he hoped they might be; and at the last moment decided to take his father and sister by surprise and join them on the morning of Christmas day. Had

[Page 17 of Trix's typescript is missing]

Irish brogue, the second verse of the song, which she had called "lovely" on board the steamer.

> "She turned to her maidens, they all looked very wild.
> 'Tare an 'ages, gurls, says she, 'which of yiz owns the
> child?"
> But take him up without fuss or flouster
> 'And we'll carry him home, and smoder him wid a boulster!

It may well be imagined that the visit so unluckily begun was not a long one, and that Thornton contrived to give as little pleasure as he received during his forty-eight hours' stay under his father's roof. If ever an elderly gentleman felt like a shuttlecock between two battledores, it was poor Colonel Thornton during that time. For his son took every occasion of reproaching him with his weakness, and his daughter lost no opportunity of imploring him to listen to no one but herself.

Had he done so, however, this story would never have been written; for she was willing to agree to her lover's proposal that they should be married at once, and leave India in the spring. But her father had the fear of his son before his eyes, and in spite of himself could not help being impressed by the contempt with which Robert invariably spoke of Blade Bone as an adventurer.

Running with the hare and hunting with the hounds is a most fatiguing form of sport, and by the end of the cold weather Colonel Thornton was forced to confess to himself that he was almost worn out with worry and annoyance. But he had temporised so long that he now found it more than ever difficult to decide upon a course of action; and it was a great relief when Sybil and Blade Bone confided to him a notable scheme which would at once settle things to their own satisfaction and relieve him of all responsibility.

It is too often the fate of very serious people to be made ridiculous in spite of themselves, and Robert Thornton played into the hands of the man he detested, as cleverly as though he had been determined that his enemy should win the game. For he also had a notable scheme which he intended should separate Sybil from her Irishman once and for all. Blade Bone had always declared that it was absolutely necessary he should return to Ireland in the spring, and had made a great point of this necessity in pleading for a speedy marriage. And Robert had decided that if his sister could be sent to the hills at the beginning of the hot weather, her lover's departure from India would comfortably put an end to everything.

He was prepared to override all opposition to a plan which he proposed to his father by letter; but, as much to his surprise as pleasure, none was made to his suggestion that he should take his sister up to Dullhouses early in May, and place her there under the care of the chaplain's wife, who was a lady of an age and character to guarantee an exceedingly quiet if not dismal time for Miss Sybil, during the whole season.

He had taken great pains to assure himself that Blade Bone was not at Ghurmabad when he made this suggestion; and it was acted upon so promptly, that there had not been time for the lovers to communicate.

If he had not been one of those very superior people who never read advertisements, he might have seen one in the agony columns of the <u>Pioneer</u>, which, if not explicit was at least suggestive. "CHOKE BORE TO BILLIARD CUE. Everything arranged. Horses at B. - Shall be there."

The beginning of the journey which ended in the discovery of the empty doolie at Dullhouses was most satisfactory; and Robert felt quite triumphant in the success of his scheme, which he felt to be already assured. This pleasant state of mind continued to increase as each stage of the weary march was safely accomplished, and rarely was a disappointment bitterer and more complete than Robert Thornton's when he discovered his sister's flight.

For as he hastened down the hill as quickly as its steepness would allow, he had a sickening conviction that he had been made a fool of by the light-hearted Irishman and Sybil. Enquiries at Babool elicited facts to confirm his suspicions, that during the few minutes in which he had left his sister's doolie to mount a fresh horse, she had escaped from that mangy conveyance to join Blade Bone, who had actually been within a few yards of him in the sheltering darkness. Angry as he might be, it was not easy to despise the skill with which the elopement had been planned and arranged. Even Sybil's luggage had been turned back at this point, and it was now perfectly clear to him that, while for twelve miles he had been doing escort duty to an empty doolie, Sybil and her lover had been gaily riding down the hill, certain of a good start which made their being overtaken impossible. It was gall and wormwood to Thornton to think how they might have made fun of his discomfiture; but in fact they had been far too well-pleased with the success of their plan to waste a thought upon his annoyance.

When Thornton reached Ghurmabad and told his story, Colonel Thornton did his best to receive the news with the surprise and indignation which would naturally be expected from him under the circumstances; but he was not a good actor, either by nature or art, and failed in representing either sentiment so signally that it scarcely needed the verbal confession, which Robert dragged from him to assure him of his father's knowledge of the affair.

Overwhelmed by the indignation which his son heaped upon him, the poor man was at first apologetic; but the timely arrival of a telegram announcing the marriage of Sybil restored his courage, and he grew bold enough, not only to defend himself, but to accuse Robert of having caused the elopement by his obstinacy.

It was clearly not from the paternal side that the younger Thornton had inherited his nature.

In due course the telegram was followed by a letter from Sybil to her father, announcing the date of their intended departure from Bombay. "tell Robert," she said, in conclusion "that by good luck we are going home in the Indus, the same steamer that brought us out. I wonder if he remembers as well as I do the day he tried to scold me in the Captain's Cabin?" The same post brought a letter for Robert from his brother-in-law. A happy impudent letter with what Thornton felt to be an insult in every sentence, though nothing had been further from Blade Bone's intention in writing it. That it was however open to this construction may be gathered from the concluding paragraph:-

"It is not your fault after all, my dear fellow, that you couldn't sympathise with us from first to last. You never were young in your life and you may take my word for it you never will be - not if you live to be as old as Methusaleh!"

:::::::::::::::::::

"A CROWNING IN."

A Story of the Black Country

["A Crowning In" and "A Sermon in Stones" show her attempting melodramatic plots; horror stories obviously attract her but she hasn't quite the sureness of touch to make them credible. The poor quality of the carbon copies meant it was unsuitable for facsimile reproduction, but we have laid out the pages roughly as the document, together with the punctuation, underlining, and spelling etc. of her original typescript.]

To any one familiar with that part of the midland counties known as "The Black Country", the mere mention of its name will bring before the mind the whole dreary spectacle, the blackness of desolation by day, the burning waste by night; while to those unacquainted with the scene, no description, however vivid, would convey a correct idea of its peculiar features.

In these days of constant railway travelling, when a distant town is often practically nearer than a neighbouring village, many who have never visited the black country have obtained a general idea of its characteristics while passing through it; and should their train have been a slow one, probably the short journey between Birmingham and Wolverhampton has given them all the acquaintance they wish to have with a scene so gloomy in the daylight, so appalling in the darkness. The flat, black ground, intersected by canals upon whose foul and muddy water slow barges laden with coal or iron are drawn by lean horses, the short wide chimneys pouring forth smoke and flame, the machinery for working coal pits, and the debris from them and from the furnaces, all go to make one of the dreariest pictures conceivable.

But the sights to which I have alluded are not the only things that render the black country terrible. It is liable to a peculiar danger of an appalling nature; and the circumstances under which I first heard of it, being in themselves not uninteresting, I make no apology for repeating them.

About five years ago I accepted an invitation to spend Christmas with a friend living in South Staffordshire. He was an iron-master of considerable position and, finding it necessary to live in the neighbourhood of his business, had built a house near to his works, and taken thither his young wife who was a cousin of mine, in the early part of the year. I had never even passed through the county, and had no idea of its aspect, and only looked forward to a pleasant week with my friends.

Professional engagements kept me in London till late in the afternoon of the 24th of December, and in the early twilight of that winter day I began my journey. There was a bitter hard frost, the clouds gathering blackly seemed to promise a heavy fall of snow before morning, and I was much annoyed to find that the only train I could take was a slow one, stopping at every station. However, it was no use to complain; and wrapping myself up as warmly as possible in my rug, I composed myself for sleep soon after we started, and was fortunate enough to have an undisturbed slumber of some length.

When I awoke it was to a novel sight. On either side

were the huge furnace fires of the black country shedding a
lurid light far into the darkness; and the heaps of refuse,
which looked grey and dead in the daylight, were now so
many glowing hillocks of red-hot embers. It was more like
a dream than any waking sight I had ever had; and more like
a vision of purgatory, or even a worse place, than like a
dream. The train stopped, and upon enquiring the name of
the station, I found that I had passed the station of -,
where I ought to have left the train, and where my friend
had arranged to meet me with a carriage. Considerably
vexed, I took up my carpet bag and asked if I could have a
conveyance to take me to my friend's house; but the place
was little more than a village, and nothing of the kind
could be had. The station-master informed me, in answer to
my impatient inquiries, that Mr - lived about three miles
off, giving me some directions as to the route, of which,
being a stranger, I could make nothing, left me to take my
chance.

I walked out of the station and then stood still
irresolutely, somewhat bewildered by the strangeness and
peculiarity of all that I saw, and dazzled by the strong
effect of light and shade, the glare from the huge fires
contrasting so sharply with the blackness of the night. I
looked at my watch and found that it was just eight
o'clock.

At this moment a man passed, and I asked him if he
could direct me to the house of Mr -. He turned at the
sound of my voice, and pointing vaguely into the darkness,
said it "lay over there."

"But I don't know the country at all" I said. "I was
never here before, and I cannot find my way unless you tell
me something more."

"Oh, if you're a stranger," he answered somewhat roughly, "you won't find it easy. You've come to the wrong station for the nearest."

"I know that" I said, "I have made a mistake."

"If that's it" he replied, more good-humouredly, "come along with me. I'm goin' a good step o' the same way, and I'll show you as far as I can."

I accepted the offer of companionship gratefully, and we walked quickly on, - now in the glare, now in the darkness, till we came to a small gate, which opened upon the canal path. It looked so dismal, and dreary as far as it could be seen, and was so impenetrably dark where it could not, that I shrank from walking along the towing-path with the contingency of walking into the water.

"Is there no other way than this?" I asked.

"Aye, there's another, but it's longer. Are you scared o' this?" was the reply.

"Well no, not exactly," I said, hesitating; "but I was never in this neighbourhood before and of course it does not look to me as it does to you, who have lived here all your life. But," I added, seeing that my companion had passed through the gate, and following his example, "if you say that this is the best way, we'll take it."

"I've not lived here all my life" he said, replying to the first part of my sentence, "and I wish to God I'd never come near it!"

I was startled by the earnestness and evident sincerity with which the words were uttered, and turned to look at the speaker; we were in the glare now, and he could be seen quite plainly. A common-place looking man enough, about forty years of age, his insignificant features deeply marked by the small-pox, and begrimed with soot and coal

dust. His dress was dirty fustian. There was nothing
remarkable about him in any way; and I concluded that he
was disappointed in wages, or had given up something better
for his present occupation, whatever it might be. He was
silent now; and though I wished to know why he had spoken
his regret so earnestly, I could not very well ask him, and
so tried to draw him into conversation.

"Are wages good about here?" I asked.

"Ay, there well enough if you work well" he said
sullenly; "they're the same here as in most places; you
earn what you get, and you get what you earn."

"Who do you work for?" I went on.

He named the friend whom I was going to visit.

"Is he a good master?"

"He's like th' rest, a hard 'un. Set his mind on
makin' his fortun' sharp, I reckon, and gettin' out o' this
cussed place."

"I suppose you'd do the same if you were he?" I
suggested.

"Like enough" he assented.

By this time we had left the canal side, and were
walking in a narrow lane, along which ran a single tramway,
and by the side of which were some of the poorest cottages
or rather hovels, I had ever seen; most of them, however,
were dimly lighted, and from some came rough sounds of
merriment and holiday making.

My guide stopped before the door of one of the cottages
which was in complete darkness, and turning to me said:

"If you keep right on for half a mile, and then take
th' road to th' left, you can't miss th' house."

"Are you not going any farther" I asked, rather anxiously,
for I greatly disliked the idea of walking on alone.

"No" he said, bluntly, taking a key from his jacket picket, and putting it into the lock of the door; "I'm at home."

"If you will show me the rest of the way I shall be much obliged" I said, at the same time slipping half-a-crown into his left hand; "and no one seems to be waiting for you."

He would not take the coin, but replacing the key in his pocket, moved forward, saying:

"No, there's no one waitin' for me."

The tone in which he echoed my words was one of such profound sadness, that I was much struck by it, and a moment after he continued:

"No, there's no one a waitin' for me; that there cottage is as empty as it is dark, there's no fire in it, and no welcome; there's no wife, nor no children; there's naught there to mak' a home of but th' four bare walls."

"You should marry", I said, cheerfully, "then you would have a wife to welcome you, and children in time, perhaps. At any rate you'd have a fire and a light."

"But I had 'em all once", he went on, not heeding my interruption, "a good wife, an' three children, an' I lost 'em all this night a year sin'. It's Christmas Eve, isn't it?"

"Lost!" I repeated, much shocked; "what did they die of?"

"Ay, lost 'em; they didn't to call die."

"Will you tell me about it?" I asked, much interested.

"This day last 'ear it was like as it is now, on'y frostier, an' blacker, 'an darker. I come home fro' work at five o'clock, and it was pitch dark by then. We lived in that same cottage, an' my wife had made it as tidy as a palace - she was a rare clean 'un - all ready for Christmas

Day, an' th' pudden was ready for boilin'; an' when we'd
had tea she foun' out that candles was forgot and wanted,
there was on'y the piece o' one that was burnin'. There's
th' shop close by there", and he indicated the direction by
pointing his thumb over his shoulder - "an' she thought no
harm o' sendin' th' youngest child - she was six 'ear old,
and sharper nor any needle I ever saw - to fetch 'em. She
didn't come back as soon as she might ha' done, and we sent
th' next 'un - she was close upon eight - after her; for
tho' it were as dark as a dog's mouth, we thought no harm,
th' shop were close to, an' them knowing th' road so well.

"She didn't come back no more nor th' first, an' we
said what we'd do when they did come, playin' away out i'
the dark, and the night so cold; an' when it come that
they'd been gone nigh half an hour, Jack - that was the
eldest of them all - said he'd go an' bring 'em in. He
stopped away too, till we was tired o' waitin', an' th'
wife says, 'Drat them children; let 'em get a playin' an'
they never think nothin' o' no errands; but I'll fetch 'em
in, "an' warm 'em too', and she puts her shawl over her
head an' off she goes. She didn't shut th' door fast, or
th' wind bursted it open, and I goes to shut it, an' just
then I thought I heerd a scream in her voice, and as she
wasn't a screeychy sort o' woman, it give me a kind o'
turn. I clapt th' candle end into an old lantern as we
had, and off I went to see if I really had heerd anything.

"It were hawful dark outside, not a moon nor a star,
and I right searched along the ground, holdin' out th'
lantern to show a light where I were goin', an' well I did.
About twenty yard fro' th' cottage I found out all 'bout it.
There'd been a crowning in, and down they was all gone,
wife, an' Jack, an' th' two other children; an' there was

me standin' on th' edge wi' th' lantern, lookin' for what wasn't to be seen, for th' crownin' in was deeper than anyone knows, an' I never saw no more of all them that had been at tea wi' me - so happy an' pleasant."

I vaguely apprehended the catastrophe, and though my ignorance of the meaning of the words "crowning in" prevented my understanding it fully, the man's voice and manner touched me to the heart.

"What is a 'crowning in'?" I asked.

"Why", he explained, "this 'ere country's all undermined wi' pits an' workin's, and sometimes the earth goes in atop, and makes a big hole; that's a 'crownin' in.'"

I comprehended the horror fully now. "Does such a thing happen often?" I asked at length.

"I've heerd on it many times. Sometimes it's under a 'ouse, an' it all goes down; but this o' mine was the worst I know."

"What did you do?" I questioned.

"There wasn't nothin' could be done, and I went back to th' cottage to think about it. The neighbours was all very good to me, an' some of 'em bided wi' me all night; an' when daylight came we went to look once again, but day or night all was dark there; and the last I ever see of my wife, an' Jack, an' the other children, was them goin' out for th' candles, one after another, an' her fetchin' 'em in."

His voice broke as he spoke the last words, and I saw him wipe his eyes with the sleeve of his jacket. I felt a rising in my own throat such as I had not known for long. A minute after he went on quietly:

"An' the next day were Christmas Day. A good woman as lives near had boiled the pudden, an' brought it an' set it

before me an' I tried to eat, but nothing never went nigher
to chokin' a man nor what that did me. I thought so of 'em
all - an' Jack, that was such a hand at a pudden - an' I
got up, an' took it in to th' neighbour as had brought it,
an' stood an' watched her children eat it; an' then I went
back to the empty cottage, an' cried out aloud, the
biggest, bitterest tears, till I were as weak as a child;
an' then I lighted my pipe, an' smoked it all alone."

"And were the bodies never found?" I asked.

"No, they was never found: there was no buryin', not
nothing. P'raps there was water at th' bottom, an' their
dead bodies was drowned; p'raps it was dry an' hard, an'
they was dashed to bits. I've thought on it every way at
one time or another, but nothing was seen no more. Take
that turn, sir", he said, suddenly resuming his old tone,
"an' it'll take you right to the 'ouse. Good night, sir",
and before I could thank him, he was lost in the darkness.

+:+:+:+:+:+:+:+:+:+:+:

"SERMONS IN STONES."

A few years ago I was travelling in the south of
England. My journey was a business one; and I had almost
completed it, when I was unexpectedly detained by some
alteration in my arrangements, and so lost my train. The
place where this occurred is a very small town, or perhaps
more correctly a large village, that but for the railway
which has been cut through it would be very much like many
other villages - picturesque possibly, and certainly of
very little interest to any but those living in it. As it
is, however, a tolerably large hotel has sprung up by the
railway-station; and the bustle of railway life has given
to one end of it an air of business, contrasting somewhat
curiously with the appearance of the rest of the village,
where the long low cottages, each with something like a
garden-farm, crowned with a small hayrick, attached, look
as if nothing about them had been changed for at least
fifty years. Even the dress of the women has a quaint old-
fashioned look in this part; the short clinging skirts and
thick white caps having a curious effect when seen at the
distance of only a quarter of a mile from the smart hats
and full dresses of the maid-servants of the hotel, who set
the fashions of the immediate neighbourhood.

There is a pretty church at the old end of the village,
its square, red brick tower almost covered with one of

those creeping-plants that are green in spring and early summer, but change slowly into golden brown and burning crimson as autumn comes on. I had once spent three hours in this village, and thought I had seen everything in it that could interest a stranger; and so was not a little annoyed when I discovered that the next train for London did not leave till six o'clock in the evening, there being but two in the course of the day. I made this discovery at about eleven in the forenoon, and was very much concerned to know how I should pass the intervening hours.

An officious waiter at the hotel, who had forced the full knowledge of this annoying detention upon me by asking what I "would please to order for dinner, and what time, sir?" and who seemed instinctively to understand my embarrassment, ran off glibly, as though it had been the bill of fare for dinner, a list of all that was entertaining and interesting in the neighbourhood; beginning with "Fine echo, sir," and ending with "church, churchyard, sir."

I smiled scornfully at the echo. It had no attraction for a middle-aged man, though I could very well remember a time, -which must have been twenty years ago, though at that moment it did not seem nearly so long,- when I had sought out an echo, and spoken words of endearment to it, that I might hear them repeated in a sweet sighing voice, which pleased me to think must be like the tone of a voice I knew and loved, if only I could induce it to speak tender words to me. And this made me think how that sweet voice had long been hushed upon earth, and I had found another, whose music had made the hushed voice only a pleasant - scarcely a sad - memory to me; and this train of thought decided me to go once again, perhaps a little sentimentally, to the old church.

It was late in the month of September, and the creeper upon the church-tower was burning gloriously golden and crimson in the mid-day sun. I walked a little time aimlessly in the churchyard, thinking, as I had not done for long, of the dear little lost love of my boyhood, the memory of whose grave had for years made all graves sacred and sorrowful to me. Then I began to read the inscriptions upon the gravestones, and I must confess that my mood changed somewhat abruptly. I read commonplaces of regret and of affection expressed in the very poorest rhythmical jingle, or in verses of Scripture curiously altered from the original text. I could scarcely forbear laughing at some of the alterations; and seeing a very old stone partly overgrown with moss, I stooped down to clear the inscription, thinking it possible I might there find something quainter and more curious than any I had yet seen. In old worn letters I read that "This stone covereth the body of Miranda, who died in her youth and beauty." The age and date I could not decipher, they were so much worn; but lower down upon the stone were two lines, which I made out thus

"I am o'erwhelmed that Death, that tyrant grim,
Should think on me, who never thought on him."

And below this were two figures rudely cut; one of Death, which seemed as if it might have been copied from one of the engravings in "The Dance of Death;" and the other of a lady sinking "o'erwhelmed" to the ground. (As I did not copy the inscription at the time, and having given it from memory, I have not attempted to preserve the original spelling, which was quaint enough.)

If I had been almost moved to laughter by the curiously

distorted and misapplied Scripture, I was more nearly moved to tears by the pathetic power of these lines; and as I turned slowly away, I seemed to see "Miramda in her youth and beauty" suddenly "o'erwhelmed" at sight of her grim and unexpected visitor; and I tried to recall the old ballad of "Death and the Ladye," which I had once read. As I walked among the graves, absorbed in thought, I struck my foot against a stone, newer and rising higher than most it its neighbourhood, and fell. As I rose, an old woman - whom I had previously noticed as being the only other person in the churchyard, and whose dress was observable as something between the quaint fashion of the old end of the village and the new fashion of the Railway part - came towards me, and asked kindly if I were hurt. I had struck my ankle, and, all tenderness and solemn thoughts put to flight by the pain, I replied that I was, and bestowed a few hearty invectives upon the stone which had been the cause of my fall.

To my surprise, the old woman said sternly, "Don't curse the grave, sir, there was curse enough before that stone was laid."

I felt a little confused by her reproof, and turned to read the inscription in order to hide that I was so.

It ran thus:

Sacred to the memory of

Mabel,

Only Daughter of Richard Bevan,

Who died July 20th, 184-,

Aged 19 years.

"Visiting the sins of the fathers upon the children"

I was interested in a moment. "Did you know Mabel Bevan?" I asked.

The old woman answered readily enough, "Surely I did, sir; I nursed her, and her mother before her."

"And will you tell me," I went on, "who put that singular inscription upon her gravestone, and why it was chosen?"

"It was put there by her father, sir; but why it was put there, is a long story, though none knows it better than myself."

"Did she live here?" I asked.
"She lived at the hall there," replied the old woman pointing to a large white house, standing in its own grounds, about a mile from the church.

I said that I should like to hear the story, if she would tell it to me; and she replied that if I would go with her to her cottage, which stood close to the churchyard gate, she would do so.

So I followed her to the cottage; and she unlocked the door, and showing me into a clean little room, offered me a seat. She left me for a moment, returning without her bonnet and cloak; and then, sitting down in a large old rocking-chair opposite to me, began to speak very slowly, and rocking herself gently the while.

"You've a kindly look with you, sir; and maybe have daughters of your own at home; and so I'll tell you how it came about in this case that the sins of the father were visited upon the children; for she wasn't the only one to suffer, though it fell heaviest upon her - as heavy as death.

"Not to make the story too long, sir, I will only say that I was her nurse from the time she was born till she needed a nurse no longer; and then I was her faithful

friend and servant till the day I laid her in her coffin,
poor lamb! You wouldn't care to hear about her pretty
baby - ways, though the memory of them is very dear to me
I loved her like as if she had been my own child; but we
see how our love can't save them we love from trouble.
Mine helped to lay her in her grave, though I meant for
the best.

My mistress (that was my poor lamb's mother) met with
Mr Bevan when she was gone to London on a visit. He had
plenty of money, and was very fond of her; and no one could
say a word against the match. He was near upon twenty
years older than her, and people did say he was very gay
when he was younger. But he was very devoted to her, and
she loved him dearly; and so they were married after a
short courtship, and he brought her down here, to live at
the hall. He gave up his London way and took to farming;
and very happy and comfortable they were.

"My young mistress, Miss Mabel, was born about two
years after they came here. Mrs Bevan had been drooping
for some time, and after that she just faded away like a
flower. My master took on sadly; and I was very glad when,
about a month after she died, he told us that he was going
abroad for some time, it might be a year. He had never
seemed to take much notice of Miss Mabel (they said he was
disappointed that it was not a son) and he just told me to
take care of her, like as if it was a thing of no
importance; and then, in June, he left England.

"He had not been long gone, when little Miss Mabel took
the scarlet fever, which was a good deal about just then,
and the doctor was very much afraid he shouldn't be able to
bring her through. I was in a great deal of trouble, for I
didn't know where to write to Mr Bevan; and for all he took

so little notice of the child, I was sure he would grieve
if she was to die while he was away, and her growing more
and more like her mother every day. Well, I nursed her
through the fever; day and night I had her in my arms; and
when she took a turn for the better, they said I had saved
her life. Oh, to think that I was so glad of it then, and
that the time came afterwards when I wished I hadn't kept
her back from the little grave that seemed waiting for her!

"In the spring of the next year, the master wrote to
say he was coming home, and ordered me to make ready to
take care of another child, a little boy, the son of his
youngest brother that was lately dead. So all was got
ready, and in the early summer he came back, bringing a
beautiful little boy about five years old, that I loved at
once, because Miss Mabel took to him, and put her little
arms round his neck, and gave him baby-kisses as soon as he
came to play with her.

The master seemed quite cheerful again, and took a deal
of notice of the baby, and indeed she was nearly a year and
half old, and was a sweet-tempered notice-taking little
thing. Little Master Walter was very like his uncle in
looks, and in some of his ways; but Mr Bevan never liked
the likeness mentioned, and once, when I said they looked
like brother and sister, he was very angry, and bade me
hold my tongue, for they were cousins. We all loved the
child; for though he was warm-tempered, he was a noble
little fellow, and you might do anything with him by
kindness. His uncle was the only one that did not seem to
be fond of him. Little Miss Mabel and he were very happy
together; from the first day he came they seemed to
understand each other. However fretful she was she would
smile when Master Walter came near her, and stretch out her

little arms for him to take her. He was wonderfully
patient with her to be sure; and any time he would leave
his work or his play to amuse her. When she grew older and
could speak plain, he used to teach her all sorts of pretty
things, and I believe he learned her to read in a kind of
game. When she was five years old, Master Walter was sent
to school, and the poor little thing nearly broke her
heart, wandering through the house and round the garden,
calling for him. I could only comfort her by saying we
could do something to please Cousin Walter when he came
back; and there wasn't a thing those words wouldn't make
her do.

"The years passed on slowly in the school-time, when
Master Walter was away, and quick enough when he was at
home in the holidays. Miss Mabel had a governess, and was
growing a very clever young lady; the master was very proud
of her, and well he might be, for there wasn't a prettier
or better for miles round.
"When Master Walter was nineteen, and Miss Mabel nearly
sixteen, he went to a great school called Oxford, where
they had a good many holidays, and one very long one that
lasted all the summer through. He was grown a fine tall
young man by this time, and he used to row Miss Mabel in a
boat on the river for hours together, and used to take her
out walking and riding. The first summer and the second
were spent in this way, and when he went back to Oxford in
the autumn, I thought my sweet little mistress seemed to
feel it more than ever; and I told her one day that it was
baby-work to fret after her cousin that would be home at
Christmas; for she let me say anything, because I had known
and loved her all her life long. And then she told me, with
the bright colour blushing all over her cheeks and neck,

down to the ends of her pretty white fingers, that she missed her cousin more than ever, because she loved him better, and had promised to be his wife when he left Oxford. I was glad of anything that made my darling happy; and she went on to say, that Mr Walter would tell Mr Bevan, and ask his consent at Christmas; and she laid her warm rosy face against mine, and whispered over and over again, 'And I am so happy, nurse; so happy, so very happy!'

It was strange that the master shouldn't have seen how things were going; he was keen-sighted enough in general; but when Christmas came, and Mr Walter asked him if he hadn't seen how he loved Miss Mabel, he said he had seen nothing of the kind, and he wouldn't see it; for it should never be! When the young man pressed for a reason, he would give none; but only swore over and over again, that he would rather see his daughter dead than married to Walter Bevan. My poor little mistress sobbed her trouble out to me, and - God forgive me - I tried to comfort her with saying, I didn't doubt her father would change his mind, and it would come right after all.

"It was the strangest thing, but though my master had said they were not to marry, he did nothing to keep them apart, and Master Walter came home for the holidays as usual, and was walking about with Miss Mabel. It was the strangest thing and the cruellest, and the wickedest, and will come up before the master surely on the Judgement Day; for he sacrificed those two young lives just that his own lies and wickedness might not be found out.

"When Master Walter came of age there was grand doings, all the same as if he had been the master's own son. There was entertainment for the country-folk, and a ball for the gentry, and Miss Mabel was the loveliest there. Everyone

said what a splendid couple her and her cousin made; for
they danced together a many times. It was the evening of
the ball that Mr Bevan met with a lady from Ireland, that
had come to visit in the neighbourhood. She was very
pretty, to be sure; but she was young and foolish, and I
never could understand how it was that the master chose her
for his wife - him, an elderly man, and so grave. But he
did, and the marriage was not long in doing; and this gay
young lady came to be mistress at the hall. Miss Mabel
felt it a good deal; but she loved her father, and wouldn't
think a thought against him, so she never complained, but
just kept out of their way a good deal, and didn't seem to
be missed. Her and me was more together than we had been
since she was my nurseling, and we used to go long walks
into the country round about; and all her talk was of Mr
Walter, and how he was going to leave Oxford in less than a
year, and then they should be so happy.

"Well, a year passed, and there was a son born to Mr
Bevan, and there was a deal of rejoicing. Miss Mabel and
her father hadn't been much together since his marriage;
but she tried to seem pleased with what made him glad, and
she took that time, poor lamb! to ask him if he wouldn't
think different about her and Mr Walter. She told me that
she never saw him so angry, and he swore, with a great
oath, that he would see her in her coffin before he would
let her marry Walter Bevan.

"It was soon after this that Master Walter came home
for good; and still the master took no notice of them being
always together, but was taken up entirely with his wife
and child. There was a new nurse for the baby, and I was
Miss Mabel's maid.

"The young people were a deal troubled at first about the

master being so determined against their marrying, but by
and by my young mistress was as cheerful as ever, and went
singing up and down like a bird. I made free to ask her
what had made the change that I was glad to see; and she
told me that Mr Walter was going to ask her father once
again, and if he refused still, they were going to be
married all unknown to him, for they were sure he would not
be angry when he found it was no use. They were determined
about this all the more, because Mr Bevan had begun to talk
of sending Mr Walter away to live. God forgive me, I was
glad to hear it; and when they found the master as set
against it as ever, and still that he would give no reason,
I helped them all I could about the secret marriage.

"It was all settled to be at a village three miles off,
and the clergyman was a friend of Mr Walter's own.

"It was such a sweet summer morning, and I dressed Miss
Mabel as like a bride as I dared, without it looking too
like, and we set off all three together, as if we were
going to take a walk.

"When we reached the church, we found the clergyman all
ready, and another friend was there to give her away; and
never was a bride looked lovelier, for all she wore a plain
white dress and a straw hat. And Mr Walter, he looked so
happy and handsome.

"It was very soon all over, and we set off to walk back
again. They were talking together how they would go
straight to the master, and tell him what they had done;
and I heard Mr Walter say, "He is my father, you know, now,
dear, as well as my uncle, and he is sure to forgive us.'
When we came to the house, we met Mr Bevan, and Mr Walter
gave me a look to go away; so I left them, and went into
the house at the back, and up to Miss Mabel's room, to wait

for her.

"I hadn't been there many minutes, when my young mistress
ran in, with her face like crimson, and panting for breath.

"'Oh nurse, nurse,' she said, 'you can't think how
angry my father is, and I am terribly frightened! He said
he must speak to Walter alone, and his face was as white as
death.' And then my dear young lady sat down, and began to
cry.

"I tried to comfort her, but in truth I was very much
alarmed, and didn't know rightly what to say. We sat there
for what seemed a very long time, and then I went
downstairs, just because I was so anxious to get to know
something, that I couldn't stay with my poor young mistress
any longer. As I got near the master's room, I heard
voices very loud, and I couldn't help but listen. I
expected to hear Mr Bevan very angry, but Mr Walter's was
the fiercest voice, and the master spoke quite low, as if
he was pleading. Then I listened, and I heard words that
turned me sick as death. That moment I heard my mistress
calling me, and I went trembling up the stairs back to her
room. I could not have spoken a word to save my life, and
I just sat down near her in silence. She didn't ask me any
thing, but she looked in my face with her large eyes very
wide open, and her face went very pale. We sat silent,
looking at each other for a long time; and when I tried to
speak, I couldn't, for my tongue was dry and stiff in my
mouth, and the words I had heard seemed to have struck me
stupid.

"The door of the room was wide open; and all at once we
heard a noise down-stairs. I sprang to my mistress, and
held her in my arms while we listened. There was the sound
of feet in the hall, and then the hall-door was opened and

dashed to again. My young lady broke from me, and ran to
the window which faced the front. I followed, and I saw Mr
Walter running away from the house very fast, without so
much as looking back. His poor little wife turned to me,
and said in a crying tone, 'What does it all mean, nurse?
oh, what does it all mean?'

The next minute the baby's nurse stood at the door, and
said the master wanted me in his room. So I kissed my poor
little mistress, and told her I'd come back directly with
good news, though, God forgive me, I had heard words that
made me sure there was no comfort and no good news for her
ever again.

"When I got to the master's door, I shook till I could
scarcely stand; and as soon as I was in the room, I sat
down on a chair without waiting for a word, - what I had
never done before in the master's presence.

"I don't remember how he began, nor what words he used;
but he told me that his sin had found him out, for Mr
Walter was not his nephew, but his own son, that was born
before ever he had seen my mistress that he married.

"I cried out at that, - no ways afraid though he was my
master, - that he was a bad man and a coward not to have
told the truth at first. I had no mercy on him, for my
heart was broken to think of the poor young thing upstairs.
He said he had told Mr Walter, and that he had cursed him
for the lie of so many years, and was gone away saying he
should never come back; and he told me that I must tell
Miss Mabel.

"But I spoke up; and said I would not, for it was part
of his punishment; that he had broken her heart; and after
all that was gone before, surely this was not a hard thing
for such a man to do. And when I said that, he rose up,

and asked me where his daughter was, with such a fierce
look in his eyes, that I cried out in terror that I would
tell her myself, and he must not go to her. So I left the
room, and went slowly up-stairs to Miss Mabel.

"I sat down, and she came and stood by me without a
word. So I drew her upon my lap as I used to nurse her
when she was a little child, and she laid her face on my
shoulder, trembling like a leaf in a wind storm. I don't
know what words I used; but as soon as I begun to speak,
she raised her head up, and sat still staring at me,
growing whiter and stiffer every moment. I held her tight,
and looked for her to faint, or to die perhaps, as her face
got whiter, and more set like death; but she kept staring
on, till I couldn't speak another word. When I stopped she
drew the ring from her finger, and let it fall upon the
floor. Then she said, 'Nurse, lay me down; for I shall
die. My heart is broken, and is bleeding to death;' and I
laid her on her bed, and kissed her cheek, that was cold
and white and stiff like stone.

"She lived three days, and the colour never came back to
her face and lips, and her poor eyes never closed but just
stared on, as if they saw some horrible thing before them.

"I never left her but once, to tell the master that he
had killed her; and I had some pity even on him when I saw
the change in him. I used to speak to her, but mostly she
took no heed; only when I asked if she would like to see
her father, she said 'No'.

"On the third day, while I was standing by her side, and
praying to see her eyes closed and her sleeping, she turned
towards me and said, 'Nurse, tell my father I forgive him;
and I send my love to my - brother;' and then her eyes
closed as I had prayed they might, and I thought she was

sleeping. But it was the death-sleep as I soon saw, though her face was no paler and colder. "I fetched the master, without saying what it was, and brought him to her bedside.

In a few days my work was ended. I laid my poor lamb in her coffin, and followed her to her grave.

"I left the hall; for though the master offered me to stay I couldn't now my dear Miss Mabel was gone. I had saved a good bit of money, and I wasn't so young, its only ten years agone - and I took this cottage, and have lived here alone ever since.

"When I saw what the master had put upon the grave I knew that he was a penitent man. The family left the neighbourhood, and went to live abroad. I have never heard of Mr Walter since."

I thanked the old woman for her sad story; and as I turned away I prayed God to have mercy upon me, and not to visit upon my children the sins of their father.

::::::::::::::::

Through Judy's Eyes

[Through Judy's Eyes *exists as a complete manuscript, and as an unfinished, edited typescript. In the manuscript, the names of the aunts were originally Grace and Lucy but have been changed in pencil to Georgie and Louie, and the cousins Jerome and Gwendolyn to Philip and Margaret, as if there was no further point in using aliases. The manuscript is undated but is on the same type of paper, and written in the same ink, that she used in 1936, so perhaps she thought, as all the principals were dead, that there was no point in keeping quiet about her view of the facts any longer. (Her Aunt Edith was still alive, but died the following year.) On the back of page 22 of the manuscript, a pencil note shows her abandoning fiction for fact:-*

'Papa had drawn a delightful picture in their Leah's (sic) book of Nonsense, of Judy pelting the chokra, while ayah held up her hands in horror - and Ruddy laughed - and he had printed this verse underneath:

> *'There was a young lady called Trix*
> *Who pelted her chokra with bricks,*
> *When they said, "No, you mustn't."*
> *She replied No I doesn't."*
> *This naughty young lady called Trix.'*

Over the page there was an even nicer verse and picture of the

> *Small Boy in Bombay*
> *Who once pon a time ran away.*

And the small boy was Ruddy in a holland tunic and red sash.

My sash's were always blue since Mother had given me a pink sash for my 3rd birthday and I took it off and walked on it saying firmly "Boo's my colour." ']

THROUGH JUDY'S EYES
(1874 - 1877)

Downe Lodge, Outram Park, Lawrence Road, Rocklington, was a small house of six rooms, not counting the greenhouse, which only Aunt Rosa remembered to call "the conservatory". It wore a shabby stucco pinafore, and had a front garden about the size and shape of a Persian prayer carpet, where nothing grew except a bank of St John's wort, which sloped down to the playroom window in the basement. That playroom was always chilly and smelt of mushrooms even in the summer, and any toys put in the wall cupboards, even Judy's best doll's dinner set, turned blue with mildew after two or three days.

At the back the ugly brickwork and mean little scullery and coalshed suggested architectural dermatitis and deformity, but there was room enough for a square grass-plot, two lilac bushes, three speckled Portugal laurels, one laurestinus, one small laburnum, and a few scentless flowers in their season; nastertiums and hollyhocks and candy tuft. Also if mustard and cress or radishes were sown in one permitted corner, they sometimes came up, and if they escaped the Rocklington snails, (a particularly hungry and, in Judy's eyes, handsome variety of mollusc,) it was possible to wash them at the tap, a privilege in itself, and have them for tea. As Aunty Rosa said, "They saved jam."

Five openwork steps of rusty iron led up from this garden into the "conservatory", which housed a number of very large millepeds and a few very dull pot plants; ferns,

white and scarlet geraniums and mauve primulas, which Judy
was forbidden to touch. Perhaps Jane's warning that, "If
you ever smelt of a primula right close up, so as the dust
came off on you, your nose would swell and swell till it
was as big as your whole head," was intended to make strict
obedience easier to her. But the greenhouse had its own
glory, for there were two green tubs of pink oleanders, and
when they blossomed, and smelt like almond pudding in
fairyland, they were all that Judy needed of true romance.

Of course there had been much finer ones in their
Bombay garden when they lived at home with Papa and Mamma,
Punch remembered them perfectly; they were taller than the
chimneys of Downe Lodge, they grew in a forest near the
well, where the green parrots lived, and where the white
bullocks were always going blindfold round & round drawing
up water in red waterpots to keep the roses alive, and
little grey striped squirrels, nearly tame enough to eat
biscuits out of his hand, used to play about in them. But
Punch was two and half years older than Judy, he would soon
be able to write his age in two figures, while she was only
seven.

Then too, as it was almost four years since Papa and
Mamma went away and left them all alone with Aunty Rosa,
who wasn't even a real aunt, like Aunt Georgie *(Grace)* in
London, or dear Aunt Louie *(Lucy)* in the country, she
couldn't be expected to "bemember much about Bombay." It
wasn't fair of Punch to call her "Silly Billy", instead of
"Jujub" which was his secret name for her, and say he
always would just because she couldn't bemember old
<u>khansamah ji</u> who made such lovely cakes and cream toffee,
or Dunnoo, who ran by the fat white pony.

What Judy remembered best, though she had tried hard to

forget it, was the leopard skin that cruel <u>budli</u> ayah had used to frighten her at night, one dreadful time when Mamma was very ill, and Judy's own kind ayah was nursing her. She had been a very little girl then, sleeping in a crib, and not able to talk properly, but ever since then when she had a cold, (and she never had nice plain colds, that could be cured by feet in mustard and hot water and black currant tea, like Harry's, but always drefful headache, and a skin so hot she could not bear to touch herself, and a pulse that looked as if something was trying to jump out of her wrist, because she had had mally-something fever before they went to Nassick) she was sure to dream of the leopard, and see him at the foot of the bed getting ready to spring, just as Radha had said he would. Then, when she screamed herself awake, which took a long time because her voice had gone away, and her throat would not work, Aunty Rosa would scold her from the right side of the big bed they shared, and say she had had too much supper, as if two little Oval Thin Captains and a cup of milk and water could give anyone bad dreams, but even a scolding was better than the leopard, and afterwards she didn't so much mind having to fall asleep with Aunty's bony arm round her, although she always hated being hugged by anyone but her own family, and wished more than anything, except going back to Bombay, for a bed of her very own.

Even Punch hadn't a room of his own, for he shared the big attic which had a nice sloping roof, like a card-house, with Harry Harrison, who was quite big, twice as old as Judy, and used to teaze them badly when Aunty wasn't there; but Judy generally managed to keep out of his way. Jane was very quick and clever in helping her to hide from him; and did not tell where she was even if Harry twisted her

arm and thumped it; a torture he was "rather good at" to
use his own words.

At any rate Punch had a bed to himself, with a red
wadded quilt he could roll up in or throw off, just as he
liked; and he could toast cheese, or roast chestnuts on the
top of the candle-lantern when he went to bed, for of
course Harry sat up quite late and had supper with Aunty.
Only bread and cheese generally Jane told her, but
sometimes on choir practise nights, there would be
sardines, or slices of red German sausage.

From the greenhouse one walked under a great curiosity,
a weaver bird's nest, that Papa had found in their Bombay
garden, and sent to Punch, into the dining room, where
there was a tall bookcase, with little side cupboards.
Judy was allowed to keep her lesson books on a shelf in one
of these, and they were very hard to keep tidy for some
were big and slippery, and some were small and limp. It
was one of Aunty Rosa's little ways, Jane used to call
them, "her nasty little ways" always to talk as if it was
very kind of her to let the children live in the house at
all. Everything was a concession. She seemed to expect
Judy to be grateful, and often to say "Thank you" because
she was let to sleep in Aunty's room. Punch too was often
told it was very good of Harry to share the attic with him.
"But there is no where else for me to go," said logical
Punch, "if you will always keep the spare room empty,
though no one ever sleeps in it."

"Punch, you know what you get when you are impertinent,"
said Aunt Rosa, in her sourest voice, and her voice was
never sweet, except when the vicar called. Judy began to
whimper, for she knew where the cane lived, and though she
had never felt it she hated it more than Punch did.

"Shut up Judy," whispered Punch with an affectionate kick. Judy heaved her shoulders once or twice, and sobbed softly, for she knew her cue.

"Don't be such a baby, Judy," snapped Aunty, "can't I say a word to your brother without your making a scene?"

I don't mind what you say to him" piped Judy, as unexpectedly brave as a desperate mother-bird; "but you are not to hit him becos its cruel."

"So I'm cruel am I?" and Aunty Rosa, who had never learnt to keep her temper with any child but her own, looked just like Red Riding Hood's Wolf. "Very well then, I had meant you to sit up to your supper, for a treat, because you learnt your poetry well today."

Judy dried her tears, and Punch managed to whisper, "She's just made that up," before Aunty went on, "But as I am so cruel I think a very rude and ungrateful little girl had better go to bed early."

"Thank you, I am rather tired," said Judy in her most grown up voice.

"Really, then as you are so tired you will be better without any supper."

Punch, as in duty bound put in an exaggerated plea for mercy, but Judy knew that Jane of the Kind Heart, was going to have dripping toast for supper, and therefore had no fear of going to sleep hungry. Moving with a good deal of deportment towards the door she declaimed,

"Glory to Thee, my God this night,
For all the blessings of the light."

in her best reading-aloud voice, curtsied to Mrs Harrison, kissed her hand to the grinning Punch and departed, with all the honours of war.

Aunty, adopting her usual tactics of trying to set little sister and brother against each other, gave Punch a kiss, as unexpected as it was unwelcome, and let him sit up to supper. There were sardines, but Judy preferred the dripping toast eaten in secret, and Punch managed to pocket two ginger snaps for her. When Aunty came up to bed she brought a cup of milk and water, and two Osborne biscuits, but the child was so unfeignedly asleep, that for once she deferred both food and scolding until next day. She thought that she had scored, and the children knew that they had, and as Punch said, it wasn't hard to get the better of her, when Harry was out of the way. Unluckily he was in the way so constantly.

To return to the dining room, where a great deal of their time indoors was spent, there was a big sideboard, with funny bits of looking-glass where you didn't expect them, and where they chiefly reflected people's feet, and over it hung a picture of the ship "Uncle Harrison", who was Harry's Papa had died in. Aunty often said she should never forget him, and Judy was sure that she could not forget him either, for there was a very big picture of him over the black marble clock on the white marble mantlepiece and it was all black and white too, and he looked very stern, though Harry had said once, that he wasn't nearly as bad as all that really. Then there was the big table for meals and doing lessons on, and Judy never liked that table, for she and Punch had learnt to read at it before she was quite four. It saved trouble to teach them both together, Aunty Rosa said, or as Jane put it, "it let one scream serve."

Judy was thought too young to be rapped over her fat knuckles with a ruler for not attending, as Punch was, so

Aunty used to lift her up, and make her stand on the table
as a punishment. The first time this happened she was so
unbroken to lessons, and Aunty's ways, that she thought it
was a game, and laughed and nearly upset the inkstand with
a light hearted dance step or two, until Aunty's bony
forefinger, which hurt quite as hard as any ruler,
convinced even her small mind, that she was very naughty
and under sentence of doom. Then she cried steadily, for
one hour and half, for though she was not habitually
tearful any real trouble made it very hard for her "to turn
the tap off" as Jane wisely said. If Jane and Punch had
been allowed to come to the rescue she would soon have been
"dood" again, but Mrs Harrison, who knew nothing of girl-
children, (and had never been young herself for one minute,
not she, according to Jane,) mistook bewildered sorrow for
impenitent sin, and scolded accordingly. It did not strike
her that Judy had never heard a woman's voice raised in
anger before, except low-caste coolies in the bazaar, and
was therefore honestly bewildered. Poor Punch's well-meant
but ill judged appeal to be "leavened by selfs with her. I
can manage her selfs all right, better nor Papa, only not
with you here. Mama used to go away when she cried that
way, Ayah and I could do, only you go away, <u>jut-put</u>."
merely served to draw down wrath on his own puzzled head.

Finally Judy, still all tears, was put to bed in deep
disgrace and Punch sent for a walk with Jane, to ensure the
culprit's complete isolation.

"You are a very naughty, badly behaved little girl,
Judy; and if you go on crying like a baby, for "Mamma!
Mamma!" I shall have to give you a good shaking."

"Then Punch will bite you; he bit bad <u>budli</u> ayah for
me once."

"Very well, if you make Punch naughty I shall whip him."

"You t'an't" cried Judy triumphantly, "only Papa may
whip Punch ever, and no one me."

"Nonsense, Punch is left in my care and when he is
naughty, I shall whip him well."

If wishes could have killed, Mrs Harrison's head, with
its frowning eyes, grinning lips, long yellow teeth, and
soiled widow's cap, would have rolled on the floor.
Happily for Judy's overstrained nerves a burst of half-
forgotten Urdu relieved the almost unbearable tension, and
she never guessed that the rosy sobbing child, whose will
she felt it was her duty to "break", consigned her to
Gehannum, in the very worst phrase she had ever heard the
<u>chokra</u> scolded for using; reviled her as a baseborn,
fittingly disfigured by the blackest of faces, and
dismissed her as beneath notice, in that she was herself an
owl, and the daughter of an owl, cursed also with owls as
grand-parents, and, (crowning insult) the miserable mother
of a dog. Even in the height of her rage Judy bemembered
Mamma, and the forbidden word "soor" (pig) was unspoken.
Mamma did not know all the words of abuse that her children
considered innocent, if not endearing, but the word "pig"
she knew and vetoed. Sometimes, after an altercation,
Punch would say, half-admiringly, "Look at that Judy. What
a name she's called me." but Mamma was only amused.

Judy's Guardian Angel, temporarily absent, must have
returned to his post in the afternoon, for the sorrowful
rebel, with spirit still unbroken, fell asleep on a
tearsoaked pillow, and while she slept her low-caste enemy
was summoned to the sick bed of an elderly cousin, who
lived at Petersfield. Jane, the ever-friendly was perforce
left in charge, and Harry, practised tale-bearer and

mischief-maker, being luckily out for tea, Judy woke to a brave new world, where faces smiled and tea was laid in the greenhouse, on a lovely tip-uppy round iron table, that clanged like a gong when mugs were set down. Her own plate was guarded by two sugar mice, one white, one pink, with yellow string tails, a present from Punch, and Jane had lent him the penny to buy them. There was treacle too instead of butter, and not treacled long before so that it sunk in, and a bun each with sweeties on it. Best of all Jane who could "take off anybody" had black cotton reels dangling from each ear, wore the red and green Afghan from the sofa as a shawl, and "did Aunty Rosa" in an inspired manner, which took the sting out of any memories of scoldings.

"It was nearly as good as a birthday," as Punch said.

Theoretically, Rosa Harrison was a good woman, respected at the Church where she attended regularly, and a regular communicant. Perhaps it was lack of imagination rather than lack of love and charity to her neighbours, that impelled her to indulge a naturally bad temper, under the guise of "Discipline" and led her, from the first, to punish an absolutely lonely little brother and sister, marooned, as it were, on the desert island of her house, by forbidding them to speak to each other. It was about this time that she interested herself in a petition for the abolition of solitary confinement in prisons; a system that her charges would have expected her to advocate as faithfully as she practised it. Unluckily for the children, the Vicar was very sympathetic to adult criminals, but being childless, had neither understanding nor interest in small sinners, whose prison walls, though invisible were very real.

II

Next day the reading lessons began again, and very soon there was another table punishment. It was really a terrible punishment, for besides the great disgrace of it, it lasted so long. Five minutes by the black marble clock, and five minutes more if she whimpered, but hours and hours by Judy's counting.

Halfway through she always felt so dizzy and so high up, that she was afraid of falling over the edge, and being dashed to pieces on the red and blue carpet; which used to sink further and further away, while she grew colder and colder, and a funny noise, like a boiling kettle, only louder, sang in her ears. She wasn't allowed to hold on to Punch's long hair, though he offered it to her as a lifeline, or even his sleeve, and if she ventured to move her feet there was danger with the inkstand and the slates.

Luckily for Judy, the Doctor, who always reminded her of Papa, because he had the same delicious tobacco-pipe smell about him, came in one day, to lance a whitlow for Harry, when she was nearing the end of a pillory punishment, and of her own small strength. She liked Doctor, but naturally expected he would be too shocked to speak to her at all, after seeing her so shamed and disgraced; but he only said, "Hullo, what's this? White as a sheet." and took her straight off the table on to his knee, holding her head low in a funny comfy way that stopped the singing and the cold feeling almost at once.

Aunt Rosa explained very fully how naughty she had been, so he said she was to shut her eyes, tight, and he would give her a dose of medicine at once and something to take after it. That was rather frightening but the medicine tasted just like the "pork-wine" they were sometimes given for a great treat on Sundays, and there was a ginger snap, and she felt warm and cozy.

Aunt Rosa looked very ugly, but luckily she did not see Punch dancing his special war dance behind her, she was too busy talking about her patience and "wise handling" and her own boy at that age, but Doctor said, "Tut, you must remember that you can't treat a china cup, egg shell china too, as if it were a tin mug. I should like a few words with you, while Punch runs up to see if Harry is ready for me, and Judy puts Jappy to sleep on the sofa. Look at poor Jappy, he can't keep his eyes open."

Jappy was the Japanese doll, almost as big as a baby, who wore a long robe of red turkey twill, and always smiled. His eyes didn't open and shut, because they were always half-shut which gave him a sleepy look, and funnily enough he was so tired that day, that he and Judy slept till dinner time.

Punch said after, that Aunty Rosa had such red eyes, and was so cross when Doctor had gone, he thought she'd been given a good scolding, and that was prime; but Punch was very "immadgytive" Aunty said so, and added usually that the less Judy believed of what he said, the better. But Punch had always been Judy's oracle, as well as her angel, so she did not love him less, only distrusted Aunty more. Strange to say Judy was never made to stand on the table again, and when Aunty tried putting her in the corner instead, it was such a baby punishment that she couldn't help laughing, and only got the usual scolding.

But that table was never like other tables to Judy; she might forget grey striped squirrels, or kind brown faces in Bombay, but anything that hurt or frightened her could not be forgotten. She was not a brooding or vindictive child, but pain or terror, especially terror, seemed to dig a groove in her brain, and she could no more efface it than she could turn her blue eyes brown.

Of course Punch soon passed her at lessons, though she learnt to read more quickly than he did. "That's because you're so little you have much less brain to see the hard things about reading," he kindly explained to her, and she quite agreed with him. Punch always understood the realness of things, and made it plain to her; but she was glad that her lesser brain let her read fluently, and for pleasure before she was five. She enjoyed taking her turn at reading verses of the psalms aloud at Prayers every morning, and was glibber at this exercise than beloved Jane, aged seventeen and very rosy in a lilac print frock. She noticed that Jane always looked shy and sulky during prayers, just as she did when Aunty Rosa was teaching her the only right way to do things; and telling her how lazy and dirty and untidy she was, which was invariably part of Aunty's teaching. Jane had no difficulty in the actual reading, for she often bought a half price, second hand copy of the "Police News", to "have something nice to read in the evenings -" but she lacked the desire to show off that was Judy's mainspring during the seven years she spent at Downe Lodge.

There was so little scope for love in her narrowed life, that it was natural for a starved, sensitive nature to long for praise, or at least for notice. She was absolutely without companions, or the chance of "making little friends". She only saw girls of her own age at Sunday school, where talking was forbidden, and when she was seven at dancing classes, where it was severely discouraged.

[This is the end of the edited typescript - from here it is unrevised manuscript - ed.]

The time that she was allowed to spend with her adored Punch - her only relative - was strictly rationed. Better acquaintance with Harry showed it was impossible to love one who was alternately bully and toady according to the company he kept, and even the beloved Jane had her limitations and barriers erected by her own sense of fitness.

When Punch grew older he used to spend lovely holidays in London with Aunt Grace, where cousin Jerome *(changed to Philip)* - two years older than he was - shewed him wonderful books and pictures, and beautiful Gwendolen, *(changed to Margaret)* only two years older than Judy, could sing "Come unto these yellow sands" and "Where the bee sucks" - and had fair hair.

"Yes, truly fair, not brownish with little red sparks like yours, and her lashes curl up and are black as black, though her eyes are blue - like stars."

"Stars aren't blue; don't be silly," said Judy.

But Punch only laughed and chanted a piece of poetry he had made up in bed:-

> "Dark hair, dark eyes, dark face are not for me!
> Margaret, Margaret, I love thee!"

"My hair and eyes and face aren't dark."

"I wasn't thinking of you."

"Then I shall go and do my knitting," and Judy went quickly out of the playroom before he saw that she was going to cry. Even Punch didn't seem to understand that she was as far from these delightful cousins as from Papa

and Mamma in Bombay - further indeed for they never wrote
to her, while Indian letters came every week - and writing
was much more difficult than reading, and took a long time.
Punch could help out his letters by pictures, for drawing
came to him by nature, even as whistling and pulling ugly
faces did to Harry, but Judy's powers of self-expression
were very limited.

She was certainly a facile talker, and could remember
the words of a song, or short poem, after once hearing it,
but Fortune had a trick of never coming to her with both
hands full, and once she could read toys lost their value,
and even her favourite dolls were emptied of delight.
Jappy and Lily Whippy, an elegant French doll, with
exquisite painted lashes on her china cheeks, and a
flounced costume of pink and brown striped moir trimmed
with "real pearl buttons", and even Arabellina, a large
Dutch doll who could assume and maintain indefinitely the
most dramatic and startling attitudes, led neglected lives
in a shadowed corner of the dank basement playroom, on a
prickly old horsehair sofa. When their mistress remembered
them, she hastily arranged them in a row, pretended to
share with them the apple she was eating, or the raw
macaroni, or cinnamon stick Jane had let her steal from the
kitchen cupboard opposite, and after a perfunctory "Now
listen my dears, sit up and attend," would read to herself
very happily until tea time. It was quite easy and natural
to make believe that she was reading aloud to them all the
time, and they seemed to enjoy it.

Experience had taught her, that if, in reply to
questioning she said, "I've been reading "Macbeth", or "No
Name", or "David Copperfield" she was told to play properly
with her toys (hadn't she two dolls' dinner sets? one white

with little green stars, and the other, a blue key pattern on white complete even to tureen, soup plates and pie dishes) and to read "Ministering Children" or "Melbourne House", if she wanted a pretty book.

It was easier to say "I've been playing with my dolls", and from her own point of view it was quite true. Aunty Rosa would probably have called her a short and ugly word in four letters, but Judy knew how often and how falsely Punch was accused of telling lies, and naturally paltered with the truth, to prevent this horrible accusation being laid against her.

Luckily for her Harry, spy and tell tale was always at school in the afternoon, and they had both learnt that any show of friendliness on his part meant that he wished to collect material for mischief making. At first it was tiresome to talk to him as guardedly as if he was Aunt Rosa herself - but it "riled him so it was quite worth it", as Punch said.

One Sunday, when successful eavesdropping behind the playroom door had enabled Harry to report, with embroidery, a talk between Jane and Judy which he hoped "in the interests of discipline" (a favourite phrase of Aunty's) would bring punishment on them both, Judy had turned the tables upon him. Punch was not there to speak for her, Harry had arranged that, and Jane was a sullen tragic mask, biting her lip not to give notice - she had promised the children to stay as long as they did - if she could stick it.

"I am very surprised and angry with you Judy. I didn't know you could be such a naughty ungrateful little girl after all my love and kindness. I thought you had a better heart and nature than to call me, - what was it?"

"Not a real Aunt at all - thank Goodness", prompted the grinning Harry.

In spite of reproof, Judy's eyes were dry for once, she was too much at bay for tears, and there was no Punch to stand in front of her and shoulder the blame.

"Would you rather I called you "Old Worrymutton", as Harry does when he wants to make us laugh or "Mother Fussbox?"

"You little liar", shouted Harry, going dark red.

"You're that - not me", said Judy.

"Be quiet both of you - Jane tell me. Is there any truth in that?"

The tragic mask nodded. Harry blustered, but his complexion was more truthful than his tongue, and his mother knew this. As Punch was not there she lacked the traditional scapegoat, and Judy was only sent to the dressing room, with instructions to perfect herself in her "Duty to Her Neighbour", and not to look out of the window at all.

"Very well, but I know how to keep my tongue from evil speaking, lying and slandering. In the interests of dishplin Harry ought to learn his "Duty to His Neighbour."

"Get away with you," growled Harry.

Judy left the room with her best dancing class curtsey "en passant", because she knew Harry would make a hideous face at her - and she wanted Aunty to see it. She did, and though they could only guess what she said to Harry he was quite endurable for nearly three days.

Perhaps Judy's behaviour was insincere - but it needs more than seven years to grow a body and soul capable of coping with unloving adults - and of learning their mysterious customs, manners and language. Under normal

conditions the budding bodies and seeking souls have
nursery blisses to help their development besides being

"Fretted with sallies of their mother's kisses,
With light upon them from their father's eyes."

but the pleasant land of Nurserydom cast Judy out before
she was four years old.

Both she and Punch, for all their natural selfishness,
were very warm hearted: "children whose very happiness was
love", and they missed Papa and Mamma far more than those
kind parents ever realized. Their trouble was that
everything had gone at once. Papa and Mamma had left them,
"deserted them, almost as much as on a doorstep", Punch
said, not because they were dead, or Papa had had to go to
the wars; Mamma was not ill, like that very peepy-weepy
Ellen Montgomery's mamma in "The Wide Wide World"; they
hadn't even lost their money. If they had Punch could have
swept a crossing, while Judy sold flowers - and it would
have been rather fun. No: they had gone back to Punch and
Judy's own lovely home, and had not taken the children with
them. As Punch said "There was no getting out of that."

They had not forgotten them, and they couldn't have
been angry with them for they said in nearly every letter
that they loved their little boy and girl and missed them
very much - ("A fat lot of good that does us", Punch
sometimes said bitterly.) But Punch could have learnt to
read every bit as well in India, if only Mamma had taught
him, and Ayah could have shown Judy how to be a "a utiful
girl", if Mamma had really wanted her to brush her own
hair, or even to wipe the cups after breakfast.

Yes - everything had gone at once, Papa, Mamma, home,

garden, sunshine, the bandstand in the evening, Ayah, Bearer, Dunnoo, the chokra who only grinned and didn't mind a bit if Judy chose to pelt him with her bricks, the broom-gharry where they sat opposite pretty Mamma in her bright frocks and drove along Back Bay, Dapply Grey, Punch's fat white pony with the ring saddle, Judy's red and green push carriage - which grew so funnily small for her, the toys, the fruit, (the first time Judy tasted a bun she threw it out of the shop door and demanded that a banana should be given her jut-put), the happy ordered routine, where the baba log were king and queen in their own country - none daring to make them afraid.

"We shall have them with us such a short time - let us make them very happy now," Mamma probably said and though Papa feared perhaps there was too much indulgence, still the children were so young, and so funny and lovable, in their different ways, it seemed impossible to begin a hardening process. Besides they would be quite happy in their new surroundings after a bit, children always were. They'd forget, children always did. Unluckily Punch never forgot, acute nostalgia made the new life difficult to him, and though Judy could and did forget details in the past, the mother want in her world was never supplied.

After the first few weeks Mrs Harrison became foolishly fond of her, and indulged her to the verge of making her quite odious - and sometimes beyond it. She had always wanted a daughter and her happy heart engulfed Judy as much as the somewhat fastidious child would allow. Her only son, with his over pomatumed black hair and narrow eyes set too near together, found his life easier when the Mater had Punch to nag at and bully, and Judy to pet and fuss over.

Rosa Harrison was thick-skinned in a double sense, and

she never realized how long it took a small sensitive creature to become accustomed to her appearance and what Jane frankly called "her nasty little ways". She was never reconciled to them. In a life so invaded and dominated by Aunty Rosa, she never ventured to phrase, even to Punch, her absolute conviction that "Aunty" was of a much lower caste than Papa and Mamma; but Punch always understood things without being told, and would comfort her in times of trouble by telling her not to mind what a no-caste woman did. Mrs Harrison was not unusual looking, she was rather of the seaside landlady type, a thin hardfaced woman, early old, with pepper and salt hair in lank loops above large ears with dangling jet ear-rings that she never took out at night. Her lips looked dry and chapped even in summer, and never hid the large front teeth and the gleaming gold wires that fastened the back ones, and her throat was long and skinny ("Just like poultry", Punch said) above her widow's collar and the string of jet beads that ended in Uncle Harrison's watch. Her dress was old fashioned, even judged by Rocklington standards, for she always wore a real crinoline, that began with a deep belt and yoke of red flannel, mysteriously supporting two shining wire hoops (on which in summer she sewed little muslin bags of rue and feverfew, to keep off fleas) and finished with a stiff full flounce of dark grey armour plate - which she told Judy was "mohair". The plainest skirt worn over this foundation stuck out amazingly and dipped and swung in a way that fascinated Judy, but it was a fascination of horror rather than of attraction. She naturally longed to dress up in it, but this was never allowed.

The bedroom was quite nice, for the toilet table wore full skirts of spotted white muslin over bright red glazed calico, which looked much prettier than Aunty Rosa's crinoline. There was a big round pincushion of red satin, with a white lace frill and "Love the Giver" worked on it in gold beads. Judy hoped for years to meet the Mrs or Miss who was so generous, and to be given a similar pincushion, only blue. On either side stood a beautiful scent bottle of red and white glass, but there was no scent in them, only a lovely smell. They were the only things that Aunty had which smelt nice, unless you liked camphorated chalk. A tray of red and white glass held Aunty's grey hairpins and the stick of white bandoline she smoothed her hair with, and there was a ring stand like a branch of red coral on a glass saucer. It never held any rings but it was very beautiful and smooth.

The brush and comb were not pretty and they lived in a white cotton bag with "Brush and Comb" worked on it in red chain stitch, as if anyone was likely to mistake them for anything else. Aunty seemed to like red letters, for "Soiled Linen" was worked very large in red cross stitch on a holland bag that hung on the dressing room door, and "Good Night" on the white case that held her scratchy grey flannel nightdress in winter, and her prickly starchy calico one in summer.

There had been a nice little bed in the dressing room when Mamma saw it, but when the children really came to Down Lodge the nice bed had gone to the attic for Punch and poor Judy had to sleep in Aunty's bed. Luckily Jane put her to bed the first night and was very comforting and full of fair promises. Some were faithfully kept the next day, such as letting her turn on both the taps in the sink, and showing her where Sprat's Kitten slept, but the most attractive of all - "A silver new nothing to hang on your arm, missee, if only you'll stop crying" - had never been fulfilled.

Jane also read her the pincushion and explained a strange picture over the mantlepiece. A very stormy sea with big waves dashing on a curiously shaped rock - which reminded Judy unpleasantly of her one visit to the "Dead Garden". A half swamped ship, with broken masts was evidently about to be wrecked - under a dark sky enlivened by lightning and spoilt, as she thought, by big gold marks all over it. But Jane said the ship was all right because the marks meant "God is Love", and looked a little shocked when Judy said "Oh yes, the same as on the pintushion."

Next morning Aunty Rosa (who both looked and sounded dreadful when she was asleep - for the mouth fell in somehow and she made little whistles in her throat) had the most surprising chota hazere Judy had ever seen. No tea - no cocoa - no hot water - but a big glass of milk that smelt very nasty, (Judy's nose was as keen as a hound puppy's) and tasted, when she was invited to sip it, worse still. "It's too good for little girls", said Aunty, who only needed a nightcap to complete her likeness to Red Riding Hood's Wolf, "my dear husband taught me to take rum and milk in the morning, when we were first married, and I have done it ever since for his sake. It sustains me."

"I'm dolly glad I'm not married!" said Judy fervently.

My Brother Rudyard Kipling

by

Alice Macdonald Fleming

[Published in The Kipling Journal in the December 1947 issue]

Rehearsal: Thursday 17th April 1947,   4.15 - 5.00 p.m.
Recording: Thursday 17th April 1947,   5.15 - 5.45 p.m.
Studio: Edinburgh No. 5.
Transmission: to be arranged
Recording No: DGW 6521

It is eleven years since my brother Rudyard Kipling died; and as the slow years lengthen I no longer dwell on the Kipling Boom of 1890 - delightful and amusing as was that diverting surprise - or on the rich and crowded years before sorrow and death came to this hearthstone. I take refuge rather in our very early days together when a sturdy little boy not quite six and a spoilt baby of three and a half - that was me - were left by their parents, who were going back to India, to face a cold world alone. And it was a <u>very</u> cold world, without one familiar face. And we were left with strangers who were very unkind to us. I think child psychology is better understood now. No kind and loving parents would leave their children for years without giving them any preparation or explanation.

As it was, we felt deserted - everything had gone at once. Mama and Papa, our home in a garden full of sunshine and birds. Dear ayah who was never cross; clever Meeta, our bearer, who made toys out of oranges and nuts, Dunnoo who took charge of the fat white pony which Ruddy <u>would</u> call Dapple Gray; and Chokra, the boy who called the other servants and only grinned and didn't mind when I pelted him with bricks. All gone at one swoop - and why? "Aunty" - as we called the woman we were left with, because she was no relation - used to tell us we had been left because we were so tiresome and she had taken us in out of pity, but in a desperate moment Ruddy questioned her husband and he said that was only "Aunty's" fun and Papa had left us to be taken care of because India was too hot for small people. But we knew better; we had been to Nassick, the Hill Station of Bombay. So what could be the real reason? We couldn't think and it worried us terribly.

I wonder if psycho-analysts are correct in their claim that early influences can poison or seriously overshadow later life. According to their gloomy theories my brother should have grown up morbid, misanthropic, narrow-minded, self-centred, shunning the world and bearing all men a burning grudge. Whereas, of course, he was just the opposite. Certainly between the ages of six and eleven, he was thwarted at every turn and inhibitions were his daily bread. I was rather spoilt - before I saw through "Aunty" - but Ruddy was systematically bullied day and night. I think "Aunty's" very worst defect was her unceasing desire to weaken the affection between the poor little people marooned on the desert island of her house and heart. She took the line that I was always in the right and Ruddy always in the wrong - a very alienating position to thrust me into, but he never loved me the less for her mischief-making. There could hardly have been a more miserable childhood.

However, we amused ourselves together. We had a sort of play that ran on and on for months, in which we played all the parts. I'm afraid there was generally a murder in it; or we ran away to sea and had the most wonderful adventures. I was the reader in those days, funnily enough, because I had more time as I didn't go to school. I remember telling Ruddy DAVID COPPERFIELD which I much preferred to MINISTERING CHILDREN. It was strange, but Ruddy only learned to read with the greatest difficulty; I think because he was too clever. I've noticed it with other clever children. A clever child will listen as long as you like while you read to him but can't be bothered with "A fat cat sat on the mat".

Now I was interested in the fat cat and wanted to follow up its story. I remember a thing Ruddy said to me quite seriously - I must have been four then, because I had been promoted to reading my verse of the psalms at family prayers while Ruddy was still spelling letters into syllables. I was probably crowing over him and he said, "No, Trix, you're too little, you see; you haven't brains enough to understand the hard things about reading. I want to know <u>why</u> 't' with 'hat' after it should spell 'that'."

In his early days Ruddy was a sturdy little boy in a sailor suit, with long straight fair hair - yes, flaxen hair - eyes like dark violets and a particularly beautiful mouth. He was thoroughly happy and genial - indeed, rather too noisy and spoilt. Mother used to say that, like Kim, he was "little friend of all the world" and that's what the Indian servants in Bombay called him before we came home. Shyness and Ruddy were never in the same room; I was shy, but he always spoke for both of us. He always looked upon me as a fairy gift and never resented my coming as some little boys would have done. When people asked him in Bombay, "Is that your sister?" he would say, "No; that is my lady."

When Ruddy was thirteen and I was eleven he went to school at Westward Ho! and I lived with mother in London. She had come home hot-foot from India because Ruddy's eyes had grown so bad that a doctor had written to her about them. I remember how at that time we all had a lovely holiday at a farm in Epping Forest; I don't know how mother survived it, we were so absolutely lawless and unchecked. Our cousin Stanley Baldwin came for a six week's visit and we infected him with our lawlessness too, even to donkey riding. He brought a bat and tried to teach us cricket but we had no time for it - it entailed too much law and order.

Then, before he was seventeen, Ruddy went off to work in India; I was left behind with three kind old ladies in Warwick Gardens. I should tell you that, for a while, Ruddy had a fancy to be a doctor; I think he regarded it from the noble point of view as an ideal profession. But a wise friend of our aunt's took him to a post-mortem. Ruddy never described it to me; all he said was "Oh, Infant", - I had become 'Infant' by then, not 'Trix' - "Oh, Infant, Mark Twain had a word for it." Dramatic pause. "I believe I threw up my immortal soul." He threw up, anyway, the idea of doctoring. He was writing verses like anything by this time. Funnily enough, just at the time when most boys cast off home life, Ruddy returned to it like a duck to its pond. I really believe the happiest time of his life - and mine - was when we all lived together after I came out to Lahore. He was eighteen then and I was fifteen. Although Ruddy and I were always devoted comrades there was never any Charles-and-Mary-Lamb or Dorothy-and-William-Wordsworth nonsense about us. We were each going to live our lives in our own way; he wasn't going to devote himself to nursing my grey hairs or anything of that kind. For instance, there was a man who wanted to marry me - a lifelong friend of Ruddy's - and he kept on writing me letters. I took one of them to Ruddy one day and said, "Here's Herbert again; what am I to do?" Ruddy shifted his pipe to the other side of his mouth and said, "Shoot the brute!" That was all the help I got from him.

By this time, of course, Ruddy was writing with both hands and a pen in his mouth, as mother used to say. Till fountain pens came in he was a persistent pen biter; in every room in our house there was a writing table and on every table was a tray of pens and father said he couldn't find a pen that wasn't bitten into a faggot at the end. So he took to dipping them in quassia. Ruddy always discussed things with me and I can still recognise "something of myself" in his writing - in DEPARTMENTAL DITTIES especially. Mother and I used to drop severely on things his women said in PLAIN TALES. "No, Ruddy, no! Not that." "But it's true." "Never mind; there are lots of things that are true that we never mention." . . . Yes, I think that was the happiest time in both our lives.

Ruddy's success in India was doled out drop by drop; people said "Clever young pup!" and talked about his awful "side". But in London success came as a flood. It amazed him; he couldn't understand it. He never got swelled head in the least, even when he received letters - extraordinary letters - from quite cultivated women who wanted to marry him, on or without sight. He came in for a fearfully foggy winter in London and he didn't like it one little bit. When I came home I went to see <u>him</u> in Embankment Chambers, now called 'Kipling House' - and he was very piano and longing for the parents again. It was about then that he sent a telegram to father in India; it just said "Genesis 45; nine". But that verse reads - and do please remember that Ruddy's first name was Joseph - "Haste ye and go up to my father and say unto him, Thus sayeth thy son Joseph, God hath made me lord of all Egypt; come down unto me, tarry not . . ." The parents did come to Egypt and for a while we had a charming house in Earl's Court Road. That was the time when Ruddy was writing THE FLAG OF ENGLAND and he was stuck at the very first line, and he said to mother "What am I trying to say?" and mother said, quick as a flash, "What do they know of England who only England know?" . . . I think it's characteristic of Ruddy that two of his best-known lines were written by his mother; the other one is "East is east and west is west and never the twain shall meet."

He loved going about and seeing things; he was always observing; he had a camera in his brain. He liked going to the docks - Limehouse and so on - and he had the golden gift of making everybody talk to him. He didn't care for games and he didn't go out much. He had strong dislikes; he couldn't stand goody-goods, for instance. But it is <u>not</u> true that he detested cats, though two months after his death a well-known Sunday paper announced with what Shelley calls the natural glee of "a wolf that has smelt out a dead child", that "Kipling always hated cats to the verge of cruelty and beyond it." If anyone can prove to me that my brother hated or was <u>deliberately</u> cruel to any animal, I will kill that animal with my own hands and eat it raw! He was devoted to all creatures and never owned a gun.[1]

---

[1] This is disingenuous of her. There is a letter from Rudyard to his son John, written in the autumn of 1912, describing how he has been out shooting with his neighbour at Burwash, Col. Feilden. "He picked up a brace of pheasants on Rye Green. I nearly stepped on one old cock who got up almost between my feet. Wish you'd been with me. I didn't take your gun. Consequence was I put up two or three coveys of partridges." This puts rather a different gloss on the matter. Trix was always quick and perhaps over-emphatic in defence of her brother, at least in public.

He always had an idea - it strengthened, I'm afraid, in later days - that people were trying to pick his brains; he became therefore very cautious. People were always wanting introductions and their stupid little stories written for them and so on. He very much enjoyed theatres and people said he should have gone on the stage; he was a curiously good character actor. He used to get the most extraordinary mail in London from quite well-known names, one very distinguished writer and critic wrote - on exquisite deckle-edged parchment - to thank "one so young and yet a Master" for "feeding him the True Bread and Wine of the Word." Ruddy's scribbled footnote was, "The old josser means SOLDIERS THREE."

About his writing he always said to the last, "I shall write something worth reading one day." I don't think he was specially pleased with anything that he had done. He liked KIM and THE JUNGLE BOOKS but the silliest little limerick he wrote would delight him - for the moment - as much as the most serious poem. Luckily the mere physical act of writing was a pleasure to him; he loved it. He was never a note-taker; he drew hieroglyphics - doodles and little funny pictures were his form of note-taking.

I am afraid you may say that I have been telling you too much about my brother's youth, but as I said at the beginning that is the part of him I find myself going back to. I married in 1889 and he married three years later and after that our paths in the world divided. He went west and I went east and the personal devil seemed to arrange that seldom the twain should meet; at any rate, our leaves in England very rarely coincided. But we wrote to each other a lot and we never lost our pleasure in exchanging the apt quotation. If he could hear me now - and, you know, I believe he is hearing me - I think he would appreciate this couplet from George Eliot -

> "But could another childhood be my share
> I would be born a little sister there."

Appendix

The following is a letter from Trix to her cousin, Florence Macdonald. We have seen in this book that Rudyard did not have any great respect or affection for Trix's husband, John Fleming. The same might be said for Trix's feelings towards Rudyard's wife, Carrie, made plain in this letter to her cousin Florence Macdonald.

14.5.39

6, West Coates,
Edinburgh.

My dear Florence,

We know – on good authority – that an odious woman, married, <u>may</u> bear a babe and mend – but what is to be done with one – to whom that remedy has been thrice applied – without success?

Also what have you done to bring that cartload of bricks down on your head? If you were writing a life of Ruddy and had applied to her for information and letters I could understand it, but – as matters stand – no.

Frankly, I think she's feeling dull and wants someone to bully. I know that Ruddy passed through a phase of almost morbid desire to throw veils over his perfectly respectable past. It used to sadden our parents a little – for after all he was not a bastard brought up in a gutter. I think it was the result of living in America and being badgered by their journalists.

I was both amused and surprised in 1901 – when I had been at home long enough to make some friends and go about a bit – to be solemnly warned by him that he had seen I had been staying with the Windsors – (now the Plymouths) at St. Fagan's – and Mother had told him that I was going to a big house-party at Hewell – and I must be careful what I said about him! "Of course you are known to be my sister, probably asked for that reason, and when they sound you about my views, you must not repeat any of the things I told you."

I told him, with perfect truth, that as my name was different, no one knew of my relationship, and I never mentioned it. He would hardly believe this till I told him once at Clouds – when talk was general at a big dinner – my partner said – though not to me – "Oh I can't stand Kipling – never could – nothing in him" – I caught Lady Elcho's sympathetic eye across the table – and no one would have said anything only unluckily dear old Mr. Wyndham – at my other side said solemnly – "I must tell you that the lady you have the pleasure of sitting next to – is Mr. Rudyard Kipling's sister – his only sister" –

I refrained from saying that on another occasion I heard my hostess explaining me to an obtuse but highborn guest – "Oh no – not <u>Miss</u> Fleming – married for years to a distinguished Colonel in India, and a sister of R.K's – but not a bit pen and inky. Quite charming and a wonderful palmist – sees auras you know!" I might have rubbed it in that another man – in a high position – who knew Rud a little – asked me if I was really his sister – he thought I could be only a half-sister – for besides being so much younger (!) R.K. didn't exactly give the impression of coming out of the top drawer" – I said I didn't follow and he rubbed it in by saying – "Well – you are so obviously upper crust – I thought any brother of yours –" I suggested he had forgotted (sic) to bring his hod –

"My hod – what d'yer mean?"
"Well, if you had it, you wouldn't drop so many bricks."

All that Rud got by this inverted vanity was the legend that he was "black – quite 8 annas in the rupee – Couldn't know so much about the natives if he wasn't" – It used to enrage us, and I fancy it still crops up at times.

Between ourselves I think its a great pit1 (sic) C.K. was made an Hon. Mem. of the K. Society. If she reads the Journals. (I suppose she _can_ read, though I have never detected any signs of it.) they must make her foam at the mouth. Quoting whole poems of his! I presume the copyright law does not control it – or she would have turned the screw long ago. You know she wrote very disagreeably to the Editor of Chamber's when my little "Memories" was advertised but not a word to me before or after.

If it comes to a matter of taste, I can neither forget nor forgive the hideous film travesties – "Wee Willie Winkie" – and "Gunga Din" – that have appeared with her sanction – wonder what she got for them. If she tries to muzzle me I fear I should say a few straight words – She is old and ill however – so if I were you I should answer smoothly and kindly regret that she feels that way – and quietly keep my own course. – Its _mortmain_ with a vengeance. After all _we_ are his flesh and blood and she is a foreigner. Do you remember the letter R. once wrote you practically covering the same ground? You bet she dictated it if it refused something – she loves the power of saying no.

Also it never seems to strike her that there is one rule for the living and another for the dead. If Rud's nervous fads, fancies and hatred of trifles are to be considered now – we might as well rail against the cruelty of shutting him up in the Abbey year after year!

Also, when I last saw her – two years ago, she talked as if all that remained of Rud was _HIS WIDOW_. I said his life's influence and all that he stood for and worked for was only beginning. – I had to bite my lip not to say – "If you *really feel like that you should have brought his ashes here — and put them to keep slugs off the fruit" —*

I'm sorry I could not write sooner but I was away for a whole day on Wednesday — the day after your letter came and very busy since. Jack is still very down and out of sorts — though his doctor thinks better of him. I hope to be in Town about June 15th. promise to come to tea and stay to dinner soon after that date — to give time for a real talk. Much love

Always your affectionate cousin

Trix.

I've kept a copy of her letter — it's so amazing — but you shall have it back if you want it.

Tx.

Bibliography

Ankers, Arthur R., *The Pater* (Hawthorns Publications, Otford, Kent, 1988)

Baldwin, A.W., (Earl Baldwin of Bewdley) *The Macdonald Sisters*
(Peter Davies, London, 1960)

Birkenhead, Lord, *Rudyard Kipling* (Weidenfeld and Nicholson, London, 1978)

Carrington, Charles, *Rudyard Kipling* (Macmillan, London, 1955)

Gilbert, Elliot L. (ed.), *"O Beloved Kids"* (Weidenfeld and Nicholson, London, 1983)

Hamilton, Sir Ian, *Following the Drums* (Faber and Faber, 1944)

Kipling, Rudyard, ed. Thomas Pinney, *Something of Myself, Etc.*
(Cambridge University Press, 1990)

Orel, Harold (ed.), *Kipling, Interviews and Recollections Vols 1 & 2*
(Macmillan, London, 1983)

Pinney, Thomas (ed.), *Kipling's India* (Macmillan, London, 1986)

Pinney, Thomas (ed.), *The Letters of Rudyard Kipling Vols. 1, 2, 3, & 4.*
(Macmillan, London, 1990, 1996, 1999)

Rutherford, Andrew (ed.) *Early Verse by Rudyard Kipling*
(Clarendon Press, Oxford, 1986)

Seymour-Smith, Martin, *Rudyard Kipling* (Macdonald, Queen Anne Press, 1989)

Smith, Michael, & Ankers, Arthur R., *Sussex Cavalcade*
(Hawthorns Publications, Otford, Kent, 1992, 1997)

Taylor, Ina, *Victorian Sisters* (Weidenfeld and Nicholson, London, 1987)

Wilson, Angus, *The Strange Ride of Rudyard Kipling* (Secker and Warburg, 1977)

Acknowledgements

The publishers would like to thank the following for their permission to reprint copyright material:

National Trust - Kipling Papers at Sussex University:-
> letters, pp. 16, 20, 27, 33-34, 37-37, 40
> excerpts from Carrie's diary, pp. 23, 38

Macmillan Ltd.
> Quotation from recollections of E. Kay Robinson, quoted in *Kipling Interviews and Recollections*, Orel, Harold Macmillan 1983

Faber and Faber
> *Following the Drums*, Hamilton, Sir Ian, Faber and Faber 1944
> p. 18

Earl Baldwin of Bewdley
> letter from Rudyard, p. 26.

The Kipling Society
> *In Memoriam Mrs Alice Macdonald Fleming* by Florence Macdonald M.B.E.,
> pp. 120-122
> *Trix* by Hilton Brown, pp. 124-125

Every effort has been made to identify and contact copyright holders. However, the publishers will be glad to rectify, in future editions, any omissions or corrections that are brought to their notice.

Index

The decorative panel (varnished paper) by Lockwood, which Trix used as a firescreen.
Trix always wanted this, and it was collected from 'The Gables', at Tisbury,
by Jack Fleming after Lockwood's death.

383

THE KIPLING SOCIETY

AN EXPLANATORY NOTE

The Kipling Society exists for anyone interested in the prose and verse, and the life and times, of Rudyard Kipling. When founded in 1927 by J.H.C. Brooking and a few enthusiasts, it met with the vehement and predictable disapproval from Kipling himself; but it quickly gained, and thereafter retained, a substantial membership. It remains today one of the most active and enduring of the many literary and historical societies in Britain. Moreover, being the only one in the world that focuses specifically on Kipling and his place in English literature, it also attracts members from many other countries.

As an essentially non-profit-making literary organisation, run on a voluntary basis to provide a service to the public as well as to its members, the Kipling Society is a Registered Charity (No. 278885) in Britain. Its overall activities are controlled by its Council, though routine management is in the hands of the Secretary and the other honorary officials.

The Society's main London activities fall into four categories. First, maintaining a specialised Library which scholars and members may consult, located in City University, London; second, answering enquiries from the public (e.g. schools, publishers, writers, and the media), and providing speakers on request; third, arranging a regular programme of lectures and a formal Annual Luncheon; fourth, publishing the *Kipling Journal*.

The *Kipling Journal* is sent quarterly to all members. Its contributions to learning since 1927 have earned it a high reputation. It has published many important items by Kipling, not readily found elsewhere, and a vast quantity of valuable historical, literary and bibliographical commentary, in various shapes, by authorities in their field. In the academic study of Kipling, no serious scholar overlooks the *Journal's* wealth of data. (The entire run since 1927 has now been comprehensively indexed.)

New members are made very welcome. Particulars of membership may be obtained by writing to The Secretary, The Kipling Society, 6 Clifton Road, London, England W9 1SS. The Society's Internet web specification is: http://www.kipling.org.uk.